COMMUNITY

COMMUNITY

Going Back to School with Television's Best Sitcom

ERIN GIANNINI

BLOOMSBURY ACADEMIC
NEW YORK • LONDON • OXFORD • NEW DELHI • SYDNEY

BLOOMSBURY ACADEMIC
Bloomsbury Publishing Inc, 1359 Broadway, New York, NY 10018, USA
Bloomsbury Publishing Plc, 50 Bedford Square, London, WC1B 3DP, UK
Bloomsbury Publishing Ireland, 29 Earlsfort Terrace, Dublin 2, D02 AY28, Ireland

BLOOMSBURY, BLOOMSBURY ACADEMIC and the Diana logo are trademarks of
Bloomsbury Publishing Plc

First published in the United States of America 2026

Copyright © Bloomsbury Publishing, 2026

Cover design: Sally Rinehart
Cover images © NBC/Photofest

All rights reserved. No part of this publication may be: i) reproduced or transmitted in any form, electronic or mechanical, including photocopying, recording or by means of any information storage or retrieval system without prior permission in writing from the publishers; or ii) used or reproduced in any way for the training, development or operation of artificial intelligence (AI) technologies, including generative AI technologies. The rights holders expressly reserve this publication from the text and data mining exception as per Article 4(3) of the Digital Single Market Directive (EU) 2019/790.

Bloomsbury Publishing Inc does not have any control over, or responsibility for, any third-party websites referred to or in this book. All internet addresses given in this book were correct at the time of going to press. The author and publisher regret any inconvenience caused if addresses have changed or sites have ceased to exist, but can accept no responsibility for any such changes.

Library of Congress Cataloging-in-Publication Data
Names: Giannini, Erin, 1974- author
Title: Community : going back to school with television's best sitcom / Erin Giannini.
Description: New York : Bloomsbury Academic, 2026. | Includes bibliographical references and index.
Identifiers: LCCN 2025022373 (print) | LCCN 2025022374 (ebook) | ISBN 9781538191897 hardback | ISBN 9781538191903 epub | ISBN 9798881865566 pdf
Subjects: LCSH: Community (Television program) | LCGFT: Television criticism and reviews
Classification: LCC PN1992.77.C64 G53 2026 (print) | LCC PN1992.77.C64 (ebook) | DDC 791.45/72—dc23/eng/20250520
LC record available at https://lccn.loc.gov/2025022373
LC ebook record available at https://lccn.loc.gov/2025022374

ISBN: HB: 978-1-5381-9189-7
ePDF: 979-8-8818-6556-6
eBook: 978-1-5381-9190-3

Typeset by Integra Software Services Pvt. Ltd.
Printed and bound in the United States of America

For product safety related questions contact productsafety@bloomsbury.com.

To find out more about our authors and books visit www.bloomsbury.com and sign up for our newsletters.

CONTENTS

Introduction: Comedy Done Right? *Community* on NBC 1

PART ONE: Greendale's Human Beings 7

1 Just a Laugh: A Brief Sitcom History 9

2 Harmon's World: Creating *Community* 31

3 The Greendale Seven 49

PART TWO: Chaos Theory: *Community*'s Characters and Narrative 71

4 "Our School May Be a Toilet, but It's Our Toilet": *Community* and Schools on TV 73

5 "I Can Tell Life from TV … TV Makes Sense": *Community* and the Likability Question 87

6 "Some Episodes Too Conceptual to be Funny": *Community* Takes on the Sitcom Genre 103

PART THREE: "Show May Be Canceled and Moved to the Internet": *Community*'s Impact 125

7 "We're Created by a Joke": Sony, *Community*, and TV on the Brink 127

8 "Six Seasons and a Movie!": *Community*'s Afterlife 141

Appendix: A Highly Subjective List of Twenty-Five Must-See Community *Episodes (in No Particular Order)* 153

Notes 170

Bibliography 199

Index 216

About the Author 220

Introduction: Comedy Done Right?
Community on NBC

Sitcoms, as a genre, are almost unique to television. While there were half-hour comedy series on radio, the term *sitcom* wasn't coined until they appeared on television. The combination of dialogue with visible action expanded the range of "situations" that could be mined for humor in that format. In many respects, it is the defining genre for US television, a durable format that stretches from *I Love Lucy* (1951–1957) to *Superstore* (2015–2021). Despite its many iterations, from "live in front of a studio audience" to mockumentary, it stands out from many other genres by having these different types of sitcoms frequently coexist—or blend—rather than replacing an older mode. The 2021/2022 US television season featured three-camera, laugh-track sitcom *Bob Hearts Abishola* on CBS, and mockumentary sitcom *Abbott Elementary* on ABC. And that's limiting it to broadcast; streaming has its own sitcoms, such as *Pen15* (2019–2021), which offered a still-rare coming of age comedy that focused primarily on young women.

Given sitcom's longevity and adaptability, the only surprise is that it took until 2009 for someone to create a series that both skewers and honors the sitcom genre: *Community*. Created by Dan Harmon based on his brief experience in community college, it appears on the outside to be a typical sitcom: lovable rogue Jeff Winger (Joel McHale) is forced to go back to college to earn the credentials he lied about, and falls in with a motley group of quirky new friends. Yet the series almost immediately deconstructs this by having the character of Abed Nadir (Danny Pudi) tie in the group dynamic to pop culture touchstones, from mafia film *GoodFellas* (1990) to bottle episodes and clip shows, commenting on its genre with a heavy metatextual bent. It aired as part of NBC's Thursday night comedy block, which dominated the 1980s and 1990s with series such as *The Cosby Show* (1984–1992), *Cheers* (1982–1993), and *Friends* (1994–2004). While branded as "Must-See TV" in the 1990s (a phrase NBC started applying to multiple nights as time went on), the quirkier, non-laugh-tracked—and lower-rated—comedies of the late 2000s and early 2010s that *Community* was a part of were called "Comedy Night Done Right," suggesting that those who weren't watching were missing out.

They were. *Community* is not merely a meta show that deconstructs pop culture; that would render it a curiosity and nothing else. Instead, it is a series that debuted on and embodies the cusp between traditional television and the streaming era. It aired in a comedy block of shows on NBC that were frequently low-rated but set the tone for the genre moving forward. It balanced the more cynical tone of *30 Rock* (2006–2013) with the more gentle humor of *Parks and Recreation* (2009–2015), with most of its humor punching up. Dan Harmon's take on story structure and particular sensibility, blending off-the-wall set pieces with grounded character development, set not only *Community*'s tone, but also that of his future projects such as *Rick and Morty* (2013–present). Particular TV writers' rooms can be packed with those who go on to have an impact in either television or film; the *Roseanne* (1988–1997) writers' room featured not only veteran writers such as Carrie Fisher and Norm McDonald, but also early career individuals such as Amy Sherman-Palladino, Chuck Lorre, and Joss Whedon. The *Community* writers' room featured individuals who would go on to shape other popular culture phenomenon like the

Marvel Cinematic Universe (MCU), with Joe and Anthony Russo directing some of the MCU's highest-grossing films, including *Infinity War* (2018) and *Endgame* (2019), and Chris McKenna writing part of the *Spider-Man* trilogy and contributing to *Captain America: The Winter Soldier* (2014). Megan Ganz would go on to write Emmy-nominated episodes of *Modern Family* (2009–2020), as well as working on *It's Always Sunny in Philadelphia* (2005–present) and *The Last Man on Earth* (2015–2018). Others, including Ryan Ridley and Alex Rubens, would follow Harmon to *Rick and Morty*.

Essentially, *Community* is a sitcom overdue for a deeper look. The writing, the characters, where it fits in the history of sitcoms, the performances, and even the behind-the-scenes drama are worth examining. Other elements worth analyzing include what it influenced and what it was influenced by, the way it differentiated itself from other sitcoms and yet embraced the genre, the comedic generational divide embodied by the escalating tension between Chevy Chase and Dan Harmon, and the ascendance of Donald Glover.

This book is an attempt to examine the cultural phenomenon that is *Community*, a series about a community college and, in the series' own words, "the goofballs who run around stirring up trouble, and the eggheads that make a big deal out of it."[1] It's a meta series with an active fandom (enough to justify a follow-up film in 2025) and features an eclectic cast. Further, it's one of a group of both comedies and dramas produced by Sony Pictures Television, who have produced several series for broadcast as one of the few studios unaffiliated with a broadcast network. I'll start out with a brief history of sitcoms on US television, from the very first one (*Mary Kay and Johnny* [1947–1950]) to *Community*'s debut in 2009. How they were structured, what they talked about, even who they did—and didn't—cast, not only show how knowledgable Harmon and company were about the form, but highlight the way that *Community* embraces or subverts the parts that have hardened into tropes. I'll then dip into Harmon's own history, from his early days at Comedy Sportz to *Community* and beyond, a circuitous journey that blends established ways to break into the industry (improv, making the right connections) and newer ones (using the internet to create and release offbeat or nonmainstream content). The Greendale Seven represent the next stop, examining the casting and development of the show, followed by deep dives into the main characters and their arcs—or lack thereof—across *Community*'s six seasons.

Part two examines the various ways that *Community* fits into three distinct areas: schools on TV, characters and characterization, and the sitcom genre. Given the fact that most viewers would have attended at least a decade's worth of required schooling, it's surprising that more series haven't used it as a setting in either dramas or comedies. That being said, "school" shows have existed on US television almost since the beginning, whether the short-lived *Mrs. G. Goes to College* (1961–1962) and the teacher-focused *Our Miss Brooks* (1952–1956; an early example of a series adapted from a film) or the more recent *A. P. Bio* (2018–2021) and *Abbott Elementary* (2021–present), as well as dramas from *The White Shadow* (1978–1981) to *Boston Public* (2000–2004), which blend stories of both teachers and students. The question of likability is up next; do characters need to be likable for a series to be successful? Series such as *Seinfeld* (1989–1998) would suggest emphatically that they do not. Yet, for the most part, NBC built its comedy brand on warm-hearted family—or friends as family—sitcoms throughout the 80s and 90s, but shifted in the mid-2000s (as they started to lose the ratings war) to series with more complicated characters and dynamics, from the self-absorbed denizens of *30 Rock* to the karma-challenged Earl Hickey (Jason Lee) trying to be a better man in *My Name Is Earl* (2005–2009), suggesting that "likable" isn't necessarily the best metric for good comedy. Finally, I'll take a look at the series' metatextual impulses, the ways in which they use their parodies and homages not just as a joke, but also to deepen story and character, as with Jeff and Abed coming to a new understanding of each other through the *GoodFellas* parody in "Contemporary American Poultry."

In the final section of the book, I'll take a long overdue look at Sony, the studio that created *Community* and one of the few big studios not connected with a network. It is, however, connected with a significant amount of television, both past and present, from its acquisition of Columbia's catalogue, as well as many of the series it has acquired since then that are frequently regarded as some of television's best. It's also an opportunity to look at *Community* as a series that looked backward (to sitcoms past) and forward (the ways it stayed on the air despite ratings and backstage drama), benefitting from both in the long run. I'll end with what happened after *Community* ended, particularly the path to fulfilling the "and a movie" promise and the ways it fits into an era of revisions and reboots.

Community, like any series, had its ups and downs throughout its six seasons, something its viewers and fans continue to debate. The Harmon-less season four struggled without him at the helm, ramping up on the parodies as well as an ill-advised pairing of Troy (Donald Glover) and Britta (Gillian Jacobs) and episodes that seemed completely at odds with how the characters had been portrayed up to that point.[2] When Harmon returned, season four's oddities are explained at the start of season five as the result of a gas leak.[3] It was subsequently dubbed the "gas leak year" by fans, something that the final episode jokes about: when Abed says "cool" six times, one for each season, Ben Chang (Ken Jeong), the most volatile character of the group, farts during the fourth one, saying, "It's an inside joke."[4] As critically reviled as it was, even season four has its defenders.[5] Which is to say, even at its worst, there was something to enjoy, whether a surprising guest star,[6] the same events shown from the perspective of a fellow classmate we'd never noticed before,[7] or a rare humanizing storyline for Pierce (Chevy Chase).[8] The way it played with the sitcom form, its extensive knowledge of pop culture, and the subsequent trajectory of its cast make *Community* worth a much longer look, and one I hope to provide here.

PART ONE

GREENDALE'S HUMAN BEINGS

1

Just a Laugh
A Brief Sitcom History

Comedy programs existed on radio, some of which, like *Father Knows Best* (1954–1960) or *The Goldbergs* (1949–1956), were eventually transitioned to television. The term *situation comedy* or *sitcom*, however, was not used until the 1950s; David Marc pinpoints its first use in an issue of *TV Guide* from 1953.[1] Still, the first television program that could retroactively claim the title was a series on the now-defunct DuMont network called *Mary Kay and Johnny* (1947–1950). Only a single episode of the series still exists—most of DuMont's programming was literally thrown in New York's East River—but it nonetheless embraced or set up several sitcom elements and tropes, including the straitlaced husband and wacky wife and the single set (the couple's apartment). (An early review of the series suggested that even in the 1940s, the "old tolerant-husband-with-dumb-wife" trope was tired.)[2] Moreover, possibly because the couple who starred in the series (Mary Kay and Johnny Strearns) were married in real life, the couple shared a bed and Mary Kay's pregnancy was written into the series almost half a decade before *I Love Lucy* debuted. While little-known today, for obvious reasons, it nonetheless set the stage for the sitcoms of its era, particularly its use of the domestic settings and a focus on interpersonal dynamics. It was filmed live, and therefore didn't use a laugh track.[3]

As a genre, sitcoms are tailor-made for television, most of which rely on humor that combines dialogic with visual humor, whether through sight gags, slapstick, or facial expression, none of which can adequately be conveyed on radio. That doesn't mean, however, that it remained static; from the 1950s to the current era, sitcoms have not only evolved their subject matter, but also characterization and formats. Understanding *Community*—and much of its humor—is aided by some knowledge of the ways sitcoms have changed, or not, throughout television's history. This chapter will briefly trace sitcoms' history, from the early "live in a front of a studio audience" to the current day. In keeping with the idea of a "brief" history, I'll be talking about the broader trends in each decade, acknowledging that not every sitcom that aired during those years fit into the wider sitcom zeitgeist.

Homecoming: Sitcoms in the Postwar 50s

If one could name a single sitcom that encapsulates the 1950s, it would likely be *Leave It to Beaver* (1957–1963). Running for six seasons (on CBS and then ABC), the series primarily featured the day-to-day misadventures of Theodore "Beaver" Cleaver (Jerry Mathers) in his suburban neighborhood, with his more responsible older brother, Wally (Tony Dow); Wally's ne'er-do-well best friend, Eddie Haskell (Ken Osmond); and Wally and Beaver's pipe-smoking dad, Ward (Hugh Beaumont), and stay-at-home mom, June (Barbara Billingsley). *The Adventures of Ozzie and Harriet* (1952–1966), which blurred the line between the real-life Nelson family and their sitcom personas, was the longest-running sitcom until it was ousted by *It's Always Sunny in Philadelphia* in 2021. And yet, during their original runs, neither ever cracked into the top 30 of the Nielsen rating. During the 1950s, it was only one of several family- and suburban-based sitcoms that defined the latter part of the era. The early 1950s focused more on what were referred to as the "ethnic sitcoms":[4] *I Love Lucy* (with Cuban American Desi Arnaz); *Make Room for Daddy*, renamed *The Danny Thomas Show* (Thomas was Lebanese American); and *The Goldbergs*, which focused on a Jewish family living in the Bronx. Not surprisingly, both in terms of population as well as where studios were located in the 1950s, all of these sitcoms took place in various parts of New York City.

Yet by the mid-1950s many of these series were gone in favor of the aforementioned family-based suburban ones. Why? They were likely considered too risky by the activities of the House Un-American Activities Committee in the US Congress, led by Senator Joseph McCarthy. *The Goldbergs*, which transitioned from radio and aired on CBS, NBC, and finally DuMont during its six-year run, was a case in point. The sitcom was dropped by CBS following costar Philip Loeb being named in *Red Channels* (a publication that purported to list famous communists); series creator and fellow star Gertrude Berg refused to fire him. It was picked up by NBC with the proviso that she drop Loeb from the cast. She finally acceded to this, but continued to pay him out of her own pocket, given the near-impossibility of him being able to find work.[5] He later took his own life.

In this earliest decade of US television, the idea of branding and a type of sitcom being particular to a certain network was not really an obvious element. Programming did not extend throughout the day in its earliest years, and would often "sign-off" and be replaced with a test pattern after midnight well into the 1980s. The networks ABC, CBS, NBC, and, until 1956, DuMont, offered a mix of family-based (*The Donna Reed Show* [1958–1966], *Father Knows Best*, *My Little Margie* [1952–1955]); couples (*Mary Kay and Johnny*, *I Love Lucy*, *Mr. Peepers* [1952–1955], *I Married Joan* [1952–1955], *The Honeymooners* [1955–1956]); and a few that didn't quite fit into either category except in the ways they suggested future programs. *The Phil Silvers Show* (1955–1959) was a workplace-type farce focused on the adventures of Sergeant Bilko, *The Morey Amsterdam Show* (1948–1950) was set in a nightclub, and *The Real McCoys* (1957–1963) was an early entry into what would be known as the "rural sitcoms" of the 1960s and early 1970s. Oftentimes, as with *The Goldbergs* or *The Danny Thomas Show*, a show canceled by one network was picked up by another, which still occurs today, but not as often as in these early days, particularly before competition for the growing number of viewers became the primary concern. DuMont, starting a tradition that new networks would employ in the 1980s and 1990s, counterprogrammed to a certain extent against the "Big Three" by offering a variety of programs aimed at an audience segment already being ignored in television's first decade: viewers of color. It was the first network to feature a Black host—Hazel Scott, who hosted a variety music program on the network (she ended up being one of the people targeted by McCarthy's committee),[6] and *The Gallery of Madame Liu-Tsong* (1951), starring silent film actress Anna May Wong as a detective involved in international intrigue, offering an early female dramatic lead and one of the only series to feature an Asian lead actress until 1995's short-lived *All-American Girl*. Unfortunately for DuMont, there were factors that limited its ability to succeed, including the dominance of NBC and CBS, the Federal Communication Commission's freeze on new station licenses, and antitrust laws that prevented it from merging with ABC, which would have given it enough affiliate stations to compete with CBS and NBC. It also, like Fox and later the WB/UPN/CW, was frequently relegated the UHF frequency (the higher-numbered stations) rather than the VHF one, which was claimed by the other three. Most TVs at the time required extra equipment to access the UHF band, and the picture quality was frequently bad. DuMont finally shut its doors in 1956, and most of its programming archive was destroyed in the 1970s to make room for other material, including the aforementioned *Gallery of Madame Liu-Tsong*, of which no filmed or scripted material remains. As television moved into its second full decade, however, the remaining three networks would start to differentiate themselves in terms of content and audience.

Magic and Meadows: The 1960s Sitcoms

The turbulence of the 1960s, with the Vietnam War, protests, assassinations, and the push for—and against—civil rights, may have been all over the nightly news, but seemed to register not at all in the sitcoms of the decade. If in the latter half of the 1950s, the sitcom abandoned the city and retreated to the suburbs, the 1960s took that a step farther: back to the countryside. Those that did stay in the 'burbs, however, did so with a more fantastical twist. Essentially, the characteristic sitcoms generally broke into two groups: rural comedies (*Green Acres* [1965–1971], *The Beverly Hillbillies* [1962–1971], *Petticoat Junction* [1963–1970]) or comedies with a fantastical twist (magic, monsters, etc.). The rural comedies themselves tended to fit into one of two modes. The first offered a lighthearted look at the follies and foibles of small-town life. The ur-version of this would be *The Andy Griffith Show* (1960–1968), with its whistled opening theme, focused on widowed father Andy Taylor, who serves as sheriff of Mayberry while trying to raise his son Opie (Ron Howard) with the help of his Aunt Bee (Frances Bavier). Despite his position as a member of law enforcement, Mayberry's "crimes" remained light and secondary to the adventures and misadventures of both the Taylor family and Mayberry at large. (Indeed, the series would be retitled *Mayberry RFD* after the departures of Griffith and Howard.) *Petticoat Junction* takes place in the fictional town of Hooterville, and centers around Kate Bradley, her family, and the Shady Rest Hotel that they run. (Creator Paul Henning apparently based Hooterville and the Shady Rest on the Shady Rest Hotel in Eldon, Missouri, run by his wife's grandmother.)[7] Henning also created *Green Acres* and *The Beverly Hillbillies*, two series reliant on the fish-out-of-water concept, with Manhattan-based couple Oliver (Eddie Albert) and Lisa (Eva Gabor) relocating to Hooterville (*Green Acres* was a "sister show" to *Petticoat Junction*), and the Texas-bred Clampetts to Beverly Hills after they strike oil. Both relied on the juxtaposition of two disparate cultures, whether it was Oliver and Lisa's adjustment to rural life, or the Clampetts' dispensing of home-spun wisdom to the more shallow and materialistic of their Beverly Hills neighbors.

The other major trend in the era was what might be called the "magic" sitcoms: *Bewitched* (1964–1972), *The Munsters* (1964–1966), *The Addams Family* (1964–1966), *I Dream of Jeannie* (1965–1970), and the one that combined the rural shows with the magic ones by featuring a talking horse, *Mr. Ed* (1961–1966). Broadly, these shows fit into two categories (with some crossover). Series such as *The Munsters* and *The Addams Family* generated comedy through the way they existed outside the norm of the usual suburban family. The Munsters, with the exception of daughter Marilyn, all appear as versions of the monsters from the 1930s Universal films: Herman (Fred Gwynne) as Frankenstein, Lily (Yvonne De Carlo) and Grandpa (Al Lewis) as vampires, and son Eddie (Butch Patrick) as Wolf Boy. While they see themselves as perfectly normal, others frequently react with surprise or fear; the first two episodes have Marilyn's dates running away when they meet her family.[8] Yet, on an episode level, the issues they deal with—school problems for Eddie, Marilyn's dating woes, or misunderstandings between family members—would not be out of place on more "normal" sitcoms, such as *Leave It to Beaver*. That's not an accident; producers Joe Connelly and Bob Mosher produced both. Further, one of the major themes of the series was to show that the Munsters, despite their oddities, were just like everyone else.

This was less the case with *The Addams Family*; there is no indication in either the series' two seasons, nor the later films and reboots, that any of the family desired to fit in. Indeed, the humor within the Addams family sprang from their own confusion with the ordinary trappings of mid-century suburban life, such as when Gomez (John Astin) and Morticia (Carolyn Jones) are caught off-guard when their son Pugsley (Ken Weatherwax) wants to join the Boy Scouts. They bring in a psychiatrist, Dr. Black (George O. Petrie), to deal with what might be wrong with Pugsley, only for Black to surmise that he merely needed to express aggression. While Black assumes that Pugsley's recounting of the various explosions and bizarre games that are a regular part of the Addams family activities is that expression, Gomez and Morticia correctly surmise that the desire to become a Boy Scout is the expression. Once that is accomplished, Pugsley returns to his (ab)normal self, much to

Black's chagrin and his parents' relief.[9] For both, however, as Stacey Abbott and Lorna Jowett point out, for all their "oddities," Morticia and Lily still fit firmly into the roles of television mothers, taking care of the home and their children while Gomez and Herman deal with the outside world on a more regular basis and that the "'real world' suburban family situation is what generates interest for the audience" despite their gothic trappings.[10]

This is rather reversed in both *Bewitched* and *I Dream of Jeannie*, which visually resemble the more typical suburban environments. Yet both the Stephens and the Nelson homes hide a secret: Samantha Stephens (Elizabeth Montgomery) is a witch from a long line of witches, and Jeannie (Barbara Eden) is a genie released from a bottle discovered by Captain Tony Nelson after a space capsule crash.[11] While both Samantha and Jeannie are literally empowered, their abilities need to be hidden from the rest of the world, and their magic is primarily used for the benefit of home and family. Indeed, the crisis at the center of these series is the potential revelation of either Samantha and Jeannie's powers to the outside world. The subtext—it's OK for women to be powerful, as long as it stays secret—is absurdly obvious. While this is something of an advance from how women were portrayed in series such as *Ozzie and Harriet*, it still positions them firmly in the home, an element that was slow to change in the first decades of television.

The 1960s were notable for at least one first: the debut of *Julia* (1968–1971), which was the first sitcom featuring an African American woman in a nonstereotypical role. Further, Julia (Diahann Carroll) was a widowed single mother—her husband's plane was shot down in Vietnam—another rarity in 1960s television. While the series was criticized for being apolitical and not reflective of the struggles in the African American community (a similar critique would later be leveled at *The Cosby Show*), it nonetheless stands as a milestone that would, unfortunately, be built upon far too slowly.

Rural versus Relevance: The 1970s

Now in television's third decade, and with the Nielsen ratings firmly established as the metric for a show's popularity, networks became more concerned with exactly who was watching. Further, the financial incentive and syndication rule (known colloquially as "fin-syn") was created to ease financial barriers for independent production companies interested in creating television. Television primarily works on deficit financing, with the costs of production, under fin-syn, shared by the network and production company until the series reached 100 episodes and thus was eligible to be sold into syndication. This opened the door to companies such as MTM and Tandem Productions, who created a number of well-regarded and award-winning sitcoms during the decade, including *The Mary Tyler Moore Show* (1970–1977) (MTM), *All in the Family* (1971–1979) (Tandem), and *M*A*S*H* (1972–1983) (Larry Gelbart), based on the book and later Robert Altman–directed film. (Its eleven-season run ended up eclipsing both its novel and film source materials.)

What this also meant, however, is that sitcoms such as *Petticoat Junction* or *The Beverly Hillbillies*, which drew large viewing audiences, were nonetheless considered failures because they appealed to the "wrong" kind of audiences: older viewers. Known as the "rural purge,"[12] CBS canceled all of the rural-based programs in favor of ones considered more socially relevant. The thinking was that shows that engaged with issues around politics, sexuality, and the generational divide would attract the younger Boomer audience as aligned with their thinking. Mary Richards (Mary Tyler Moore) could discuss birth control,[13] *All in the Family* expose working-class challenges (and bigotry), and *M*A*S*H* provide commentary on the Vietnam conflict, despite the fact it was set during the Korean War. Perhaps more importantly to the networks than artistic and political quality, however, was that advertisers felt the same way; that is, willing to accept a smaller audience if that audience had money. ABC went in a different direction, with its most popular sitcoms the nostalgia-laden *Happy Days* (1974–1984) and *Laverne & Shirley* (1976–1983). Series such as *Barney Miller* (1975–1982) and *Soap* (1977–1980) touched on more serious topics, including featuring TV's first out gay main character (*Soap*), and music-driven (and more kid/teen-oriented) series such as *The Partridge Family* (1970–1974) offered blended families and single parents, still comparative rarities on television. While neither cracked the top 10 in Nielsen ratings, *The Brady Bunch* (1969–1974) in particular found its audience in syndication, particularly among Gen X viewers. Indeed, a late 1980s sitcom called *Day by Day* (1988–1989), cocreated by Andy Borowitz (*The Fresh Prince of Bel-Air* [1990–1996]), about two former yuppies who quit their high-powered jobs to run a daycare center, featured a dream sequence in which their son Ross (Christopher Barnes) is transported into an episode of his favorite show, *The Brady Bunch,* as long-lost Brady son Chuck (a likely reference to Chuck Cunningham, the eldest son on *Happy Days* who disappeared near the end of the second season, never to be referenced again). It featured nearly all the actors from the original series.[14] (Barnes would later be cast as Greg Brady in the 1990s *Brady Bunch* feature films.)

NBC, however, struggled with comedy through the 1970s, with only two of its sitcoms—*Sanford and Son* (1972–1977) (Tandem Productions) and *Chico and the Man* (1974–1978) (James Komack)—lasting more than a season or two. It was only in the 1980s that NBC would start dominating the field, a feat that lasted into the 2000s.

Women, Misfits, and NBC's Big Comeback: The 1980s

While CBS dominated the 1970s with its MTM and Tandem production sitcoms, these shows had all taken a bow by the early 1980s. With the Vietnam War in the rearview and Reagan in office, sitcoms in the 1980s seemed less inclined to deal with heavier or more controversial subjects (outside of a few very special episodes). Not that CBS strayed entirely from either controversy or progressive messages; *Murphy Brown* (1988–1998), which debuted in 1988, became a political talking point in the 1992 presidential election, when VP Dan Quayle took the fictional Murphy (Candice Bergen) to task for choosing to be a single mother. Making the premise of the show a television newsmagazine (à la *60 Minutes*) allowed the series to comment on any number of issues of the day, from gun control to feminism. Indeed, throughout the 1980s, the most buzzworthy and popular shows on CBS were both created by and heavily featured women. *Murphy Brown* was created by Diane English. *Kate & Allie* (1984–1989), about two single mothers and best friends sharing a brownstone in Greenwich Village and attempting to reinvent themselves after divorce, was created by Sherry Coben. *Designing Women*, about four women running an interior design firm in Atlanta, Georgia, was created by Linda Bloodworth-Thomason, who created several successful series for CBS from 1986 to 1995.[15] While characters such as Murphy and Julia Sugarbaker (Dixie Carter) were known for their forthright attitudes and strong opinions (Julia's rants against sexism, racism, and homophobia were legendary throughout the series), the quieter lives of Kate (Susan Saint James) and Allie (Jane Curtin) as one attempted to earn respect at work (Kate) and the other to figure out what she wants beyond homemaking (Allie) were progressive in a medium that even as late as the 1970s took issue with featuring divorced characters (e.g., both Carol and Mike Brady were widowed).

Taking a different tack, ABC's biggest (or most remembered) sitcom hits of the 1980s derived their humor from various "fish-out-of-water" scenarios. *Who's the Boss?* (1984–1992), *Growing Pains* (1985–1992), and *Full House* (1987–1995), all family-based sitcoms, featured men as the primary caretakers, either through spousal death (*Full House*) or simply changing work and economic dynamics. Jason Seaver (Alan Thicke) moves his psychiatric practice into the home to parent their three kids while his wife returns to work as a reporter, while Tony Micelli (Tony Danza) accepts a job as a live-in housekeeper in Connecticut to provide a better environment for his daughter, Samantha (Alyssa Milano), than he feels his native Brooklyn can offer. Not only is Tony marked as an outsider because of his working-class roots, but also his job maintaining the household and nurturing both his own daughter and his boss Angela's (Judith Light) son, Jonathan (Danny Pintauro), more effectively than her was a slight bit of progress in upending the expected gender roles on TV. *Bosom Buddies* (1980–1982), while not a huge ratings success, was nonetheless a career-launcher for Tom Hanks, taking a page from 1959's *Some Like It Hot* to tell the story of two guys in New York who end up having to dress as women to rent in an affordable building that is women-only. *Perfect Strangers* (1986–1993) paired up straitlaced Chicagoan Larry Appleton (Mark Linn-Baker) with his recently transplanted distant cousin from a small island in Greece, Balki Bartokomous (Bronson Pinchot), in a small apartment as they navigate big-city life. *Webster* (1983–1987) resembled NBC's *Diff'rent Strokes* (1978–1986), with George (Alex Karras) and Katherine Papadopolis (Susan Clark) taking in the orphaned son of one of George's teammates from his pro-football days, and *Head of the Class* (1986–1991) mixed the laid-back energy Howard Hesseman brought to *WKRP in Cincinnati* (1978–1982) to a Manhattan public high school's gifted class.

NBC, however, started a domination of the sitcom genre in the 1980s that would last until the early 2000s. After languishing at the bottom of the ratings for a good portion of the 1970s, by 1985 NBC had a Thursday night comedy block that mixed family-based sitcoms (*The Cosby Show* and *Family Ties* [1982–1989]) with fairly unconventional takes on the workplace sitcom: a bar (*Cheers* [1982–1993]), and a Manhattan municipal night court (*Night Court* [1984–1992]). While a rudimentary version of this lineup existed before 1984, it was the debut of *The Cosby Show* in 1984 that solidified the night of programming. While its legacy has been tarnished by the allegations against and subsequent trial of Bill Cosby, *The Cosby Show* had an unprecedented six-year run as the number one show in the Nielsen ratings, buoying up the other shows within the Thursday night NBC lineup. Focused on an upper-middle-class family in Brooklyn, *The Cosby Show* mixed typical sitcom family situations (e.g., one of the kids wrecking the house with a party when his parents are out)[16] with more than a few educational moments, particularly around Black history.[17] This was a particular interest of Cosby's; witness his documentary *Black History: Lost, Stolen, or Strayed*, which aired on CBS in 1968, only a few months after Martin Luther King's assassination, in which he emphasizes the importance of Black children knowing their own history. The *Cosby Show* spin-off, *A Different World* (1987–1993), had more leeway to tackle contemporary (and historic) issues facing its Black students at Hillman, a historically Black college based on institutions such as Morehouse, including the LA Riots, HIV/AIDS, and even the discovery of Black ancestors who owned slaves.[18] The four-comedy block followed by a drama worked well for NBC, as did front-loading the family-based sitcoms in the early prime-time block, allowing family viewing followed by the more adult-oriented shenanigans of *Cheers* and *Night Court*. There were, however, changes on the horizon, which came to fruition in the 1990s.

Broadening the Spectrum: The 1990s

Although it launched in 1986 with a focus on teen dramas (among other things), the Fox network really came into its own in the early 1990s with the debut of *The Simpsons* (1989–present). The first prime-time broadcast cartoon since *The Flintstones* went off the air in 1966, it was originally a small part of British comedian Tracey Ullman's sketch comedy show. These shorts did well enough during Ullman's three-season show to be spun-off into its own series. Fox offered other sitcoms during the 1990s, usually with an off-beat premise. *Get a Life* (1990–1992), with Chris Elliot as a thirty-year-old paperboy who still lives with his parents, was a surreal gem; *Herman's Head* (1991–1994) split its running time between the titular Herman and the embodied emotions in his head, a premise that predates *Inside Out*'s similar structure; and in *Parker Lewis Can't Lose* (1990–1993), the surreal and cartoonish visual and aural shots eventually led to it being referred to as the "Julliard" of television production for up-and-coming writers and directors. *The Simpsons*, however, became the dominant sitcom of the network by blending typical family sitcom dynamics, self-awareness, and a touch of the surreal and irreverent. Indeed, its second most successful sitcom during the 1990s was *Married ... with Children* (1987–1997), which was constantly criticized by both moral crusaders and parents for its raunchy content and low-rent aesthetic. Both set a trend for the successful sitcoms of the Fox network pushing against the boundaries of their particular era, whether in terms of content or style. Combined with ABC's *Roseanne* (1988–1997), however, *The Simpsons* finally ended *The Cosby Show*'s dominance in the ratings, suggesting a cultural shift between the family sitcoms of the 1980s, which tended to feature upper-middle-class families, to more working-class, "realistic" (for TV) situations.

By mid-decade, however, two new networks were added to the broadcast spectrum: the WB and UPN, both, like Fox, connected to established studios (Warner Brothers and Paramount, respectively). Both needed, like Fox, to differentiate themselves from the Big Three, and for both, they initially started by programming for audiences underrepresented on television, particularly people of color. The WB's earliest successes were sitcoms, including *Sister Sister* (1994–1999), *The Parent 'Hood* (1995–1999), *The Wayans Bros.* (1995–1999), *The Jamie Foxx Show* (1996–2001), and *The Steve Harvey Show* (1996–2002), some of which fit into the family genre (*The Parent 'Hood* and *Sister Sister*), while the others blended the family and workplace genres (*The Wayan Bros.* and *The Jamie Foxx Show*). Only *The Steve Harvey Show* remained primarily a workplace sitcom, one of the (relatively) few TV sitcoms based in a school (see Chapter 4). Many of them were also fronted by actors who were already something of known quantities at the time their shows debuted; Jamie

Foxx got his start on Fox's sketch comedy series *In Living Color* (1990–1994), created by Keenen Ivory Wayans, whose brothers Shawn and Marlon starred in *The Wayans Bros.*, and who cowrote the script for *Hollywood Shuffle* with Robert Townsend, who anchored *The Parent 'Hood*. Steve Harvey was a well-established stand-up comedian by the mid-1990s. Yet by 2001 only Harvey's sitcom remained; the others had been canceled in favor of the teen dramas the network became known for. UPN had slightly better luck; both *Girlfriends* (2000–2008) and *Everybody Hates Chris* (2005–2009) ran for multiple seasons; indeed, it was the Black-led sitcoms that did best on the channel, including: *Moesha* (1996–2001); *Malcolm and Eddie* (1996–2000), which starred Malcolm Jamal-Warner, previously on *The Cosby Show*; and *The Parkers* (1999–2004).

This discussion, however, would not be complete without mentioning a series about six friends and their romantic and professional interactions in New York City. I'm talking, of course, of Fox's *Living Single*, which debuted in 1993. Like *The Cosby Show*, which ended the year before, most of the action takes place in a brownstone in Brooklyn, but the interpersonal dynamics between Kadijah (Queen Latifah), Max (Erika Alexander), Regine (Kim Fields), Synclaire (Kim Coles), Overton (John Henton), and Kyle (T. C. Carson) are at the center of the narrative. The series did not shy away from issues around work (e.g., Kadijah's attempts to keep her magazine, *Flava*, afloat) and, in particular, offered three female leads who did not fit into the particular body types generally seen on TV, without sacrificing their attractiveness or sexuality. It was also the first sitcom to be created and showrun by a Black woman, Yvette Lee Bowser, opening the door for more creators of color. Warren Littlefield, when asked if there was a show he wished he'd optioned, he said *Living Single*; a year later, *Friends* debuted with a remarkably similar premise—and a blindingly white version of New York.[19]

Friends, which would go on to run for ten years (as opposed to *Living Single*'s five), debuted in *Family Ties*' old timeslot in 1994, between *Mad About You* (1992–1999) and *Seinfeld*. Dubbed "Must-See TV," NBC on Thursday nights dominated over its competitors for the next decade. Frequently, newer sitcoms would debut on Thursdays as a test run before being moved to other nights, expanding NBC's scope of sitcoms across multiple nights, with series such as *Wings* (1990–1997), *Cheers*' spin-off *Frasier* (1993–2004), and *Will & Grace* (1998–2006). With a couple of exceptions, most of these sitcoms (even those that were short-lived) took place in major metropolitan areas, including Seattle (*Frasier*) and St. Louis (*The John Larroquette Show* [1993–1996]), with New York and its boroughs the primary setting (*Will & Grace, Mad About You, News Radio* [1995–1999], *Friends, Seinfeld, Caroline in the City* [1995–1999]). The success of these series did not prevent NBC from using promotional gimmicks, including 1994's "Blackout Thursday," in which a city-wide power outage affected the characters of *Friends, Mad About You*, and the short-lived *Madman of the People* (1994); filming sequences of the first season finale of *3rd Rock from the Sun* (1996–2001) in 3D; or the "supersized" episodes of shows like *Friends* and *Will & Grace* both to avoid channel surfing and potentially outfox the still-nascent DVR technology in the early 2000s.

If *Friends* popularized, while not inventing, the "hang-out" comedy, ABC in the 1990s relied heavily on comedian-led series, likely due to the popularity of *Roseanne*, featuring the working-class Conner family, whose relatable financial and interpersonal challenges were the first to knock *The Cosby Show* from its number one spot at the end of the 1980s. While its star, Roseanne Barr, was mired in controversy from the beginning (e.g., her off-key rendition of the national anthem infuriated a number of public figures), it also (briefly) brought back stories set around the working class that Norman Lear had championed in the 1970s. Aside from *Roseanne*, comedian-led sitcoms included *Home Improvement* (1991–1999), with Tim Allen; *Grace Under Fire* (1993–1998), with Brett Butler; *These Friends of Mine*/*Ellen* (1994–1998), with Ellen DeGeneres; and *The Drew Carey Show* (1995–2004), with, obviously, Drew Carey. *Roseanne* (in its earlier seasons), *Home Improvement*, and *Grace Under Fire* based much of their premises on either the life of or comedic persona of the star, such as Tim Allen's macho throwback/goofball Tim Taylor on *Home Improvement*. *Ellen*, originally titled *These Friends of Mine*, was based on DeGeneres's brand of laid-back observational humor, although it ended up having a much different impact as the series went on. *The Drew Carey Show* mixed the hang-out and work comedy with a touch of the surreal, including fantasy sequences and a few musical numbers. Mixed with these series was the continuation of their TGIF (Thank God It's Friday/Thank God It's Funny) family-friendly comedy block of—at various times—*Full House*, *Family Matters* (1989–1998), *Step by Step* (1991–1998), *Boy Meets World* (1993–2000), and *Hangin' with Mr. Cooper* (1992–1997), which started as closer in spirit to the other comedian-led series on the network before reformatting itself as more family- and kid-friendly when it moved to the Friday night block.

Yet the ABC series that made the biggest splash in the 1990s was *Ellen*. A hang-out comedy in the style of *Friends*—although, like *Living Single*, it debuted before *Friends*—it was originally called *These Friends of Mine*, changing its title for the second season after *Friends* debuted. Like the other comedian-led comedies on the network, it focused on the gentle observational humor and light quirkiness of DeGeneres's comic persona, but this eventually was overwhelmed by speculation around DeGeneres's sexuality. This question was worked into the narrative of season four, with winking references to Ellen possibly coming out of the closet, until the two-part episode "The Puppy Episode" (so named as a reference to the network's suggestion that her character get a puppy rather than come out) in which she did, featuring a cavalcade of celebrities as both characters (Laura Dern, Oprah Winfrey) or themselves (Melissa Etheridge, Billy Bob Thornton). It was the highest rated episode of the series, and yet the series sank in the ratings following that, finally being canceled following its fifth season. Much of the critical conversation around the series at the time was that, following "The Puppy Episode," the series got "too gay" because it focused on Ellen's dating life, an element that had been part of the series all along.[20] The message at the time seemed to be that it was fine for Ellen's character to be gay, as long as she didn't do anything about it. Why *Will & Grace* succeeded in having a gay main character only a year later—albeit with a certain degree of nervousness on NBC's part[21]—while *Ellen* didn't, or experience the same level of backlash, might have been due to the fact that not only did *Will & Grace* not feature a same-sex kiss until its second season, but that Eric McCormack, who played Will Truman, was not gay himself.[22] That is, the line between character and actor was distinct in a way that some may have thought was not between Ellen Morgan (character) and DeGeneres herself. (This wasn't limited to sitcoms; shows such as *Dawson's Creek* [1998–2003] and *Buffy the Vampire Slayer* [1997–2003] had to fight for any displays of affection between gay characters.)

While NBC was dominating the landscape and ABC breaking new ground, CBS seemed to reach backwards a bit, with sitcoms featuring stars from previous successful sitcoms, including Harry Anderson (*Dave's World* [1993–1997]), Ted Danson (*Becker* [1998–2004]), and Bill Cosby (*Cosby* [1996–2000]), although often playing against the type they played on NBC, with Danson as a misanthropic physician rather than affable bartender, and Cosby as a more working-class man working in customer service forced into early retirement, although casting Phylicia Rashad as his wife was clearly inviting comparisons to his previous work. While *Murphy Brown* and *Cybill* (1995–1998) offered female leads (Candice Bergen and Cybill Shepherd, respectively) that built on their predecessors (such as *The Mary Tyler Moore Show*), its other series offered a more old-fashioned take on the genre, with the fish-out-of-water comedy of *The Nanny* (1993–1999), which paired Queens-born-and-bred Fran (Fran Drescher) with an elite British theater producer in Manhattan; the crazy in-laws trope of *Everybody Loves Raymond* (1996–2005); and the schlubby guy/hot wife pairing of *The King of Queens*, later mercilessly skewered on AMC's dramedy *Kevin Can Fuck*

Himself (2021–2022). Sticking with this classic sitcom structure, however, would prove successful for CBS in the 2000s.

Niche versus Mainstream: The 2000s

In 2004, the long-running sitcoms *Friends* and *Frasier* wound up their runs on NBC. While NBC attempted to keep things running with a spin-off centered around Joey Tribbiani (Matt LeBlanc), it was panned and ran only for two seasons. With no big hits for fall 2004, NBC dropped in the ratings as other networks rose. Most of them, including Fox, focused on the same multicamera setup that had characterized the sitcom for most of its life, as well as relying on traditional setups with (somewhat) updated trappings. CBS, in particular, went in this direction, with hang-out comedies *How I Met Your Mother* (2005–2014) and *Rules of Engagement* (2007–2013), as well as their biggest hits (created by Chuck Lorre): *Two and a Half Men* (2003–2015) and *The Big Bang Theory* (2007–2019). *Two and a Half Men* was "family-based" in the tradition of *Married ... with Children* in that while it was focused around two brothers, Charlie (Charlie Sheen) and Alan (Jon Cryer), and Alan's son, Jake (Angus T. Jones), the humor and situations would not be considered family-friendly in the traditional sense. *The Big Bang Theory*, with its group of friends (some of whom were coworkers) living either in the same building or nearby, borrowed some elements from *Friends* while focusing on a group of well-educated if socially awkward guys (that is, nerds).

For ABC, it offered a mix of the comedian-led—or at least known quantities—sitcoms that had brought it success in the 1990s, with *According to Jim* (Jim Belushi) (2001–2009), *8 Simple Rules for Dating My Teenager Daughter* (John Ritter) (2002–2005), and *George Lopez* (the title says it all) (2002–2007). The only other sitcoms that lasted longer than a season were workplace sitcom *Less than Perfect* (2002–2006), which got a significant amount of press for casting Sara Rue in the lead, as she was, at the time, considered "full-figured," and *Better Off Ted* (2009–2010).[23] *Better Off Ted* was the outlier on ABC, a corporate satire in which the main character, Ted Crisp (Jay Harrington), regularly breaks the fourth wall to comment on the essential horrible-ness of his workplace, Veridian Dynamics, a corporate conglomerate. The narrative was also interspersed with ads for Veridian Dynamics, usually related to the theme of the episode, that highlighted exactly how terrible they were.

Fox's schedule in the 2000s offered a combo of both traditional three-camera sitcoms, such as *That '70s Show* (teen hang-out/family) (1998–2006) or *'Til Death* (married couple) (2006–2010), with single-camera and more experimental fare, including *Malcolm in the Middle* (2000–2006), *The Bernie Mac Show* (2001–2006), and *Arrested Development* (2003–2006). (*The Simpsons*, of course, is ongoing.) All three of these broke the mold in different ways. For *Malcolm in the Middle*, centered around Malcolm (Frankie Muniz)—a certified child genius—and his dysfunctional family, the show not only broke the fourth wall (like the aforementioned *Better Off Ted*), but was a single-camera series shot on film, using no laugh track but plenty of sound effects, musical cues, odd camera angles, location shooting, and fast cuts, not unlike 1990s sitcom *Parker Lewis Can't Lose*. The comedian-led—and inspired—*The Bernie Mac Show* would also occasionally break the fourth wall so he could comment on the absurdities and issues in front of him, captions would appear to provide more information, and the character's celebrity position created a deep bench of guest stars that appeared on the series, from Chris Rock and Billy Crystal to Charles Barkley and Matt Damon, among many others. *Arrested Development*, with a film-based pedigree (Imagine Entertainment produced the series; Ron Howard served as narrator), was a critical darling despite its low ratings, offering a documentary aesthetic (without necessarily being a documentary) in a satire about wealth and privilege, with a dizzying array of musical, visual, and narrative gags that could perhaps best be appreciated through re-watching.

As for the so-called fifth and sixth networks (the WB and UPN), they closed their doors and merged into a single channel, the CW, in the summer of 2006. Before the shutdown, UPN debuted *All of Us* (2003–2007) in 2003, cocreated by Will and Jada Pinkett Smith, loosely based on their own lives, and *One on One* (2001–2006), about a sportscaster single dad, which offered the opportunity for a roster of guest stars, including Smokey Robinson and Solange Knowles. *Girlfriends* took up the mantle from *Living Single* to create a series focused on Black women's experiences in the workplace, home, and with one another, even with their differing backgrounds and experiences. Finally, *Everybody Hates Chris* (2005–2009), loosely based on Chris Rock's upbringing in the Bed-Stuy neighborhood of Brooklyn, debuted for UPN's final season as a network. Of these, only *One on One* was not brought over to air on the CW, giving the new network a decent roster of sitcoms as they started out. Neither of the two sitcoms that debuted during the WB's final year (*Modern Men* or *Living with Fran*) survived the merger.

For NBC, however, the ending of *Friends*, *Seinfeld*, *Will & Grace*, and *Frasier* led to a precipitous drop in their ratings; during the 2004/2005 season, they dropped behind Fox to become the fourth-rated network. Conversely, this offered the network the opportunity to be a bit more experimental, as evidenced by their best-received (if not highly rated) series of the 2000s. *The Office* debuted as a mid-season replacement in 2005, but failed to make much of an impression. An adaptation of the popular British mockumentary series, the first season made the same mistake as 2003's *Coupling*, in that it recycled the scripts from its UK source with only minor changes. (*Coupling*, created by Steven Moffat, was essentially the British version of *Friends*—although raunchier—which made adapting it for the United States while *Friends* was still airing a bit ridiculous.) In its second season, however, it began to form its own identity, making Steve Carrell's Michael Scott a warmer—if not less cringey—character than Ricky Gervais's David Brent. *My Name Is Earl* debuted in the fall of 2005, focusing on a ne'er-do-well named Earl Hickey (Jason Lee) who wins $100,000 on a lottery ticket and almost

Earl and his brother, Randy, try to fix Earl's karma. NBC/Photofest © NBC, Photographed by Paul Drinkwater.

immediately gets hit by a car. As he recovers, he hears Carson Daly on TV talking about karma, and decides to use his winnings to make amends to all the people he's hurt.

Scrubs debuted in 2001, an early entry into the single-camera, no laugh track sitcoms that NBC would embrace throughout the decade. Its fairly realistic hospital stories were aided by medical consultants, and the creative use of cutaways (main character J. D. [Zach Braff] frequently imagines various scenarios) and visuals owe an acknowledged debt to *Parker Lewis* as well as inspiring later series such as *Brooklyn Nine-Nine* (2013–2021). (*Scrubs* was also one of the few remaining series during the 2000s that did not air on the network whose studio produced it; it was produced by ABC's Buena Vista Television but aired on NBC.) By 2006, *30 Rock* was added to the lineup, a backstage comedy satirizing both TV tropes and creator Tina Fey's own experiences as head writer at *Saturday Night Live* and NBC more generally. Rounding out the roster was *Parks and Recreation* and *Community* (2009–2015), both of which debuted in 2009. *Parks and Recreation* was co-created by Greg Daniels (who had adapted *The Office* for US television) and Michael Schur as a gentle satire on local government. Like *The Office*, it debuted mid-season with six episodes and a similar mockumentary format; its main point of view character, Leslie Knope (Amy Poehler), also initially came across as a female Michael Scott. With its second season, however, Leslie was re-conceived as a competent, if overly enthusiastic and a bit bossy, administrator. The final series to debut was *Community*, created by Dan Harmon and, as I'll discuss throughout this book, incorporating many elements of the sitcom throughout its history. What all of these sitcoms airing on NBC have in common was their eschewing of traditional sitcom tropes and/or norms, either by skewering them (à la *30 Rock* and *Community*) or avoiding them in favor of new forms of address, such as the mockumentary. Critically lauded but low-rated, these series not only spoke to the increasingly fragmented viewership of broadcast TV going forward, but suggested new ways of looking at the format as it moved to platforms such as streaming.

2

Harmon's World
Creating *Community*

Every series has an origin story. Some are relatively simple: *Sanford and Son* and *All in the Family*, both created by Norman Lear, were adaptations of British series *Steptoe and Son* (1962–1974) and *Till Death Us Do Part* (1965–1975), respectively, although Lear and his team put their own stamp on the narrative and characters. (The dangers of not doing this were clear in the adaptation of Steven Moffat's *Coupling*, which simply repurposed the original scripts with a few changes to indicate the change of location, and to a lesser extent, the first season of the US version of *The Office*. *The Office* corrected itself by going its own way in season two; *Coupling* was canceled after four episodes.) With the greater focus on creators in the twenty-first century, viewers and fans can hear these stories through interviews or DVD extras in ways seemingly unavailable or unwanted for earlier shows like *Leave It to Beaver* or *The Facts of Life* (1979–1988). Indeed, with the internet and social media allowing fans to "talk back" to writers, actors, directors, and producers, television showrunners seem to have their own kind of celebrity, which can range from simply watching whatever they produce to cult followings like that which grew up around Joss Whedon. Or, in fact, Dan Harmon.

This chapter focuses on Harmon himself, from his brief stint at community college and start with the improv group Comedy Sportz in Milwaukee, to his collaboration with Rob Schrab to create Channel 101, a Los Angeles–based short film festival in which participants submit films in the form of television pilots, both of which informed his writing style (the "story circle") for his subsequent projects and provided opportunities in terms of learning to create pilots and making the connections that led to *Community*'s eventual debut. It will also touch on why showrunners like Harmon, despite some problematic behavior toward other writers or cast members, have a fandom of their own. Put simply, this chapter will focus on their interaction and openness with their fans and the potential consequences of this symbiotic relationship.

Comedy and Other Sportz: Dan Harmon before *Community*

In an interview not long after being ousted from *Community*, Dan Harmon connects his need for television to his own past: "I grew up watching it, and I connected to my own mother through it. We would sit side by side not looking at each other watching 'Cheers' and what my mom laughed at taught me what was funny. This box in our living room was babysitter, surrogate and ultimately God" and thus he "wanted to go out to L.A. and make the people on it talk."[1] While Harmon did in fact do just that, it was not a straight line, although not an unfamiliar one. That is, like many actors and writers since the 1970s (e.g., Eugene Levy, Jordan Peele, Chris Farley), Harmon's first foray into the industry was through improv. In 1996, he joined Comedy Sportz, an improvisational comedy organization started in his hometown of Milwaukee, although it currently has licensed organizations in twenty-eight cities, including in England and Germany. Unlike more traditional improv groups such as Second City, which functions as a theater troupe, Comedy Sportz is a competition between two teams of improvisors, judged either by a panel or the audience. There is an annual tournament, the "Comedy Sportz National

Tournament," held every year since 1988 on a rotating system of host cities (held online during the Covid-19 pandemic). Like Second City, it does have notable alumni; aside from Harmon himself, there is Jessica Williams (*The Daily Show* [1996–present]); Jason Sudeikis (*SNL*, *Ted Lasso* [2020–2023]); and Wayne Brady (*Whose Line Is It Anyway?* [1998–present]), among many others who would go on to work with Harmon on other projects.

Perhaps the most notable connection that Harmon made during his time with Comedy Sportz, however, was Rob Schrab, a fellow Wisconsinite. While Schrab's acknowledged first love is drawing and illustration, he early on branched into other creative areas, including improv comedy.[2] Harmon and Schrab connected through Comedy Sportz, although they gravitated to the Dead Alewives, a separate improv group spun off from Comedy Sportz and not beholden to their more family-friendly rules.[3] (There's a brief reference to it when Abed sports a Dead Alewives T-shirt in the episodes "Basic Story" and "Basic Sandwich" in season five.) One of the group's most memorable and well-regarded skits was based around a game of *Dungeons and Dragons*, a premise Harmon would revisit in two episodes of *Community*.[4] Yet it was Schrab's artwork that would end up being the duo's entrée into the entertainment industry: Schrab's comic book series *Scud: The Disposable Assassin*, debuted in 1994 and ran until 1998, with a four-issue finale released in 2008 (by Image Comics; original publisher Fireman Press had folded in 1998). The series blended humor and science fiction in its futuristic story about a world in which robots are available for purchase out of vending machines. Both Schrab and Harmon wrote issues, and in 1997, *Scud* was optioned by Oliver Stone's Illusion Entertainment. The pair traveled to Los Angeles in an attempt to convince the production company to let them write the script; however, they were turned down, and *Scud*'s option lapsed in 2000. (MTV later optioned it for a series, but it never made it beyond casting.)[5]

In 1999, the pair got the opportunity to create a pilot for Fox, one produced by Robert Greenblatt, who had already developed two of Fox's signature shows in the 1990s, *Beverly Hills, 90210* (1990–2000) and *Melrose Place* (1992–1999), among others. *Heat Vision and Jack* (1999), cowritten by Harmon and Schrab, also got Ben Stiller to direct the pilot, fresh off his Emmy win for his recently canceled Fox series *The Ben Stiller Show* (1990–1993), and starred Jack Black as Jack Austin, an astronaut overexposed to the sun and thus granted superintelligence (but only during the day), and his roommate, Doug (Owen Wilson), accidentally turned into a sentient motorcycle (Heat Vision) by Jack's nemesis, Ron Silver (Ron Silver), a NASA-trained killer intending to eliminate Jack. The penchant for meta reference and parody that *Community* would be known for is evident even in this early work, particularly the way it recalls the high-concept series of the 1970s and 1980s, like *The Six Million Dollar Man* (1973–1978) or *Knight Rider* (1982–1986). While well-known today, Black, Wilson, and Stiller—as well as Harmon and Schrab—were still on the cusp of the larger successes that would characterize their careers. While Fox elected not to go to series with it, it's interesting to contemplate what would have happened with their subsequent careers if it had, particularly since for Black, Wilson, Stiller, as well as Harmon and Schrab, their biggest successes were still in the future.

The failure of *Heat Vision and Jack* to go to series, however, sent Harmon and Schrab in a different direction. With neither *Scud* nor *Heat Vision* moving forward—or, as they put it, "banished from legitimate television"—the two initially decided to make their own content.[6] In 2001, Schrab invited friends over to watch *Jaws: The Revenge* (1987), with a caveat that anyone attending would create something that would predict the film's plot, in whatever medium they chose (i.e., short film, mixtape, etc). This ended up growing over the next two years, with more entries and a larger audience; they initially called it the Super Midnight Movie Show, and they held it at Improv Olympic West (in Los Angeles). Yet the space would prove to be too small and the amount of entries too overwhelming, so Schrab suggested it be held monthly, that entries be no longer than five minutes, and the audience would vote on which of these "pilots" were the best. It would thus be named Channel 101 (after the numbering convention for television episodes), an imaginary network for content that didn't fit on broadcast television.[7] It proved popular enough for a version to launch in New York (Channel 101: NY) with Harmon and Schrab's okay. These pilots also drew in notable names, including Drew Carey, Jack Black, Flavor Flav, Felicia Day, and Aziz Ansari. Acceptable.TV, an entry by Harmon and Schrab, was picked up for eight episodes on VH1, with Jack Black as executive producer, and was comprised of mini-episodes created by the Acceptable.TV writing staff and one from a viewer; the cast was also made up of Channel 101 contributors. It was also notable for a few skits written by Justin Roiland, who would go on to co-create *Rick and Morty* with Harmon after *Community* ended.

They did continue to try to break in to more mainstream productions, and after writing some scripts on spec, one was seen by director/producer Robert Zemeckis. He signed the duo to a two-film deal, out of which came the film *Monster House* (2006). *Monster House*, an animated horror comedy feature for younger audiences, ended up being released by Sony, who would later go on to produce *Community* for NBC. While the film was reviewed positively, including being nominated for Best Animated Feature at the 2007 Academy Awards, and featuring the voice talents of Catherine O'Hara, Jason Lee, Maggie Gyllenhaal, and Steve Buscemi, among others, Harmon and Schrab's script was revised by screenwriter Pamela Pattler, something Harmon seemed fairly upset about even years later, writing to a kid—at the behest of the child's mom—who'd been terrified by the movie, that "the movie you saw was not the story I wanted to tell you" before going on to diss both director Gil Kenan and executive producer Steven Spielberg.[8] In 2007, they did get the opportunity to cocreate, along with Sarah Silverman, *The Sarah Silverman Program* (2007–2010) for Comedy Central. Harmon, who was in charge of the writers' room, was let go after six episodes, attributed not to his writing skills but rather clashes between him and Silverman over the direction of the show and their respective positions within it; that is, that he alone could make it work. Harmon later put it like this: "When you're working on the Lucille Ball show with Lucille Ball, that's a pretty unprofessional attitude to take."[9] Schrab stayed with the series, which ran for three seasons, and Harmon and Silverman, by his account, remained friends. The firing also ended up being beneficial in the long run; unemployed, he began approaching network executives with an idea to do a sitcom about a study group at a community college, based on the semester and a half he spent in 2003 taking courses (Spanish, biology, and psychology) at Glendale Community College in Los Angeles, doing so, in his own words, to save his relationship with his then-girlfriend, also attending Glendale.[10] As Harmon puts it, while *Community* doesn't attempt to accurately replicate the community college experience (no one is using the series as a recruitment tool), the open admissions policy and variety of individuals attending were ideal from a creative standpoint, particularly for a television series that requires twenty-two stories a season.[11]

To write these stories, Dan Harmon developed what he called "story circles," a distillation of Joseph Campbell's hero's journey informed by his large consumption of television and film throughout his life. The circle works as follows: "1. A character is in a zone of comfort, 2. But they want something, 3. They enter an unfamiliar situation, 4. Adapt to it, 5. Get what they wanted, 6. Pay a heavy price for it, 7. Then return to their familiar situation, 8. Having changed."[12] He used these "story circles" for everything from sight gags to seasons, as well as individual episodes, and it is easy to see the structure from the pilot onwards.[13] Indeed, the pilot features Jeff thrown out of his comfortable situation (a cushy job as a lawyer), entering the unfamiliar world of Greendale in order to regain that life, and decides the fastest way to do so is to cheat his way through as he did to become a lawyer in the first place. Yet, when he seems to get what he wants, having manipulated former client/Greendale professor Ian Duncan (John Oliver) into giving him test answers, he realizes Ian double-crossed him, giving him nothing but blank pages. Having walked away from the nascent study group he had formed, they come to him, drawing him back to the group a (slightly) changed man.[14] On a season arc level, Pierce's story in season two also broadly follows this pattern, from his trampoline injury that broke his legs, caused because he didn't want to be left out, leaving him wheelchair-bound, which he adapts to by becoming addicted to painkillers. He eventually kicks the habit with the group's help, but by the end of the season, both he and the study group struggle to "return to their familiar situation" because of the changes wrought by Pierce's behavior.[15] In that instance, the change is a negative one; as the narrator says in "Advanced *Dungeons and Dragons*," where Pierce hits new behavioral lows: "And so it was that Pierce Hawthorne saved the life of Fat Neil while learning very, very little."[16] As showrunner and writer, Harmon had input on every script for the first three seasons, making adjustments as needed. Yet as a self-avowed perfectionist as well as a procrastinator, scripts would frequently be late and shoots would run long, exhausting both cast and crew.[17] Things finally hit a breaking point near the end of the third season, amid an ongoing feud with Chevy Chase (including playing one of Chase's expletive-filled voicemails aloud on his podcast *Harmontown* and having the crew chant and swear at him during the season three wrap party)[18] and Harmon's admittance to being a "ninja of alcoholism,"[19] leading to his ouster by both NBC and Sony, to be replaced by Moses Port and David Guarascio, who had created the multicamera sitcoms *Happy Endings* (2011–2013) for NBC and *Aliens in America* (2007–2008) for the CW. Harmon was brought back for the fifth season, following fan outcry and Joel McHale applying pressure behind the scenes. Despite the challenges of late nights and Harmon's often erratic behavior, the cast seemed to take it in stride, with Allison Brie suggesting that the show felt "rudderless" without him, and that Harmon would be the one to challenge the network on their behalf.[20] Harmon was able to see the series through its final two seasons.

With Great Power: The Rise of the TV Showrunner

On May 3, 1948, the Supreme Court ruled on the case *United States v. Paramount Pictures*, brought against Paramount by the Southern District of New York for violation of antitrust laws. Basically, because Paramount, and the major Hollywood studios more generally, not only owned studios but the theaters that exhibited the pictures, meaning since they had sole determination which films were shown in which theaters (controlling both production and distribution), they constituted a monopoly. This became known as the Paramount Decree, and essentially broke up the studio system. Prior to this, studios wielded an enormous amount of power over actors, directors, and writers, including what was known as the Hays Code, which put strict controls on content deemed offensive. Forced to divest themselves of their theaters, studios had less of a say in what films would be shown; it also brought about the rise in independent theaters, which could show either studio-produced, independent, or foreign films. They also began opening their lots to filmmakers and studios not affiliated with the majors, and ceased the long-term contracts that bound casts and crew to a single studio. They were free to negotiate, making films for multiple studios rather than being held to one (or, in some cases, loaned out to another studio at an executive's behest). Further, this gave directors more creative freedom, leading to the rise of the director auteur that came to fruition in the 1970s, including Francis Ford Coppola and Martin Scorsese (both of whom got their starts with the B-movie superstar company American International Pictures) and Michael Cimino, among others. Steven Spielberg and George Lucas also came of (professional) age during this era, although their work—particularly Lucas's—pointed in the direction of the blockbuster-ridden 1980s rather than the character studies of their contemporaries. This shift put more emphasis on the producing side, with blockbusters such as *Jaws* (1975) and *Star Wars* (1977) pointing the way forward, a trend that continued throughout the 1980s, and in many respects, never truly went away. It also helped that certain high-profile failures, such as director Michael Cimino's *Heaven's Gate* (1980), ended with studios again exerting more control over directors and spelling the end of the director auteur phase to a great degree.[21] The 1984 film *Irreconcilable Differences*, while focusing primarily on the breakdown of the marriage between aspiring—and then successful—director Albert (Ryan O'Neil) and his wife, writer Lucy (Shelley Long), and its effect on their neglected daughter, Casey (Drew Barrymore), parodies this type of runaway production helmed by a megalomaniacal director with Albert's film *Atlanta* (2016–2022), which bombs and destroys his career. The film was loosely based on the breakdown of the marriage of another 1970s director auteur, Peter Bogdanovich, with his wife, producer Polly Platt, after he had an affair with Cybill Sheppard,[22] which Platt herself suggested "got more right than wrong."[23]

Television's trajectory has somewhat mirrored that of film. Once the studio system broke down, one solution presented itself in the advent of television, which initially separated itself from its more critically regarded sibling by focusing on live programming, although the live era didn't last long. Film studios saw an opportunity to create content along the lines of B-movies; that is, featuring less well-known actors, writers, and directors; using sets often built for film but going unused. (As per example, an area of Warner Brothers backlot known as "Midwest Street" can be seen in *Rebel Without a Cause* [1957] and *The Music Man* [1962], as well as *Gilmore Girls* [2000–2007] and *Pretty Little Liars* [2010–2017]. The reconstruction of the house from *The Waltons* [1972–1981]—the original was lost in a fire but rebuilt for the follow-up TV films—also served as the Dragonfly Inn on *Gilmore Girls*.)[24] Given the ubiquity of television in homes by the mid-1950s, and the possibility of children watching, it is probably no surprise that Disney was an early studio to get involved with television, with series such as *The Wonderful World of Disney* (1954–present) and *The Mickey Mouse Club* (1955–1996).

Yet, unlike film, independent productions got a much earlier, and successful, start in television history than in film. In particular, Desilu Productions, the independent production company started by Lucille Ball and Desi Arnaz, not only produced *I Love Lucy*, but also dramas and sitcoms, some of which, such as *The Untouchables* (1959–1963) and *Star Trek* (1966–1969), were critically successful and/or culturally significant. During this early television era, however, it was the studios as producers that tended to garner the most attention; that is, insofar as the average viewer paid attention to those behind the scenes, programs were produced and distributed by studios such as Warner Brothers, Universal, or Disney and starred particular individuals, with less attention paid to writers, episode directors, or showrunners. These affiliated studios could thus produce programs, and air them on their stations, making independent production companies, such as Desilu, a rarity; the cost barrier to entry was too high for smaller companies to compete.

This changed, however, with the adoption of the financial incentive and syndication rule, known as "fin-syn," in 1970. While, as noted above, independent production companies could do well, before the implementation of fin-syn, networks tended to own a majority of the programs they aired, meaning that they got the larger share of the profits. Fin-syn changed this. Networks could only air fifteen hours of their own created programming per week, opening up opportunities for independent productions because the studio/network programs would have to compete with them on the open market (e.g., NBC/Universal could create a sitcom, but it would likely have to air on ABC or CBS; they would "license" it to the other network). It also allowed the independent companies to retain ownership of their work; networks could run it no more than twice (initial broadcast; first syndication) and the producer would then be free to sell it into syndication themselves and keep the profits.[25] While it took time to fully implement, the 1970s and 1980s ended up being the high point for independent companies, including Norman Lear's Tandem Productions, MTM, Stephen J. Cannell, and Aaron Spelling. Some of these were associated with particular channels, with many of Lear's and MTM's programming debuting on CBS, or Aaron Spelling Television's near-exclusive relationship with ABC. These production companies frequently had many series airing, with producers such as Spelling or Lear staying primarily on the production side rather than the writing or showrunning one. Some blended both; Stephen J. Cannell wrote episodes for many of his series, such as *The Rockford Files* (1974–1980) or *21 Jump Street* (1987–1991), and Sherwood Schwartz served as showrunner (and occasional writer) for both *Gilligan's Island* (1964–1967) and *The Brady Bunch*.

If there was a single series, however, that brought the role of showrunner to prominence over that of producer, it was likely *The X-Files* (1993–2002). That's not to say it was the first; US television's earliest fandom, as we understand it today, with conventions, ancillary products, and fan-created work, was *Star Trek*, making its creator, Gene Roddenberry, the first fan-known showrunner. Further, *The Twilight Zone* (1959–1964) was not only created by Rod Serling (although owned by CBS/Paramount), but Serling wrote ninety-two of the original series' 152 episodes and served as host; he is inextricably linked with the series. Yet *The X-Files* had the advantage of debuting in 1993, just as the internet was coming into use, which would become an easier way for fans to communicate with creators and actors as well as one another than the fanzines and (occasional) conventions that characterized fan meetups in the past. *The X-Files* is often considered the first internet fandom.[26] Because Chris Carter himself did not have either a website or social media presence—and did not attend a huge amount of conventions—discussion about *The X-Files*, its characters and storylines, and Carter himself was more one-sided than would be seen with later showrunners.

The combination of the internet coming into general use, and the revoking of the fin-syn rule, which led to the creation of the first new broadcast channels since DuMont went off the air in 1954 (Fox in 1986; the WB and UPN in 1995), were surprisingly instrumental in ushering in this new era. In order to set themselves apart from the "Big Three," all three channels initially targeted underserved TV demographics, including audiences of color and teen viewers. On Fox, that led to groundbreaking programs such as *Living Single*, which former NBC president Warren Littlefield listed as his biggest regret in not picking up, as well as sketch show *In Living Color*, created by Keenan Ivory Wayans and featuring an almost-entirely Black cast. It not only launched the careers of most of the Wayans family, but also Jamie Foxx and Jim Carrey.[27] Both the WB and UPN also offered opportunities to creators and actors of color, including Steve Harvey (*The Steve Harvey Show*, see Chapter 1), Robert Townsend (*The Parent 'Hood*), Marlon and Shawn Wayans (*The Wayans Brothers*), and Jamie Foxx (*The Jamie Foxx Show*) on the WB, and Will and Jada Pinckett Smith (*All of Us*), Mara Brock Akil (*Girlfriends*), D. L. Hughley (*The Hughleys* [1998–2002]), Ralph Farquhar/Sara V. Finney/Vida Spears (*Moesha/The Parkers*), and Chris Rock/Ali LeRoi (*Everybody Hates Chris*) on UPN. Yet, on the WB in particular, this turn toward attracting a more diverse audience was overwhelmed by the possibility of attracting a teen one; the surprising success of mid-season replacement *Buffy the Vampire Slayer* meant that WB shifted its focus to teen/young adult drama rather than the sitcom format where creators of color had dominated. Shows like *Dawson's Creek*, *Roswell* (1999–2002), and *Charmed* (1998–2006) followed in its wake, but none had as active a fanbase as *Buffy*.

Essentially, *Buffy*, and its creator/showrunner Joss Whedon, arrived at a fairly ideal time for it, and Whedon, to succeed. Debuting as a mid-season replacement for the short-lived *Savannah* (1996–1997, a prime-time soap produced by Aaron Spelling) and based on a film from 1992, it seemed unlikely *Buffy* would last beyond those first twelve episodes. Both *Savannah* (the WB's first hour-long drama) and *Buffy* were considered cross-programming, meant to appeal to female audiences the way Fox's Monday comedy block during that time was oriented toward male audiences. Its blend of comedy, drama, and horror resonated with audiences—Emily Nussbaum called it a "mythic, feminist-inflected meld of horror, comedy, and teen drama"—and the relationship between Buffy (Sarah Michelle Gellar), destined to kill vampires and demons, and Angel (David Boreanaz), a vampire with a soul who loses it when he and Buffy consummate their relationship and he reverts to his soulless alter ego, Angelus, was a significant factor in cementing the series as a cult classic.[28] While long story and character arcs weren't unknown on television, they tended to be limited to the daytime and prime-time soaps. *Buffy* embraced that aesthetic, with both its stories and characters able to develop throughout the series' seven seasons. That this followed the era of the "very special episode," in which sitcom characters could go through horrific trauma (death, assault, etc.) only for the next episode to continue as if nothing happened made the series' focus on actions' consequences all the more resonant.

Yet Whedon's engagement with fans made him a celebrity in his own right, connected to but separate from his work. He was the first third-generation television writer, with his grandfather John working on early series such as *The Donna Reed Show* (1958–1966) and *Leave It to Beaver*, and his father, Tom, on *The Golden Girls* (1985–1992) and *The Electric Company* (1971–1977), among others. He and others such as David Chase were considered television auteurs in a structurally similar way to the director auteurs of the 1970s, although the difference in medium means that "a television auteur must be seen at once as an effective boss and an inspired genius."[29] Whedon's professions of being a feminist—not a common claim even in the 1990s—and support of causes like Equality Now seemed to mark him as a different breed of creator. The website Whedonesque, created in 2002 to keep fans up-to-date on *Buffy* and other Whedon productions, ended up attracting attention from Whedon and staff writers, who started posting as themselves and engaging with viewers. Indeed, Whedonesque, and Whedon's posting on it during the 2007–2008 Writers Guild strike, kept fans updated on the strike's progress and even led to pro-strike activity on their part, such as sending pizza to the striking writers and contacting the Alliance of Motion Picture and Television Producers on the writers' behalf. *Star Wars* fans disappointed by the release of the first prequel film in 1999 made up T-shirts reading "Joss Whedon Is

My Master Now" through sites such as CafePress. He would give speeches and interviews underscoring his feminist leanings. Coming on the heels of the backlash in the late 1980s against female-led sitcoms such as *Roseanne*, whose star was excoriated for what were considered uncouth behavior and a loud mouth or *Murphy Brown*, whose storyline where she elected to have a child without marrying, drew criticism from President George H. W. Bush and Vice President Dan Quayle, among many others—a series featuring a teen girl who could fight for herself, make mistakes, and grow and develop, along with those around her, still seemed revolutionary.

While perhaps not as prominent, other showrunners during this time (1997–2015) also garnered fans of their own, including: Eric Kripke (*Supernatural* [2005–2020], *Timeless* [2016–2018], *The Boys* [2019–present]); Rob Thomas (*Veronica Mars* [2004–2007], *Party Down* [2009–2010, 2023]); Amy Sherman-Palladino (*Gilmore Girls*, *The Marvelous Mrs. Maisel* [2017–2023]); and Shonda Rhimes (*Grey's Anatomy* [2005–present], *How to Get Away with Murder* [2014–2020]), willing to watch new series they created, or even, in the case of Thomas, help fund a follow-up film to his signature series, *Veronica Mars*, canceled after its third season. What many of these showrunners share is, like Whedon, a signature style, as with Sherman-Palladino's rapid-fire dialogue and pop-culture savvy as an element of all of her series. Of them, however, Dan Harmon likely shares the most with Whedon in terms of garnering his own fanbase connected to and yet separate from his signature series. Aside from his earlier work, and *Community*, Harmon also started the podcast *Harmontown* in 2012, in which he shared any number of details about his work and life; in his words, "I can't trust therapists, but I've always worshipped audiences."[30] This cuts both ways, however; by making himself open to his fans, it can at first empower them, only to morph into entitlement. In an interview with *GQ*, Harmon says: "I'll go, 'I ate a cupcake today,' and they're like, 'Stop eatin' cupcakes and write the fuckin' show, you piece of shit!'"[31] This is referring specifically to *Rick and Morty* fans, the same ones who lost their minds over McDonald's bringing back Szechuan sauce for a single day, which ran out quickly, after the episode "The Rickshank Redemption" referenced the short-lived dipping sauce.[32]

Like Whedon or Sherman-Palladino, the ways in which he wrote *Community*, even on episodes on which he was not credited, reinforce his particular vision, making him the focus despite others' contributions. And like the aforementioned other two, his absence from the series he created in the fourth season was reflected in the writing and characterization to the show's detriment (according to its viewers and fans). Sherman-Palladino in particular is a good corollary; after leaving, following *Gilmore Girls'* sixth season due to a contract dispute with the network, most of the show's fans felt its seventh season was not the same show, given how much of its writing she did. She later claimed never to have watched the seventh and final season of the show, a fact apparent when the show was briefly revived in 2016, which either made no reference to or ignored the developments of the final season.

Yet this level of control, combined with adulation from fans, can frequently cover a multitude of sins. As Maureen Ryan writes in her analysis of the

Harmon's follow-up had even more rabid fans. Adult Swim/Photofest © Adult Swim.

toxic power dynamics in Hollywood, too many people were allowed to "do whatever they wanted, no matter how counterproductive, time-consuming, money-draining, or damaging" because "[t]heir bad behavior was considered a necessary accessory to their creativity, passion, drive, dedication, artistic boldness, and vision."[33] This is descriptive of a wide range of individuals, but within television, revelations regarding the toxic nature of sets ramped up in the late 2010s and early 2020s, on series such as *Buffy the Vampire Slayer/Angel* (1999–2004), *Lost* (2004–2010), and *Sleepy Hollow* (2013–2017), among others. (*Saturday Night Live* (1975–present) has been a long-term offender in that regard, with reports of bad behavior in almost every era of the series.) Perhaps what sets Dan Harmon apart is that it was well known—mentioned by both the actors and Harmon himself—about the long hours, Harmon's procrastination leading to last-minute scripts or rewrites,[34] and his struggles with alcohol, by the time Harmon was fired after the third season.[35] Yet, like so many other "genius" TV showrunners, he was allowed, for a time, to get away with it because of the idea that "difficult" and "creative" are inseparable, and was rehired for the final two seasons of the show. Nor was this the end of it; in 2018, Megan Ganz came forward to indicate she'd been mistreated by Harmon, although she did not share details. Instead, it was Harmon who confessed what he had done: he'd asked her out, she'd turned him down, and he, in his own words, decided to "teach her a lesson" for that rejection. "He owned up to having had a lack of 'respect for women on a fundamental level' and berated himself for getting away with it 'by not thinking about it'" when he discussed it on *Harmontown*; Ganz not only accepted his apology but called it "a master class in How to Apologize."[36] Still, this culture is too often left to fester; as Annemarie Navar-Gill writes in her analysis of the relationship between fans and creators: "In an era where large coalition audiences are a thing of the past, and narrower, deeply engaged active audiences have increased value, the ability to inspire fan community makes Harmon exceptionally valuable to corporate television producers, forcing them to overlook other issues with his management."[37] That one could replace Harmon's name with so many others speaks to a continuing toxic culture in entertainment that too frequently encompasses both showrunners and fans.

Harmon's career leading up to *Community*—and, one could argue, beyond it—does suggest the expected dose of luck that characterizes anyone's career success, but also the ways in which Harmon, and those he collaborated with, made use of the opportunities that arose out of their work. Like many before him, improv offered a foot in the door, but when things didn't work out as expected, he made use of tools unique to this particular era: the internet. When Harmon and Schrab's pilot for *Heat Vision and Jack* was rejected, there was Channel 101, which combined a live film festival with an internet community that opened doors for both. For *Community* itself, the fanbase around both the series and Harmon himself kept it alive when in other television eras, its viewing numbers would not have merited a full first season. Harmon, and his career, in many respects embodies the shifts in television discussed above, not only the shifts in viewing habits, but also the ways in which television itself has mirrored the progress of film, from production-led media to the showrunner auteur. That this consists of both positive developments (an increase in variety of and outlets for programs) and negative ones (the numerous reports of bad behavior left unchecked across multiple levels of the industry) is, sadly, par for the course.

3

The Greendale Seven

A series lives and dies on its cast and the characters they embody. Based on Harmon's community college past, this chapter will focus on the process of casting the series, from early hire Chevy Chase and what each character was meant to embody versus what actually made it on screen. As the series jokes about throughout, despite the setting, the stories and characterization revolve around the dynamic between the seven community college students and the world of Greendale; this chapter will focus on both the process of casting the series and arcs of these characters through the series' run.

"Casting Was 95% of Putting the Show Together": Building *Community*

While in the streaming era, it's become almost commonplace for film stars to appear in series (limited or otherwise), even in 2009, it was still fairly rare for a film actor to appear as a main cast member on a weekly television series. In the case of Chevy Chase, who got his start on TV (*Saturday Night Live*), it was perhaps even more surprising, given his last ill-fated foray on the medium: *The Chevy Chase Show* (1993). Created in the wake of Johnny Carson's retirement from *The Tonight Show* (1962–1992), with all the networks hoping for a slice of the late-night pie, Chase's talk show lasted all of six episodes and the reactions were brutal, including calling it the "sort of disaster TV fans will recall for their grandchildren" and a "mind-deadening, Chevy-centric rut."[1] Chase would later say that what aired was not what he conceptualized it to be: "What I wanted had a whole different feel to it, much darker and more improv. But we never got there."[2]

That type of reaction could certainly give one pause about doing episodic television again, but in an interview, Chase suggests he was won over by Harmon's writing. "Speaking with him, you can see that he's very articulate and thoughtful and confused ... about anything outside of himself. But his writing was so funny."[3] Like the prime-time soaps of the 1980s, which offered late-career opportunities to actors such as Lana Turner, Diahann Carroll, or Rock Hudson, *Community* was an opportunity for Chase, whose last box-office success had been *Christmas Vacation* (1989). While other actors were considered for the role of Pierce Hawthorne, including John Cleese, Fred Willard, and Patrick Stewart, Sony, the series production company, insisted on Chase, as he had significant name recognition.[4] (Willard would later appear as an alternate reality version of Pierce in the series finale.) That being said, the blending of Pierce as a character with Chase's own persona makes the casting seem inevitable.

As for the rest of the cast, Harmon indicates he had "no juicy answers for this"; that is, it ended up being a combination, like many series, of luck and good auditions. This was likely aided by Harmon's flexibility in conceiving the characters, with Jeff as "a handsome version of me," Abed based on a friend he nearly cast before Danny Pudi auditioned for the role, and Troy a "teenage Woody Harrelson" until he saw Donald Glover at work. While he admits to ripping off the character of Tracy Flick (Reese Witherspoon) in *Election* (1999) for conceptualizing Annie (which Brie suggests fairly well), the idea of a Mary Steenburgen–type for Shirley went out of the window, as he thought, "Yvette's [Nicole Brown] versatility was more valuable to me."[5] As for Britta, Gillian Jacobs was not how he conceived of the character (he suggests "Jo from *Facts of Life*") but thought Jacobs was "an obvious natural dramatic talent" that would work for the character. Harmon also admits he was lucky, as they had foregone a "chemistry" read with the whole cast before filming, and yet the cast meshed together well. This would prove to be vital because, as discussed in Chapter 2, the challenges of Harmon's working style would lead to long hours due to late scripts and last-minute changes. Nevertheless, *Community* became one of the new crop of sitcoms in the 2000s that eschewed not only the laugh tracks but the static characterizations of the multicamera era. The study group can thus be viewed as evolving, devolving, or remaining fairly consistent.

Evolving

Jeff Winger: Typical Protagonist?

As discussed earlier, the premise of the series was based on Harmon's own experience of community college as an adult, down to starting a study group in order to spend time with a woman he was interested in. In that respect, Jeff Winger could be seen as a Harmon avatar. Yet, as with many protagonists on long-running series, he is a reflection of those he surrounds himself with, and they reflect aspects of his (potential) character. He is introduced in the pilot episode as an amoral grifter, needing to return to college to earn his bachelor's degree after he is outed to his law firm as not having obtained it. That is, as former client/Greendale professor Ian Duncan (John Oliver) says: "I thought you had a bachelor's from Columbia," Jeff can only reply: "Now I have to get one from America."[6] Indeed, his first goal is basically to pressure Duncan, whom he got off a DUI when he was still a practicing lawyer, to help him cheat his way to finishing quickly so he can return to his former life. While Duncan thinks it over, Jeff meets Britta (Gillian Jacobs), a fellow student in his Spanish class, and asks her to study with him as a way to get closer. Britta seemingly sees through Jeff, and invites several others to join them, all of whom will make up the bulk of the core group through the first four seasons. Yet for Jeff, these new people are disposable; once Duncan comes through, Jeff leaves the group, only to find that Duncan has tricked him. In order to pass his language requirement, he needs this group. This is the first moment of change for Jeff; not only must he rely on others and actually do the work to finish his degree (to an extent, at least), but he is no longer a part of his old life, in which his amorality is normalized, celebrated, and present in almost all of his old colleagues.[7]

Jeff characterizes himself, particularly in the early seasons, as wanting nothing more than to get out of Greendale and back to his former life. And yet, the numerous times when this is offered as an option, he turns it down. The most significant one occurs during "Introduction to Finality," when he goes up against Alan (Rob Corddry), his rival at his old law firm (and the one who turned him in to the state bar for not having a bachelor's degree).[8] Shirley and Pierce are at odds over the ownership of a sandwich shop they were planning to open together in the school's cafeteria. Pierce, who is wealthy, is a client at Jeff's old firm. Shirley asks Jeff to represent her interests. Alan, who has a more powerful position at the firm in Jeff's absence, promises him his old job back if he sells out his friends, not wanting the firm to lose "cash cow" Pierce. Jeff eventually elects to do the right thing, zealously defending Shirley's interests; this impresses Pierce, who agrees to work with Shirley and fires Alan.

One trait Jeff never loses is the assumption that he is in charge of the group, and he rarely reacts well when that's challenged. In "Contemporary American Poultry" (a riff on *GoodFellas*), his plan to ensure the study group gets the chicken fingers everybody loves but the cafeteria always runs out of (they get the fry cook, Alex [Dino Stamatopoulos] replaced by Abed) eventually gets him pushed out of the group when Abed uses his power as chicken finger producer to give the study group everything they could possibly want. When they start to take it for granted, however, Abed and Jeff eventually come to an understanding, and the balance seems to be restored.[9] In season three, Jeff finds himself on the outs again, when he is kicked out of the biology class they are taking that semester for using his phone. Pierce, who had been on the outs for the latter half of the previous season, gets Jeff's place in class, and Jeff slowly morphs into a younger version of Pierce, both in his rage at being left out and making a racist assumption. (Pierce eventually takes the blame, telling Jeff he's used to being the bad guy.)[10]

Jeff, as a young white guy, thinking he's in charge by default is, in many ways, part of the series' overall metatextual take on the sitcom genre, particularly in the ways Jeff grows and changes throughout the series. Putting aside the fourth season, which had different showrunners who brought their own take to *Community*, Jeff's attempts to maintain an ironic distance from both his friends and the various shenanigans in which they all engage, become increasingly difficult to maintain. After he graduates at the end of season four and returns to his law practice, he maintains contact with the study group. Abed produces and directs the commercial for Jeff's new private law practice, which he has dedicated to helping those in need, rather than reaching for money or power.[11] (Abed portrays him as a superhero in the commercial.) Within a year, his practice is forced to close; he is broke and jobless. Alan reappears, offering him the opportunity to recoup his losses by suing Greendale. While Jeff initially goes along with this, convincing the reconvened study group that Greendale has left them worse off than before they arrived, the interaction itself reignites their connection. Jeff takes a job teaching at Greendale, and the group's new mission is to save the ailing school, a mission that will take the series through to its conclusion.[12]

Jeff's arc throughout the series is all about the ways in which Greendale changes him. By the end of the series, although its members have changed and shifted since the fifth season, it is Jeff who has the hardest time letting go. There are fears about growing older (more so after Pierce dies, making Jeff one of the oldest members of the study group); his fortieth birthday inspires a meltdown that involves him overdosing on herbal medication and hallucinating himself and the study group in an episode of the 1980s *G.I. Joe* (1983–1986) cartoon.[13] And while he still makes noises about leaving Greendale, it's actually Annie and Abed who leave in the final episode, while Jeff imagines increasingly complex "plots" to keep them as part of the group and leave the dynamic (mostly) unchanged.[14] His journey is essentially about learning to be part of the group, rather than the leader, and the final shot of the remaining group seems to underline that, as they share drinks and chat around a table in a bar.

Troy: Embracing Your Inner Nerd

Troy's arc, until he leaves near the start of season five, is subtler than Jeff's, but they do share some similarities. For both Troy and Jeff, Greendale is a significant shift from where both of them thought they would be: Jeff's legal career is (temporarily) over, and Troy went from a star football player (and prom king) in high school to (in theory) just another student among many at Greendale. An injury derailed his final year of playing; it is soon revealed that Troy injured himself on purpose.[15] In the first few episodes of the series, however, Troy still clings to his identity as a jock and star (including wearing his letter jacket), and consequently is frequently paired with Pierce in these early stories. (Pierce also struggles with his relevance, or lack thereof.)

It's Troy's connection with Abed, however, that marks the first big shift in his character. While they appear together in Professor Duncan's psychology experiment, it is the next episode that truly represents the start of their friendship.[16] "Advanced Criminal Law" shows Troy teasing Abed by telling him obvious lies (e.g., that he's Barack Obama's nephew); he eventually comes clean, and Abed, more amused than offended, attempts to make a few jokes of his own, like pretending he is an alien. The amount of work Abed puts into the illusion unnerves Troy, and they come to an agreement not to prank one another anymore. The mark of things to come really shows up in the stinger at the end of the episode, a scene in which Troy and Abed compete to see how many pencils they can cram into their mouths.[17] These stingers, featuring Troy and Abed, become a regular thing as the series continues. Abed, who unashamedly appreciates what might be considered "geeky" things, including *Dungeons and Dragons*, 1980s-era B-movies, and the series' riff on *Doctor Who* called Inspector Spacetime, allows Troy to start embracing those things too. There is a sense that he is torn between Jeff's detached, cool approach and Abed's unsubtle enjoyment of things, which comes to a head in "Epidemiology." One of the few Halloween episodes of the series, the episode plays out at a Greendale costume party, where Abed and Troy dress as the xenomorph and Ripley in the P-5000 Power Work Loader, respectively. When he is rebuffed by two girls he tries to hit on, Jeff suggests Troy isn't coming across as a prospect but rather reminding them of "taking their little brothers to Comic-Con." He changes out of his costume into one he calls "Sexy Dracula." When the party takes a dark turn—that is, everybody starts turning into zombies—it is Abed and Troy's knowledge and embrace of horror movie tropes and geeky interests rather than Jeff's cool detachment that help him to survive and reverse the effects.[18] Troy viewing Jeff as a role model is possibly dealt a fatal blow in "Mixology Certification," when the group takes Troy out for his twenty-first birthday. Annie, Jeff, Britta, and Abed all get drunk, with Jeff and Britta not only making out on the way home, but realizing the bar each mocked the other for liking was actually the same bar. Troy, who ended up remaining sober, realizes that, despite being older, Jeff has little to teach him, a fact Jeff himself acknowledges. "You're a man now," he tells Troy. (This, of course, is followed by a stinger featuring Abed and Troy trying to figure out how many T-shirts they can put on.)[19]

While Jeff and Troy do butt heads on who is in charge, most notably during the paintball battle at the end of season two, he does still occasionally look to him for lessons on how to be a man.[20] Despite that, Troy increasingly embraces his geekier side with Abed and softer, more emotional approach in several situations. He "sacrifices" himself (that is, he gives in to the pressure of the dean of the Air Conditioning Repair School, who doesn't allow their students to fraternize with other Greendale students) to save the study group, followed by Troy forcing them to integrate their classes and students with regular Greendale.[21] Season four, however, seems to stall all the characters' growth, leaving behind the more arc-based structure of the first three seasons for a more typical sitcom's one-and-done stories. Troy does embark on a relationship with Britta, a story that had been teased in a few episodes, but in practice comes across as awkward and forced, and is over by "Basic Human Anatomy," when they agree it's not working (via a Freaky Friday tribute in which Troy and Abed pretend to switch bodies).[22]

Troy's final turn comes when Pierce dies. After putting the study group through a grueling lie detector test, he bequeaths them various items, but to Troy, he leaves his boat and the bulk of his fortune. The caveat is that Troy live out Pierce's dream to sail around the world, since he never did. After some debate, Troy realizes this is an opportunity to, as Pierce suggests, discover himself. While his decision causes Abed a significant amount of distress, they get around it by deciding that Troy, Abed, and the rest of the study group have been reborn as clones, and therefore are stronger, braver, and less sad at Troy's departure.[23] Troy sails off with LeVar Burton (there to make sure Troy completes the mission); his "clone" is no longer afraid either to leave or to talk to LeVar Burton, a personal hero he'd met once before and was incapable of interacting with.[24] As the emotional heart of the group, however, Troy's departure also represents a shift in the series itself; his absence represents the shifting dynamics that will characterize the remainder of the series.

Annie: Growing Up

While only a year younger than Troy, Annie initially comes across as much younger. Like Troy, with whom she went to high school and harbored a crush on, her life took an unexpected turn in her senior year: she became addicted to Adderall in an attempt to maintain her academic standing and ended up in rehab. After losing scholarships and being cut off by her parents, Annie tries to rebuild her life. She keeps the competitive spirit that led to her earlier achievement, and yet tends to keep quiet about the challenges she faces, including living in a dangerous neighborhood with limited financial resources. It takes Pierce following her home when he catches her collecting aluminum cans to recycle for cash for her to admit to anyone she is struggling; he offers her financial assistance, but soon reveals an ulterior motive for his generosity that makes her regret it, and she doesn't open up to anyone about it again.[25] Indeed, it's only after Troy discovers a gun in her purse, which she bought for protection, that her living situation becomes clear to the entire study group.[26] (Troy and Abed suggest she move in with them, and she takes them up on their offer, although not without some initial challenges as they try to adjust to living together.)[27]

For much of the early seasons, Annie is still negotiating the transition from childhood to adulthood, at least psychologically and socially. Part of this is internal and part external; that is, she will, for instance, throw a tantrum during a Model UN session when she doesn't get her way, and her interactions with Jeff after they kiss at the end of the first season are designed to make both Jeff and the audience uncomfortable in the way they underscore the pair's age difference.[28] The external factors, however, relate to the way that the group as a whole—minus Troy, who knew her before Greendale—tend to treat her as the "baby" of the group. In "Romantic Expressionism," Britta and Jeff elect to take on the roles of the group's "parents" by preventing Annie from dating Britta's ex-boyfriend, a hacky-sack player named Vaughn (Eric Christian Olsen). In Jeff's words: "Her taste in men is still being established. Creepier and creepier dudes will start thinking of her as an option, and it all starts with Vaughn. He's a gateway douche bag." They try to enlist Troy, whom Annie had a crush on in high school, to date her instead, but it all goes wrong, and Annie is furious that they don't respect her enough to make her own decision. Both concede that Annie is capable of making her own decisions, and she dates Vaughn until he is recruited for a hacky-sack team out of state.[29] She debates going with him, but ultimately decides to stay at Greendale, and she and Jeff share a kiss as the episode ends, something he tries to disavow at the start of season two.

The dynamic between Jeff and Annie remains fraught until the end of the series, as the age difference between the two (approximately fifteen years) troubles Jeff enough to keep her at arm's length. Annie, however, spends this time figuring out precisely what she wants from her professional life, even as her personal life remains in limbo. She takes health administration classes to see if that might be a viable option, before settling on criminal justice, which the show subtly suggests in their parody of *Law & Order*.[30] At the end of the series, she accepts an internship with the FBI, and her departure finally leads to an honest conversation between the two of them, in which they seem to realize their attraction may be based on Annie's longing for maturity and Jeff's missing of his youth, freeing her to seek out her own path and make her own mistakes.

Devolving

Pierce: Old White Man Says ...

Airing almost three years before the debut of *Community*, the *Law & Order* episode "In Vino Veritas" offered Chevy Chase a role markedly different from the comedic ones that made him famous in the 1980s. Based on the July 2006 arrest of Mel Gibson for driving while under the influence, during which he launched into an anti-Semitic tirade, Chase plays Mitch Carroll, a washed-up actor arrested for driving under the influence, who not only harasses the female officer (calling her "sugar tits") but accuses her of spearheading a Jewish conspiracy to make him look bad. Chase plays it as both angry and clueless as to what he's done wrong; later, when his son is implicated in a hate crime, he shrugs off any idea that he was responsible for his son's behavior.[31]

This is a similar energy to that Chase brings to Pierce Hawthorne. The heir to the Hawthorne moist towelette empire, Pierce is a mainstay at Greendale, taking various classes with no seeming plans to graduate. The oldest member of the study group by a considerable degree, Pierce comes across as out-of-touch, both in thinking he is younger (and hipper) than he is, and in his interactions with others, which tend to border on—and often cross into—racist and sexist ideas that he seems completely unaware are such. (Had the series aired more recently, Pierce would be the one decrying "wokeness" ruining comedy.) These include his assumption that Abed is a terrorist because he's Muslim, and mixing up Shirley with other Black women on campus. He occasionally shows flashes of self-awareness; when Jeff points out that his ex-stepdaughter is only spending time with him to get money, he not only confesses that he knows, but also comforts Jeff over his recent breakup.[32] When he is temporarily kicked out of the study group after trying to keep up with Troy and Abed's race to pull pranks by pantsing Shirley, the two of them actually end up bonding over how they feel left out due to their ages and different circumstances. Pierce, who won't apologize, instead tells her: "I respect you more than anyone else in the group ... you are a strong, dignified woman who's raising a family, a bigger accomplishment than anybody else in that room. And nobody can ever strip you of that, not even me."[33]

Instead of building on this, however, Pierce as a character takes a darker turn in season two, becoming addicted to painkillers following an accident brought on by his own paranoia at being excluded.[34] The painkillers only sharpen these tendencies, and with a few exceptions (he helps Abed through his holiday meltdown when Abed's mother cancels their Christmas plans), he sinks deeper into villain territory, particularly in "Advanced *Dungeons and Dragons*."[35] His rage at being excluded (mostly because the group was worried

Pierce's outdated views infect even his fantasies. NBC/Photofest © NBC.

he'd say something insensitive to the troubled Greendale student, Neil [Charley Koontz], they were attempting to help) leads him to take over the game and direct his nastier remarks at the one he feels is usurping his place in the group. While he does actually ending up helping Neil, both by revealing who gave him the "Fat Neil" nickname that caused Neil so much distress, as well as giving Neil something to fight against, Pierce learns nothing.[36] Later, while he's recovering in the hospital for a near-overdose on his pain medication, he decides essentially to torture nearly every person in the study group (with the exception of Annie), including telling Jeff he's contacted Jeff's long-lost father, giving Britta a check for $10,000 to see if she'll live up to her espoused principles and donate it, and giving Shirley a CD he claims is the study group talking about what they really think about her. When he is confronted, he rages at the group for ignoring him and not taking him seriously.[37] In the final episode of the season, he finally admits that he has trouble keeping friends, and therefore sabotages his relationships, before leaving the group entirely.[38]

The third season does add some nuance to his character, when it becomes clear his upbringing, particularly his racist, distant father, is responsible for many of Pierce's flaws.[39] His father's death does free him a bit, and the revelation of a half-brother, Gilbert (Giancarlo Esposito), offers him a new family dynamic.[40] Unfortunately, real-life events behind the scenes, including the growing tension between Harmon and Chase, lead to Harmon's ouster and new showrunners to be brought in for the fourth season. Chase, however, was still dissatisfied with the direction of Pierce's character as a bigoted old man, which led to him walking off the set during the filming of "Advanced Documentary Filmmaking." (He also used the *n*-word before storming off. As episode director Jay Chandrasekhar makes clear, however, this was not directed at anyone but rather "political"; i.e., that the direction they were taking Pierce in meant Pierce saying [even worse] racial slurs was inevitable.) While he does graduate from Greendale at the end of the season, he remains perpetually stuck as the aging, attention-needing Baby Boomer, appearing as a hologram in "Repilot" before the reveal that he has died after masturbating himself to death, suggesting that he learned little throughout his time at Greendale after all.[41]

Britta: Getting Britta-d

One element that tends to be downplayed throughout the run of *Community* is that it is, in fact, Britta who brings the study group together during the pilot. Jeff, noticing Britta early in the episode, offers himself up as a tutor, claiming that he is good at Spanish, as a pretext to being alone with her. It's obvious Britta sees through this ploy, and tests Jeff by inviting several other people in their shared class to form a study group. In the early episodes, she is generally the first to speak up about social causes and human rights abuses, although she struggles with taking action. When Shirley and Annie take action after she talks about imprisoned Guatemalan journalists, organizing a protest and vigil,

Britta at first disparages their efforts before recognizing her own limitations (she talks but doesn't act) and joins in.[42]

The Britta of season one is sometimes a killjoy, occasionally a hypocrite, but generally on an upward character arc. While often over-the-top—she compares being asked to empty her bag when Annie's pen goes missing to the abuses of the PATRIOT Act and "Gitmo"—she isn't actually wrong; it is a violation of privacy and breach of trust.[43] She sees through Jeff's ploys to get her attention, is willing to admit when she's wrong, and undermines her own "cool" image to do something she enjoys, such as taking a modern dance class and performing in front of the school.[44] When she cheats on a Spanish test, she comes forward when Ben Chang (Ken Jeong), their Spanish teacher, threatens to fail the entire class.[45] It's Britta, along with Jeff, who tries to help Abed when he starts to see everything in Claymation.[46] In the first paintball episode, "Modern Warfare," in which the prize is priority registration, she vows to give it to Shirley if she wins, so Shirley can spend more time with her kids, despite Jeff accusing her of being performative. Indeed, she ends up being one of the last two standing, sacrificing herself so Jeff can confront the dean about offering a prize he couldn't make good on. Seemingly inspired by this, Jeff actually does what Britta promised, and gives the priority registration to Shirley.[47]

This, unfortunately, is the high-water mark for Britta's character, and "Modern Warfare" also represents the start of this downward spiral. Trapped in the study room, the two jokingly give in to the sexual tension the study group has noticed between them and sleep together. While both seem inclined to dismiss it as a fluke, the end of the season has Britta confessing her love to Jeff in public when he seems inclined to get back together with an ex.[48] At the start of season two, she is embarrassed to face Greendale—and the study group—again, only to find a significant group of people who praise her for being brave and loathe Jeff for leaving her exposed to ridicule. Both trapped in their own anger at the other, they end up almost getting married in a game of one-upmanship.[49] Things don't improve for Britta after this; Troy and Abed accuse her of "ruining" guys they like to hang out with by dating them and then sharing things about them with the pair.⁵⁰ She gets jealous of a friend arrested for protesting in Syria and pulls several stunts at Greendale in an attempt to keep up.⁵¹ Her decision to major in psychology leads to numerous attempts to use her limited knowledge to diagnose or treat other members of the group.⁵² The combination leads to the group coining the term *Britta-d* to describe making a huge mistake based on bad judgment.

Yet Britta's lowest point might actually come in season six, when we finally meet her parents, George (Martin Mull) and Deb (Lesley Ann Warren). When she elects to move in with Annie and Abed, a new couch is delivered to the apartment under the name "Perry," and she deduces that it is a gift from her parents. Abed and Annie then reveal that her parents have been giving them money for years either to get Britta things she needs or loaning her funds, so she would not know it was from them. At this point in the narrative, Britta's reaction is not surprising; she confronts her parents, who come across as

Britta struggles to act maturely in front of her parents. NBC/Photofest © NBC.

kind and well-meaning. When she realizes Annie and Abed are already there, she storms out, and, unable to start her car to leave, steals a tricycle from a neighborhood child and rides off.

While her parents reveal to Annie that they overprotected her as a child, and are trying to keep their distance and allow her independence, none of this reflects well on Britta, and is a far cry from the character who called out Jeff in the pilot episode.[53] (It should be noted that Harmon himself did not think that Britta was dumbed down, but was in fact "one of the most sophisticated characters in TV comedy.")[54]

Slight Shifts

Abed: "Self-Esteem Falling Out of My Butt"

In other sitcoms, a character like Abed, who admits he's "on the spectrum," might be subjected to a story in which he learns his value despite being "different" from others, or learns how to fit into social situations.[55] Instead, within *Community*, his friends in the study group simply make allowances for the ways his reactions or thoughts differ from theirs. Not without some degree of conflict; at one point, Jeff yells at him to "stop being meta": "Why do you always take whatever happens and shove it up its own ass?"[56] In season five, new group member Buzz Hickey (Jonathan Banks) has little patience for Abed's behavior, at least until Abed helps him reconnect with his son.[57]

Essentially, Abed likes television, creating imaginary worlds, and having fun with Troy, most of which doesn't change throughout the series. He will frequently create personas for himself based on popular culture suited to the situation, allowing him to, as per example, put on a Don Draper persona to be suave, or cosplay Harrison Ford as Han Solo in "For a Few Paintballs More."[58] While Troy is almost always willing to go along with these scenarios—or create a few of his own—the rest of the study group also seem to enjoy playing along. Annie plays Leia to Abed's Han Solo as well as joins him in what he and Troy dubbed the "Dreamatorium" to act out scenes from the in-universe show *Inspector Spacetime*. Even Jeff happily plays Hawkeye to Abed's Radar when Abed re-conceives Jeff's role as editor-in-chief of the school paper as a *M*A*S*H* tribute, down to Jeff dressing the part and drinking martinis from a home-made still.[59] Indeed, despite his occasional grouchiness at Abed's behavior, he plans an elaborate *Pulp Fiction*-themed birthday party for Abed and even buys him a pricey replica of the briefcase from the film.[60]

He struggles to adapt to change, whether it's relatively minor, like changing clocks for Daylight Savings Time, or more serious (usually involving Troy).[61] When Troy agrees to cut off contact with the study group in exchange for the Air Conditioning Repair School helping them out of a sticky situation, Abed adopts the persona of the Abed from the "darkest timeline," first by reducing Britta to tears and then going after Jeff.[62] When Annie tries to set up Britta and Troy, Abed retreats into the Dreamatorium. Annie follows him there, only for him to use their imaginary scenarios to enact a brutal takedown of why she did it.[63] While he admits he has trouble reading expressions and nuances, he is good at analyzing individuals and generally knows how to approach particular situations. In "Introduction to Film," when Britta finds out Abed can't take a film class because his father forbids it, she pays for it. Abed spends the episode filming both Britta and Jeff in different situations, driving them crazy, before cutting it into a film in which he superimposed his parents' faces over Britta and Jeff's. His father, Gobi (Iqbal Theba), understands immediately that the film is implying that Abed believes his father blames him for the divorce (something they'd never discussed). Gobi realizes that this is the best and easiest way for Abed to communicate and agrees to let him pursue film studies.[64] The study group becomes briefly convinced Abed can predict the future when they see his short films that seem to mirror what they've done, but were created before the events they portray. Abed shrugs this off, indicating that he knows them well enough to predict their reactions.[65]

Abed remains remarkably consistent throughout the series. That is, sharply observant, confident in himself, and most comfortable viewing life through the lens of popular culture. It is not surprising, then, that in the final episode he reveals he's gotten a job as a production assistant for a television series, and will be moving away. Perhaps the biggest indicator of Abed's growth is yet another meta moment, when he speaks to both his friends and the audience about television:

> It's TV, it's comfort. It's a friend you've known so well, and for so long you just let it be with you and it needs to be okay for it to have a bad day or phone in a day. And it needs to be okay for it to get on a boat with LeVar Burton and never come back. Because eventually, it all will.[66]

He doesn't change much, but in the end becomes a bit more comfortable with the process.

Shirley: "That's Nice"

As a character, Shirley should have provided numerous storylines for the writers of *Community*. She's got a compelling backstory revealed across multiple episodes, including a hard-drinking past, a recent divorce after her husband leaves her for a stripper, and taking business classes at Greendale with an eye to opening her own baked goods business.[67] She is overtly Christian, going so far as attempting to covertly convert both Annie, who's Jewish, and Abed, who is Muslim, and frequently openly disdainful of the morality of others in the study group. She speaks in a soft voice that masks a deep-seated rage.

And yet few stories, particularly when compared with Jeff, Britta, Troy, and Abed, revolve primarily around Shirley. There is the ongoing saga of her ex-husband, Andre (Malcolm Jamal Warner), whom she reconnects with offscreen in season two, only for her to discover she'd slept with Ben Chang during the Halloween party nobody remembered.[68] When she discovers she's pregnant, she is unsure if Ben or Andre is the father, and tries to hide that ambiguity from him. It, of course, is eventually revealed, and Andre storms out, seemingly for good. Yet Jeff discovers him just outside the school, and in a surprising turn, Andre reveals that what happened between Shirley and Chang never would have occurred if he'd not cheated himself, and commits to raising the child whether or not he's the father.[69] The two eventually decide to remarry in season three, although Shirley's desire for more independence clashes with Andre's for things to return to normal, and the wedding nearly doesn't happen. It takes Jeff and Britta acting ridiculous for Andre and Shirley to come to an understanding, and they go through with the wedding.[70] She does open a sandwich shop on campus, fulfilling part of her dream; unfortunately, the start of season five reveals that Andre left her—and took their kids—because she was neglecting them in favor of her business. In what might be the final indignity, when Yvette Nicole Brown leaves at the end of the fifth season to care for her ailing father, Shirley as a character doesn't even get a send-off episode in the vein of Troy's sailing away or Pierce's hologram and the reading of his will.[71] Instead, her fate is relegated to a stinger at the start of season six; Abed indicates she was "spun off," followed by a promo for a (fake) new series called "The Butcher and the Baker," in which Shirley becomes the personal chef of a depressed police detective in Atlanta and helps him solve the murder of his wife.[72]

Shirley doesn't get as much nuance, beyond her religiosity and her relationship with Andre, throughout the series. One stand-out is the reveal of her past in "Foosball and Nocturnal Vigilantism." When a group of German students take over the rec center at Greendale, noisily playing foosball, Jeff confronts them; they agree to stop if Jeff can score a point off of them. He fails; they mock him. More determined to beat them, Jeff practices there late at night, which is where Shirley finds him. She shows him some moves, and he

Shirley briefly gets the spotlight. NBC/Photofest © NBC.

begs her to teach him. Reluctantly—as she doesn't like what the game brings out in her—she agrees, only for that same competitive streak to emerge again. Later, the two discuss why foosball is important to them; Jeff because he was humiliated at it as a kid, not long after his father walked out, and Shirley because it was a release at a time when she was being teased for developing early. She quit when she made an opponent pee his pants after she won by jamming the foosball bar into his crotch, earning him the nickname "Tinkletown." That, of course, was the humiliation Jeff was referring to; contrary to a season four episode that purports to explain the backstory of what brought the group to Greendale, Shirley and Jeff actually met as kids (Shirley was "Big Cheddar" to Jeff's "Tinkletown").[73] They hash out their long-buried rage in an anime-style foosball battle, and when they face the Germans again, manage to work together to defeat them, before walking off hand-in-hand (shown as their child selves rather than adults).[74] Sadly, this episode was the exception rather than the rule when it came to Shirley. Even an episode set at her house on

Thanksgiving barely features her, as the study group hides out from her family in the garage.[75] While she does become (slightly) more tolerant and (slightly) less passive-aggressive throughout the seasons, the series didn't take enough advantage of the stories her character could have offered.

As suggested above, *Community* came out during a time when sitcoms were drifting away from the multicamera setup and employing more of a "memory" in terms of plot and character; that is, plot development and character growth weren't limited to a single episode but could have repercussions that played out over multiple seasons. Even when the characters steadfastly refused to grow and change, like the Bluths on *Arrested Development*, the show was filled with callbacks, Easter eggs, and joke setups that could take episodes or even seasons to pay off. The series that surrounded *Community* on the schedule—*The Office*, *30 Rock*, and *Parks and Recreation*—all evinced these changes to varying degrees, particularly *Parks and Recreation*, which recalibrated its main character, Leslie Knope (Amy Poehler), following its short first season, and continued developing her and those around her throughout its run. Indeed, cocreator Michael Schur took this idea further in *The Good Place* (2016–2020), by structuring it like a novel, down to naming each episode "Chapter [Number]." The blending of casting and plot in *Community* allowed a particular flexibility in how the story developed and helped cement this newer breed of sitcom as the way forward.

PART TWO

Chaos Theory: *Community*'s Characters and Narrative

4

"Our School May Be a Toilet, but It's Our Toilet"

Community and Schools on TV

Given the fact that, in the United States, one of the most common shared experiences is at least eight to twelve years of attending school, it's surprising that school, as a setting, is not more common on television. Or, rather, one in which the school is the primary setting; teen dramas, from *Buffy the Vampire Slayer* to *On My Block* (2018–2021), frequently split stories between school, home, and social lives. School-based series, from grade school to college, are not the most common genre on US television, but nonetheless have been a part of each era, whether through dramas such as *Mr. Novak* (1963–1965) or mockumentary (*Abbott Elementary* [2021–present]). Surprisingly few of them, however, take place primarily on college campuses, and *Community* may be the first to be set entirely in a community college rather than a four-year institution. This chapter will offer a brief trip through school series on television, which tend to fit into two broad categories—student-focused and teacher-focused—and the way *Community* plays with, and occasionally subverts, that structure.

Still Learning: Teacher-Focused Stories

Can US television be educational? In other countries, such as England, the first stations to broadcast were public service stations, such as the BBC, and it was written into their charter that they must include an educational element in their programming.[1] The United States, however, started with a commercial service transitioned from radio, with only National Education Television, which would offer five-hour blocks of documentaries and imported programming (as well as distance learning classes), launched in 1954 as a noncommercial network. (It was later replaced by PBS in 1970.)

Yet US TV's focus on commercially supported programs doesn't mean that there can't be an educational element to any number of series outside of either public broadcasting or news. The Ad Council, created in 1941 by James Young, cofounder of the Young and Rubicon ad agency, has been providing free public service announcements (PSAs) for both radio and television since the Second World War, including Smokey Bear's warnings about forest fires (first airing in 1944), Nancy Reagan's "Just Say No" antidrug campaign, and 2015's "Love Has No Labels" focus on diversity and inclusion (and the first PSA to win an Emmy). What came to be known as "Very Special Episodes" also attempted to educate viewers, particularly younger ones, about the dangers of drunk driving (such as *Growing Pains*' "Second Chance," in which Carol Seaver's [Tracey Gold] boyfriend Sandy [Matthew Perry] drives drunk and dies) or stranger danger/predatory behavior (*Diff'rent Strokes*' (1978–1986) "The Bicycle Man" two-parter was notorious among 1980s kids).[2] These episodes were frequently followed by cast members providing information to the audience about hotlines and other resources for those who might need help. In the late 1990s and early 2000s, network executives, advertisers, and the Office of National Drug Control Policy (ONDCP) colluded to create antidrug and -drinking content that could be subtly—or not-so-subtly—incorporated in teen sitcoms' and dramas' narrative, particularly those on the WB.[3]

There are other, less obvious ways that TV shows offer information or education through their stories. Series such as *Bones* (2005–2017) or *The Good Place* will often employ a subject-matter expert to ensure that there is at least some degree of accuracy in the portrayal of forensic science (*Bones*) or philosophy (*The Good Place*). Within individual shows, the "knowledgeable" character will often be paired with one who knows little of the subject and is thus educated—along with the audience—when he or she explains about bone fractures or Immanuel Kant. In that respect, setting a series in a school seems to be an ideal venue for "educating" audiences about any number of things, although most of the time what the audience learns is more about the job of teaching rather than particular subjects. This was the case from one of the earliest teacher-based TV series: *Our Miss Brooks*, which transitioned over from radio, ran from 1952 to 1956, and even spawned a film. The stories on the series shifted between issues within the school, particularly around money or supplies, and Connie Brooks's (Eve Arden) personal life, including her feelings for fellow teacher Philip Boynton (Robert Rockwell), and relationships with other teachers and administration. In many respects, the series set the standard for future school sitcoms, including featuring a few memorable students who occasionally get their own side stories (Walter Denton [Richard Crenna] suggests future teen characters such as Steve Urkel [Jaleel White] on *Family Matters* and Arnold Horshack [Ron Palillo] on *Welcome Back, Kotter* [1975–1979].) *Mr. Peepers*, which debuted the same year, offered a similar structure while focusing on Robinson J. Peepers (Wally Cox) as he starts a new job as a junior high science teacher in Jefferson City, Missouri. He deals with the challenges of teaching science in a comedic way and develops a crush (that eventually ends in marriage) on school nurse Nancy Remington (Patricia Benoit). *Mr. Novak*, a drama rather than a sitcom, offered a blend of stories built around teachers and students, although most of it was filtered through the perspective of new teacher John Novak (James Franciscus), and was lauded for dealing with topics rarely touched on in other series, including racism, drug abuse, and anti-Semitism; it later won a Peabody Award for its realistic take on the profession and education content. *Room 222* (1969–1974), an early dramedy, was also noted for not only featuring an African American lead (Lloyd Haynes) and a diverse cast (extremely rare in late 1960s/early 1970s television) but also focusing on topical stories (as did *Mr. Novak*), including the war in Vietnam, school violence, teen pregnancy, and drug use. *The Bill Cosby Show* (1969–1971) featured Cosby as Chet Kincaid, a physical education teacher, marking it as the first of the "named" sitcoms to feature an African American lead. As with the others, the series' two seasons offered a mix of Chet's school and home life, although it differed from other sitcoms of the era in two significant ways: the use of earlier African American stars such as Rex Ingram and Lillian Randolph in supporting roles, and Cosby's insistence that no laugh track be used. (*Everybody Hates Chris* would later adopt a similar policy, with recurring characters played by past sitcom stars such as Todd Bridges [*Diff'rent Strokes*] and Ernest Lee Thomas [*What's Happening!!* (1976–1979)], among others.) While the stories tended toward gentle life lessons, a few focused on more serious subjects, including the final episode, in which a kid on Chet's Little League team has to decide between playing or sitting out due to his religious beliefs (i.e., a game played on the Sabbath).

The life lessons approach used by *The Bill Cosby Show* eventually won out. By the late 1970s, however, the school-based series tended to be less politically motivated (with the exception of *The White Shadow* [1978–1981], which was one of the earliest dramas to feature a majority Black cast) and more focused on pranks and generation-gap-motivated hijinks. *Welcome Back, Kotter* focused on both Gabe Kotter (Gabe Kaplan) as teacher and the students in his remedial education class (known as the Sweathogs), one that he had been a part of when he was in high school. The generation gap is not between Kotter and his students, who became a big part of his personal and professional life, but between Kotter/the Sweathogs and the school administration, particularly

Vice Principal Michael Woodman (John Sylvester White). *Head of the Class* took a similar tack, although in this instance it was a group of gifted rather than remedial students, anchored by the laid-back Charlie Moore, who inspires them to look beyond their individual skills and abilities and engage more with the world, although it fits better into the student-based sitcoms, as the viewer sees little of Mr. Moore's personal or home life (unlike Kotter, whose wife was a supporting cast member and whose apartment is a second set). While many of the situations on the series were typical (worries about grades or dating), the series is notable for being the first US television series to film episodes in Moscow.[4]

This lack of focus on the real-world issues of teaching that series like *Room 222* or *The White Shadow* dealt with continued into the 1990s and the early 2000s, even on dramas like *Boston Public*, which frequently showcased spectacle (e.g., a student who wants to be a stripper) rather than the challenges of funding, supplies, or political interference.[5] *Hangin' with Mr. Cooper* was part of ABC's TGIF lineup, airing for most of its run after *Full House*; Mark Cooper (Mark Curry) was a former NBA player who becomes a substitute teacher/coach, with episodes switching between his work at various schools and his personal life. *The Steve Harvey Show* followed a similar format to *Our Miss Brooks*; that is, Harvey's character, Steve Hightower, forms friendly relationships with a few students at Booker T. Washington High, but most of the stories revolve around the adults in the series and their professional and romantic entanglements. That his character is a former musician does allow the series to work in guest appearances by a number of then-contemporary musicians, including Snoop Dogg, Sean Combs, Busta Rhymes, and Brian McKnight. *A. P. Bio* offered a mix of *Head of the Class* (substitute teacher in charge of gifted students) and *Community*, in that Jack (Glenn Howerton) takes the job only after he loses his dream job to a rival, and uses his students' intelligence to run scams that primarily benefit him, a move that the early version of Jeff Winger would have approved of. Indeed, it wouldn't be until the debut of *Abbott Elementary* in 2021, which focuses on a majority Black school in Philadelphia and uses a mockumentary format akin to *The Office*, where a teacher-focused sitcom would explicitly and frequently address such issues, including having to purchase their own school supplies, outdated equipment, borderline unsafe conditions, and the rise of charter schools siphoning money and students from the public school system.[6] Indeed, the charter school storyline was a significant part of the series' first season, allowing a fairly nuanced discussion over numerous episodes as to whether they were destructive to public schools or offering more opportunities to students. As with the other series, the students don't generally get much of the spotlight (with a few notable instances, as when one doesn't show up for school for several days), but rather the effects of these issues on the teachers' abilities to provide education for them.[7] *English Teacher* (2024), which aired on both cable and streaming (FX), blends comedy and drama in the half-hour format, while touching on some of the same socially relevant topics that *Abbott* does.

Learning and Growing: Student-Based Stories

Given the dramatic physical and emotional shifts that comprise adolescence, it's perhaps not surprising that a majority of series about school from the students' perspective tend to be dramas. The 1990s, in fact, were a high-water mark for teen dramas, with the debut of *Beverly Hills, 90210* in 1990, and the formation of the WB netlet channel, which offered series such as *Buffy the Vampire Slayer*, *Dawson's Creek*, *Roswell*, and *Felicity* (1998–2002; a rare college teen drama) as a significant part of their programming. (UPN got in on the trend with *Veronica Mars*, whose first two seasons were based in high school.)

But earlier shows did not always have the same division between student and teacher stories; shows like *Head of the Class* and *Welcome Back, Kotter*, as discussed above, offered a blend of plots that featured either or both. Many still also blend school and home life, with teachers often serving as supporting characters both in and out of the classroom. One of the earliest examples, representing a move away from teacher stories such as *Our Miss Brooks* and *Mr. Peepers*, was *The Many Loves of Dobie Gillis* (1959–1963). While Dobie (Dwayne Hickman) and his friends graduated from high school at the midpoint of the second season, the story continued through a brief stint in the army with his best friend Maynard G. Krebs (Bob Denver) and on to college for the remainder of the series, something later dramas such as *Dawson's Creek*, *90210*, and *Buffy* would adopt.[8] As evidenced by the title, regardless of setting, Dobie's main focus was finding the right woman—or the right-now woman—that would make him happy, with most of the classroom stories focused on how they affect his love life. While not discussed as much as other 1950s/1960s sitcoms like *Leave It to Beaver* or *The Addams Family*, *Dobie Gillis* actually served as the inspiration for both *Happy Days* and *Scooby-Doo, Where Are You?* (1969–1970, 1978), with Fred as Dobie; Daphne as Dobie's long-term crush, Thalia; Velma as Zelda, who nursed a long-term crush on Dobie; and Shaggy as beatnik-inspired Maynard.[9] Even the transitioning of high school teacher Mr. Pomfritt (William Schallert) to the university when Dobie and friends start college is echoed in the later series *Boy Meets World*.

The 1970s and 1980s school sitcoms have primarily been discussed above, although there are still a few that focused more on students. *Square Pegs* (1982–1983), created by Anne Beatts, who wrote for *National Lampoon* and *Saturday Night Live*, lasted a single season on CBS, but its legacy stretched beyond that. The series opens with Patty (Sarah Jessica Parker) and Lauren's (Amy Linker) first day as freshmen at Weemawee High School, where it becomes abundantly and immediately clear that they are misfits (i.e., "square pegs") in the high school hierarchy. Many of the episodes revolve around their attempts to fit in with the cooler kids, as well as developing their own circle of friends outside of it. Like *The Bill Cosby Show* in the 1960s, *Square Pegs* broke new ground by virtue of having a female showrunner and a primarily female writers' room and directors (still a rarity in television). It also offered an extensive list of guest stars, both from *SNL* (Father Guido Sarducci, Bill Murray) and then-contemporary music (Devo plays a bat mitzvah; The Waitresses play a school dance as well as the series' theme song).[10] The combination of music, guest stars, and a focus on the "misfits" of high school predate John Hughes's *Sixteen Candles* (1984) by almost two years. Beyond that, shows such as *Freaks and Geeks* (1999–2000) could be considered *Square Pegs'* direct descendants. *It's Your Move* (1984–1985), itself a series a bit ahead of its time with its teen antihero protagonist, was fairly equally split between Matthew Burton's (Jason Bateman) home life, with an older sister and a widowed mother, and school, in which Matthew enacts various schemes, including creating a fictional band out of biology class skeletons to play a school dance to cover for his friend Eli (Adam Sadowsky) losing the money to hire a musical act; it ends up so successful that Matthew has to fake the band's death to maintain the secret.[11]

Before leaving the 1980s entirely, there was one series that did not air in prime time, but had a significant amount of popularity and pop culture longevity either way: *Saved by the Bell* (1989–1993). It originally debuted on the Disney Channel as *Good Morning, Miss Bliss* (1988–1989), featuring Hayley Mills as the titular Miss Bliss at John F. Kennedy Junior High in Indianapolis. Following the structure of shows like *Head of the Class*, it focused on both teacher and students, as well as the occasional interaction with Principal Belding (Dennis Haskins). When Disney canceled it after a single season, NBC, which had produced the series, reclaimed, relocated, and renamed it to *Saved by the Bell*, eliminating the Miss Bliss character, transitioning it to high school, moving the location to Los Angeles, and refocusing the stories on the teen characters almost exclusively, with Zack Morris (Mark-Paul Gosselaar) as the main point-of-view character. Unlike the *Miss Bliss* years, classroom scenes were overwhelmed by the teens' stories, particularly Zack's various plans and schemes, a character who owes an unacknowledged debt to Bateman's on

It's Your Move, with the primary adult character Principal Belding, who seemed to vacillate between putting a stop to Zack's actions and participating in them. The series did make some prime-time viewings, with a couple of "vacation" specials and a short-lived college-based spin-off, before going off the air, only to be resurrected for streaming in 2020. Unlike the source material, the spin-off actually garnered some critical respect before being canceled in 2021.

It was in the 1990s, though, that teen sitcoms and dramas set in schools really took off. Aside from the aforementioned teen dramas, the WB also offered *Smart Guy* (1997–1999), about a boy genius who starts high school, as well as picking up the final season of *Sabrina the Teenage Witch* from ABC, which featured the eponymous Sabrina (Melissa Joan Hart) attempting to navigate high school, home, and her magical powers, which she will occasionally use to make her high school experience more palatable (e.g., turning resident mean girl Libby [Jenna Leigh Green] into a pineapple on her first day of school).[12] They picked up *Sister, Sister* (1994–1999) from ABC as well, airing four additional seasons about twins separated at birth (à la *The Parent Trap* [1961, 1998]) reuniting and getting to know one another and their new circumstances. *Boy Meets World*, which was part of the same ABC programming block as shows like *Full House*, focused on Corey (Ben Savage) and his best friend Shawn (Rider Strong) and friend turned love interest Topanga (Danielle Fishel), with Corey's neighbor/teacher Mr. Feeney (William Daniels) offering them lessons both in and out of school; like the aforementioned *Dobie Gillis*, Mr. Feeney also follows them when the show transitions to a college setting for its final seasons. The other netlet, UPN, picked up syndicated show *Sweet Valley High* (1994–1997), based on the book series, for its final season to air in prime time, but would not pick up another school-focused series again until the debut of *Veronica Mars* in 2004, with *Everybody Hates Chris* debuting in UPN's final year and subsequently transferring to the CW. While *Everybody Hates Chris*, based on Chris Rock's childhood, did divide its time between school and home life, following the challenges Chris (Tyler James Williams) faces when his family moves to Bedford–Stuyvesant, Brooklyn, touching on elements similar series didn't, particularly the challenges of being the only Black kid at a predominantly white school, meaning Chris dealt with both aggression (class bullies) and micro-aggressions (the assumption he can play basketball well due to his color).[13] (Williams, who played the young Chris, would go on to play teacher Gregory Eddie on *Abbott Elementary*.)

It's significant that the majority of these series did not air on the Big Three networks, which tended to default to seeking a broader audience. When they did try to air series skewed to a particular demographic (like teens), it tended not to be successful, as when NBC attempted to adapt 1985's *Ferris Bueller's Day Off* into a half-hour sitcom in 1990. While it represented an early role for Jennifer Aniston, the series did not get off to the best start by suggesting the "film version" of *Ferris* was a lie, followed by the TV Ferris (Charlie Schlatter) chainsawing a cardboard cutout of Matthew Broderick.[14] Its thirteen-episode run focused primarily on the high school setting, and the hijinks in which Ferris, his best friend Cameron (Brandon Douglas), and love interest Sloan (Ami Dolenz) can get away with under the watchful eye of Principal Rooney (Richard Riehle). It was not well-reviewed, and is still discussed today as a poor adaptation of a popular film.[15] The other factor was the Fox network's more successful gloss on the material: *Parker Lewis Can't Lose*.

In *Parker Lewis*, the students of Santo Domingo High School spend precious little time in actual classes; the main focus is Parker (Corin Nemic) and his friends Jerry (Troy Slatten) and Mikey (Billy Jayne), and the various schemes they pull, as well as avoiding the wrath of Principal Grace Musso (Melanie Chartoff). It was less about the educational system than the social matrix of high school overall. While such a plot doesn't break any new narrative ground, *Parker Lewis* was notable for the ways it mixed various film and television influences (including cartoons), and the risks it took with both its self-aware style (Parker addresses the audience regularly) and its cinematography (e.g., mounting a camera on a guitar). They managed to bring in guest stars such as Ziggy Marley, Kool Moe Dee, Young MC, Weird Al Yankovic, and even director Robert Zemeckis within its first two seasons. Later showrunners such as Bill Lawrence (*Scrubs*) cite the series as an inspiration for their own work, particularly in terms of directing. The series' awareness of contemporary pop culture was evident, with episodes built around the movie *Heathers* (1988; "Heather the Class") and the animated version of *Beauty and the Beast* (1990; "Beauty and the Kube"), as well as meta touches, like an episode focused on writing a short story ending with a nod to the production card for Stephen J. Cannell Productions ("Write or Die").[16] There was also one in-universe crossover between Fox's popular teen drama *Beverly Hills, 90210*, featuring the cast commenting on one of the characters in *Parker Lewis* as if he's a real person;[17] promotional commercials for the third season of *Parker Lewis* also featured Jason Priestley (Brandon on *90210*) popping into the promos unexpectedly, offering a boost for the lower-rated series. Following the show's cancellation in 1993, and the end of high school adjacent series *21 Jump Street* in 1991, Fox focused primarily on an older demographic, or a family audience, with series like *The Simpsons* and later *Malcolm in the Middle*. With a few notable exceptions, teen sitcoms, whether based around school, home, or social life, tended to move to cable, from the brightly colored Disney and Nickelodeon sitcoms like *iCarly* (2007–2012) to MTV's *Beavis and Butthead* (1993–2011) spin-off *Daria* (1997–2002), which did frequently tackle school issues relevant to the era, such as the corporate sponsorship of public schools.[18] Before leaving the 1990s entirely, there is one more series, in what became known as the "dramedy" category where series such as *Gilmore Girls* resided: *Freaks and Geeks*. Set in 1980, the series revolves around a group of teens, with Lindsey Weir (Linda Cartollini) as the primary protagonist, attempting to navigate the social structures of their high school. It was a series that both embraced and satirized the conventions of the genre, not unlike *Community* would do less than a decade later. The narrative splits its perspective between Lindsey, a college-bound mathlete who decides to hang out with the slackers and stoners (known as "freaks" in the social hierarchy of the school), much to the horror of both teachers and her parents, and the "geeks" represented by Lindsey's younger brother Sam (John Francis Daley). It takes surprising turns for the era, including an episode dealing with gender identity and dating, or, less seriously, one of the "freaks," Daniel (James Franco), bonding with the geeks over *Dungeons and Dragons*.[19]

Possibly the longest-running school series would be the Canadian Degrassi franchise. Starting in 1979 with the *Kids of Degrassi Street*, a series of short films that later became a series, the original focused more on young kids and the neighborhood they lived in. *Degrassi Junior High* (1987–1989) aired on PBS in the United States, and while the series used the thirty-minute format more akin to sitcoms, the tone and stories in *Degrassi* were more serious, including teen pregnancy, child abuse, shoplifting, and coming out. It used a rotating cast of more than fifty kids, which offered a more realistic environment than most shows' focus on a core group. Most of the cast transitioned to *Degrassi High* (1989–1991) before the series went on hiatus for a decade. *Degrassi: The Next Generation* debuted in 2001, and would end up running for fourteen years, with older cast members reappearing and a continued focus on serious topical stories. (This version did not air in the States but was released on DVD and later was available on streaming.)

Before turning to the *American Horror* and *Feud* franchises, Ryan Murphy created two series in the 2000s that focused on high school: *Popular* (1999–2001) and *Glee* (2009–2015). *Popular*, another WB dramedy, was nominally about the newly blended McQueen and McPherson families, whose daughters Brooke McQueen (Leslie Bibb) and Sam McPherson (Carly Pope) are on opposite sides of the popularity spectrum at their high school. Yet the series was as much about the school, and the quirky characters in it, as their new blended family. His later series, *Glee*, would focus more intensely on the school setting, and according to Murphy, had more leeway than *Popular* to touch on more serious subjects (sex, disability, teen pregnancy) and provide greater

LGBTQ+ representation. (He was told by WB executives to make certain characters on *Popular* "less gay" and chided for coded gay references in the series.[20] *Grosse Pointe* [created by Darren Star], a backstage comedy about a teen show, which aired on the WB at the same time, highlighted the other side of the WB's reaction to gay characters; that is, the potential ratings boost if the "gay" content appeals to straight men.)[21] Despite being *Community*'s competition on the schedule (and winning the time slot most weeks), the two series share a particular focus on both the school setting (high school versus community college) and a select group of individuals in that setting with a varying level of self-awareness of the unreality of what's going on around them.

While series about schools—grade, junior high, and high school—are represented in every decade of US television thus far (including streaming), shows based in colleges are far more rare. *Mrs. G. Goes to College*, which ran for a single season in 1961, was a quasi-spin-off of the early TV sitcom *The Goldbergs* (the character of Sarah, played by Gertrude Berg, was very similar to her earlier Molly Goldberg). The premise was the newly widowed Sarah, now in her sixties, decides to make a new start as a college student, an option presumably unavailable to her when she was younger. Later dramas, including *Felicity* or the short-lived *Bedford Falls* (2006), took place on college campuses, but the college series seemed to have greater critical and commercial success as sitcoms, including *Undeclared* (2001–2002), *Dear White People* (2017–2021), *Grown-ish* (2018–2024), and *A Different World*, the *Cosby Show* spin-off that frequently touched on subjects that the parent show avoided.[22] Yet whether comedies or dramas, the college shows offered an acceleration of their high school siblings, focusing not only on finding one's identity but also one's (eventual) place in the world as an independent adult (even, as with the case of Mrs. G., if that occurred later in life).

Community both fits into and satirizes the ideas, life lessons, and structure of the school-based series, not the least of which is through its setting in a community college. (As of 2025, the only other series that features a community college is a

Class time in Community *is minimized in favor of shenanigans.* NBC/Photofest © NBC.

documentary program on Netflix called *Last Chance U* [2016–2020].) While I'll discuss the way that *Community* plays with the sitcom genre in Chapter 6, on an episode level, it also plays with the pedagogical nature of school-based shows, both in obvious ways (Jeff's speeches that frequently summarize an episode's theme) and less obvious ones (the way Mr. Rad in "Regional Holiday Music" plays on the study group's weaknesses to get them to do what he wants, or Jeff's nonsense speech in "Paradigms of Human Memory").

The community college setting, which is often a kind of liminal space by its nature—it can be a gateway to a four-year college course or a place to learn new skills or trades to foster a career change, and thus offers a wider age range of students—reflects both the characters (most of whom are at a crossroads of a sort) and the narrative, which frequently shifts between sincere to metatextual, sometimes in the same scene. In those respects, *Community* manages both to honor and mock its forebears.

5

"I Can Tell Life from TV ... TV Makes Sense"

Community and the Likability Question

There is something of a cottage industry on places like YouTube, in which commentators will revisit old films and television shows and "discover" that certain characters were terrible, actually. Ross Geller (David Schwimmer) from *Friends* seems to hold a commanding lead, with Zack Morris from *Saved by the Bell* a close second. And, in retrospect, certain behaviors or plots of older films and movies, once viewed as funny or quirky or at least breezed over, are troubling and uncomfortable to watch years later (see most of *Revenge of the Nerds* [1984] or large swathes of *Sixteen Candles*). Yet the goal of US television from the 1960s until likely the debut of *The Sopranos* in 1999 was to create shows and characters that appealed to a wide audience. This was known as "least objectionable programming" by an NBC executive named Paul L. Klein, which boiled down to the idea that audiences rarely found anything they really liked on TV, so the goal was not to create shows that appealed but rather those that didn't offend.[1] A program could be successful as long as it captured at least a third of the viewing audience; even better if they stayed and watched a single network's block of shows. Yet, as cable started to cut into broadcast viewing audiences, with HBO making its first tentative steps into original programs like *The Larry Sanders Show* (1992–1998) or *Arliss* (1996–2002), broadcast networks had to regroup, deciding to target particular segments of the audience. This was especially true of the kind of audiences that advertisers liked: young people, and people with money.

The NBC network struggled, especially with sitcoms, in the 1970s; it tended to be the low point of the three-network triangle. Unlike CBS, which had a productive relationship with Norman Lear and MTM and their more socially conscious sitcoms, or ABC's with Aaron Spelling, NBC could only claim two sitcoms that lasted more than a season throughout most of the decade: *Sanford and Son*, a rare Lear series that didn't air on CBS, and *Chico and the Man*, created by James Komack, who'd previously had hits with *Welcome Back, Kotter* and *The Courtship of Eddie's Father* (1969–1972) for ABC. (Unfortunately, *Chico and the Man* came to a premature end with star Freddie Prinze Sr.'s suicide.) Starting in the late 1970s, however, NBC started to recover from a long, low-rated slump through the power of its comedies, including *Diff'rent Strokes*, *The Facts of Life*, and *Gimme a Break* (1981–1987). It was its Thursday night block, however, where NBC really shone. Indeed, NBC dominated this timeslot for more than twenty years, with its family-oriented comedies of the 1980s (*The Cosby Show*, *Family Ties*) followed by the friends-as-family series of the 1990s (*Friends*, *Will & Grace*). Yet the departure of long-running stalwarts such as *Friends* and *Frasier* in 2004 returned NBC to the ratings doldrums they occupied in the 1970s, deepened by audiences segmented by demographics and increased choice. Rather than returning to the more warm-hearted three-camera series of the past, however, NBC created a new comedy block—*30 Rock*, *Parks and Recreation*, *Community*, and *The Office*—of single-camera series featuring characters not always easy to like and a heavy dose of cringe comedy. This chapter examines how *Community* fits in with these other not-quite-antiheroes and the single-camera aesthetic of the 2010s on NBC.

The Good Guys? NBC Sitcoms in the 1980s and 1990s

If Norman Lear's Tandem Productions and MTM ruled the 1970s (and CBS) with shows like *All in the Family, Maude* (1972–1978), and *The Mary Tyler Moore Show* (plus their associated spin-offs), a new player, created in 1981, finally gave NBC its own special relationship: Carsey-Werner Productions. Formed by television producers Marcy Carsey and Tom Werner, they created a wide variety of family-friendly (or at least family-based) content that produced numerous hits. While they did have successful shows on CBS (*Grace Under Fire*; *Cybill*), ABC (*Roseanne*), and Fox (*That '70s Show*), they had a mutually beneficial arrangement with NBC, raising their own profile and the network's rating with *The Cosby Show*, its spin-off *A Different World*, and *3rd Rock from the Sun*. *The Cosby Show*, for all its problematic legacy, was the anchor of NBC's Thursday night lineup, which offered two family-friendly sitcoms during the early part of prime time (*Cosby* and *Family Ties*), followed by the more adult-oriented *Cheers* and *Night Court*. While *The Cosby Show* took place in Brooklyn and *Family Ties* in Ohio, both shared the same feature of the multicamera sitcoms in that the majority of the action took place within their homes, and mostly featured situations that could be resolved within the half-hour framework. While fitting more into the friends-as-family style, *Cheers* and *Night Court* were similarly set-bound; that is, a bar and a Manhattan municipal court. All were filmed in front of a studio audience, which had fallen out of favor in the 1960s but made a comeback in the 1970s.

However they might come across now, the main characters of these shows were supposed to be relatable, or at least charming. Alex P. Keaton (Michael J. Fox) was a Ronald Reagan fanboy, but this is framed as a response to his hippie parents. Sam Malone (Ted Danson) was a womanizer, but also a recovering alcoholic who owned a bar; his relationship with the intellectual and uptight Diane Chambers (Shelley Long) was contentious but monogamous. *Night Court*'s premise depended on the quirks both of its main characters and those brought into the court; while Dan Fielding (John Larroquette) is a suck-up and an unrepentant Lothario, his behavior is generally the butt of the joke, rather than aspirational. (And even he gets his better character moments, as when he hires himself out as a date for wealthy older women, and helps one of his clients deal with the grief of losing her husband.)[2]

This element was true of all the Big Three networks during the 1980s, from the family moments on *Growing Pains* to the acerbic but supportive interactions between Blanche, Rose, Sophia, and Dorothy on *The Golden Girls*. The sitcom lead as antihero, or at least morally questionable, tended to be doomed in this environment. A case in point was 1984's short-lived *It's Your Move*, cocreated by Ron Leavitt and Michael G. Moye and starring Jason Bateman, fresh off the sweet-natured father/son sitcom *Silver Spoons* (1982–1987), as Matthew Burton, a scam artist who was not above cheating, blackmail, or other underhanded maneuvers to get what he wanted. In the series' most memorable episode, "The Dregs of Humanity, Parts 1 and 2," he even creates a fake band made of skeletons filched from the school's biology lab to cover for his friend Eli losing the money for the school dance. The band ends up taking off, and Matt is forced to fake their death.[3] No lessons are learned, and Matthew's actions seem to have minimal negative consequences for him. In the family-friendly environment of 1980s TV (at least on sitcoms) and the conservative bent of the era, it's perhaps not surprising that the show was canceled after numerous (parental) viewer complaints, mostly centered around fear that their children would emulate them. Such reactions might sound familiar to older viewers of *The Simpsons*; during his reelection campaign in 1992, George H. W. Bush stated he wanted a return to family values, "more like *The Waltons* and a lot less like *The Simpsons*," at a press conference on January 27, 1992. Bart Simpson was considered a bad role model, and several schools banned wearing Bart T-shirts in the early 1990s.[4] (Bush went on to lose the election to Bill Clinton.)

Indeed, it was on Fox, debuting as a fourth network in 1986, where the cracks started to show. Wanting to differentiate itself from the Big Three, Fox in its early years focused on series that could potentially appeal to different demographics than the other three. These included teen cop show *21 Jump Street* and teen drama *Beverly Hills, 90210*; a sketch comedy show anchored by British comedian Tracey Ullman; and the show that spun off Ullman's: *The Simpsons*. An institution now, in 1989 it was the first prime-time animated series since *The Flintstones* ended in 1966. Series like *Parker Lewis Can't Lose*, *Herman's Head*, and *Get a Life* offered quirky premises; sketch comedy show *In Living Color* and sitcoms *Roc* (1991–1994), *Living Single*, and *Martin* (1992–1997) offered casts and creators of color that the Big Three didn't. The cynical worldview of *It's Your Move* was reflected more successfully in Leavitt and Moye's next project for Fox: *Married ... with Children*. The more working-class and—for the time—edgier sitcoms such as ABC's *Roseanne* and *The Simpsons* knocked *The Cosby Show* out of the top spot it had held for the first five years it aired.

Despite this, NBC continued to feature sitcoms in which its protagonists might be flawed, but not unlikable or un-relatable. They did expand their focus beyond the family sitcom (with some exceptions, such as *Empty Nest* [1988–1995], which featured a widowed father and his two daughters, or *The Fresh Prince of Bel-Air*, initially a fish-out-of-water story about Will [Will Smith] moving from West Philadelphia to escape violence and crime to his aunt and uncle's posh Bel Air home) to also offer several "friends as family" or workplace comedies, including *Friends*, *Will & Grace*, *Frasier*, *News Radio*, and *Just Shoot Me!* (1997–2003). The exception to this, and the one that points to NBC's future, was *Seinfeld*. The famed "show about nothing" was peopled with four characters not meant to be either kind or relatable; indeed, its controversial series finale ended with Jerry, Kramer, Elaine, and George being jailed for a year for violations of the Good Samaritan Law by refusing to help a man being carjacked. The trial consists of numerous character witnesses who testify to the four's history of selfish behavior, and after sentencing, they are shown to have learned nothing from the experience.

Single-Camera and Complicated: NBC's New Thursday Nights

In those respects, *Seinfeld* sets the template for the direction of NBC sitcoms in the 2000s. After the endings of the long-running *Friends* and *Frasier* in 2004, as discussed in Chapter 1, NBC dropped in the ratings, and seemed to scramble to find replacements that could match the ratings of their predecessors. (*Scrubs*, which debuted in 2001 but frequently struggled in the ratings, nevertheless lasted for seven seasons on NBC, and served as a harbinger for the comedy shifts of the network as the decade progressed.) A new head of programming, Kevin Reilly, who'd worked at Brillstein-Grey Entertainment (producer of shows like *The Steve Harvey Show*, *Just Shoot Me!*, and others), was appointed in 2003, which meant that he oversaw the departures of NBC's big-name shows but also ushered in a new direction for comedies at the network through his support of *The Office*, which debuted in 2005, and *My Name Is Earl* (which he picked up despite pushback from other NBC executives).[5] Both series signaled the network's new direction, with *The Office* adopting the same cringe-comedy aesthetic of its British originator, and *My Name Is Earl*'s titular hero a man who describes himself as "the kinda guy who does nothing but bad things and then wonders why his life sucks? Well, that was me."[6] Their position at the bottom of the ratings conversely allowed the network to be a bit more bold in the types of programs they chose. While CBS leaned into the multicamera/laugh track style with shows like *Two and a Half Men* and *The Big Bang Theory*, NBC slowly rebuilt its Thursday night with a single-camera series of different types. Keeping *The Office* (mockumentary) and *My Name Is Earl* into the 2006–2007 season, they added *30 Rock* to the lineup, a backstage series of an *SNL*-type show created by Tina Fey, who had served as the first female head writer of *Saturday Night Live*. *Parks and Recreation*, cocreated by Greg Daniels and Michael Schur, came out of new programming head Ben Silverman's desire to capitalize on the popularity of *The Office* with a spin-off. Daniels, who had adapted *The Office* from its UK source material, brought fellow *Office* writer Michael Schur onto the project, with both concluding fairly quickly that the new series should be its own thing; maintaining the mockumentary format and some of the character tropes (e.g., sarcastic, disaffected employee [Jim Halpert/Mark Brendanawicz], clueless boss [Michael Scott/Leslie Knope]) in a different setting: local government.[7] The final addition to the lineup came in the fall 2009 season with the premiere of *Community*. This schedule would hold until 2013, when both *The Office* and *30 Rock* ended their run and *Community* and *Parks and Recreation* were paired with new shows that did not last beyond a single season. In May 2014, *Community* was canceled on NBC (later picked up for a final season by the short-lived Yahoo! streaming service), and *Parks and Recreation* was moved to Tuesdays in the fall for its final season.

On a production level, *The Office*, *30 Rock*, *Community*, and *Parks and Recreation* all used the single-camera aesthetic in particular ways. *The Office* and *Parks and Recreation* adopted the mockumentary style, although unlike *The Office*, there was never actually any explanation for the presence of cameras or the "talking head" asides. As a "backstage" series, *30 Rock* blended the antics of the writers' room, the actual sketch show, and the personal lives of its main characters, giving it a broader canvas than many, more set-bound series. While of these four, *Community* offers the least amount of diverse settings, the main one of Greendale Community College itself creates a degree of variety; season three and beyond also offer Troy and Abed's apartment as a secondary hub of action. There was no laugh track. (There was also a bit of crossover, as Donald Glover worked as a story editor, writer, and [occasional] actor on *30 Rock*, mostly in its first two seasons.) All four shows garnered critical respect, but viewership remained far below the more conventional shows on other networks. As Saul Austerlitz writes about *30 Rock*: "Its humor and its mediocre ratings stemmed from the same root cause; it was a sitcom about the exhaustion of sitcoms, a summing-up and parodying of all television's tired appeals. The sitcom was triumphing by acknowledging its failings. And who would want to watch that?"[8]

One of those failings/triumphs for *30 Rock*, *The Office*, *Community*, and the first season of *Parks and Recreation* is abandoning, as did series such as *Married ... with Children*, *Arrested Development*, *Seinfeld*, and *Roseanne*, the idea that the characters had to be relatable, likable, or both. Many if not most of these shows did this by emphasizing, through their characters, that they were well aware how they came across. Near the end of *Arrested Development*'s broadcast run, the episode "S.O.B.s" is nominally about the Bluth family's legal troubles, but primarily about how the Bluths as characters are perceived by audiences and its effect on viewership. Michael (Jason Bateman) ends up giving a speech that sums it up as the show neared cancellation: "I was going to say that you don't know who my father really is and that what has happened to us is a great injustice, that we were never really given a fair chance. But that's not the truth. We've been given plenty of chances. And maybe the Bluths just aren't worth saving, maybe we're not that likable, you know."[9] For *30 Rock*, its status as a parody of the excesses of both sitcoms and television in general suggests that the viewer isn't meant to see themselves in Liz Lemon or Jack Donaghy; moreover, they'd likely mock you if you did. Michael Scott's (Steve Carell) desperation to be liked on *The Office* is the source of its cringe-comedy style, and the conceit of these ordinary workers being constantly filmed suggests that their actions and reactions are, confusingly, both real and staged simultaneously. While not a spin-off of *The Office*, the first season of *Parks and Recreation* took a similar approach to the character of Leslie Knope (Amy Poehler) as they did Michael Scott, portraying her as well-meaning but ineffectual and suggesting she failed upward into her job as deputy director of the Parks Department in her mid-sized Indiana town, while characters such as Mark Brendanawicz (Paul Schneider) served as the straight man to the antics of those around him in the tradition of Jim Halpert. The first season's reviews skewed negative, including calling the series "worse than *Joey*," the short-lived *Friends* spin-off, and suggesting that it was too close to *The Office* but lacked its charm.[10] The series would regroup with its second season, making Leslie less the butt of the joke and integrating the rest of the cast into more of a community; of the four Thursday night series of the era, *Parks and Recreation* subsequently became the most optimistic and least cynical of them.[11]

And how does *Community* fit into this? It's not a mockumentary, like *The Office* or *Parks and Rec*, which frequently expose the gap between what the characters say is happening and the reality of the camera, and it's definitely not a parody of 2000s-era network television like *30 Rock*, although, as I'll discuss later, it does satirize particular tropes. They are not the self-absorbed denizens of *Seinfeld* or angry working class of the Bundys (or the Bunkers). They range in age from 19 to 60+ years old, and come from a variety of backgrounds. But are the Greendale Seven—and those around them—likable? And, in the end, does it matter?

As perhaps the only US series set at a community college, *Community*'s setting allows the opportunity for a wide variety of recurring and one-off characters of faculty, staff, and students by its very nature. Because community colleges offer different opportunities than four-year institutions, including two-year associate degrees, graduate equivalency courses, trade and technical training and certification, and continuing education programs, their student populations are not limited to the expected eighteen- to twenty-two-year-old demographic. Aside from the study group, students range from Magnitude (Luke Youngblood), who is approximately the same age as Troy and Annie ("Heroic Origins" shows him at the fateful high school party in which Annie had her Adderall-induced breakdown and Troy his football career–

ending keg stand) to Leonard (Richard Erdman), whose precise age is never given but who has been attending Greendale since the 1970s, when it was known as Greendale Computery College.[12] They can be decorated war heroes, like the much-put-upon Todd (David Neher) or thieves and wannabe-meth-makers like Alex "Star-Burns" Osbourne. Dean Craig Pelton (Jim Rash) plays favorites with the study group, has a tendency to look down on Greendale at certain points, and often fails to respect boundaries (see the season four storyline in which he moves into the apartment next to Jeff's). To a greater or lesser degree, these characters, as well as ones like Fat Neil, Garrett (Erik Charles Nielsen), and Professor Ian Duncan (John Oliver), get some degree of backstory or facets throughout the series.

For both the main cast and the supporting players, then, the series employs a high degree of nuance. Jeff, as a main point-of-view character, presents as aloof and lies easily. His first order of business at Greendale is to manipulate Duncan into giving him test answers, so he can cheat his way to a degree and return to practicing law. He lies to Britta in order to get her attention, claiming he is fluent in Spanish and can serve as her tutor.[13] He relishes his role as leader of the group and can get petty or downright psychotic when it is threatened.[14] Yet, as much as these episodes show Jeff's darker side, "Contemporary American Poultry" also features the entire study group growing increasingly selfish and entitled when they are given whatever they want, and Jeff's feeling of exclusion after he's kicked out of biology class is exacerbated by exposure to a gas released in the vents. Annie is smart and driven, and good at making the best out of bad circumstances (as when her parents kicked her out after she went to rehab), but those same qualities also led to Adderall abuse. She is also not above manipulation to win arguments, or throwing tantrums when she either doesn't get her way or feels wronged.[15] Shirley defines herself by being born again, but can frequently weaponize it against others by denigrating their own religion or setting herself up as the misunderstood but morally superior member of the study group, often verging into uglier sides of religion, such as homophobia;

"Horror Fiction in Seven Spooky Steps" has her tell a morality tale in which the rest of the study group is damned to a hell ruled by Dean Pelton as the devil, the only openly queer regular character, while she is raptured.[16] Yet she was also abandoned by her husband and struggled with alcohol, so much that she was a cautionary tale at a local bar.[17] The sense of moral superiority that her religion gives her not only helps her rebuild her life and confidence, but also serves as a mask for her justifiable anger at her circumstances. Abed admits to being on the spectrum and struggling with change, whether big or small. Yet he also sometimes struggles to consider the consequences on others as important as doing what he wants, whether it's ruining Buzz Hickey's (Jonathan Banks) cartoons or running up a debt hiring celebrity impersonators that his friends are forced to work off and his seeming anger—suggested by the appearance of "Evil Abed" at the end—that Troy puts a stop to him hiring more.[18]

While Troy, Britta, and Pierce are given somewhat less nuance, there are still layers to each of them. Troy struggles to redefine himself after high school and can be overemotional and gullible. He is rarely mean or cruel; perhaps the closest he comes is developing a Twitter feed called "Old White Man Says," a jab on Justin Halpern's feed "Shit My Dad Says," in which he quoted the various politically incorrect or offensive things his father said; Halpern parlayed it into a book deal and later short-lived TV series that debuted the night "Anthropology 101" aired. Given that he is living with Pierce at the time, he eventually feels guilty and tells Pierce he'll delete it. Once Pierce finds out how many followers it has, however, he suggests leaving it up.[19] Troy also "sacrifices" himself to save the study group by agreeing to join the Air Conditioning Repair School, which does not allow fraternization, when they are trapped by Ben Chang.[20] Britta is frequently motivated by political outrage, and yet often struggles to back that up with knowledge and can gatekeep other ways of expressing protest or solidarity, as when Shirley and Annie put together a candlelight vigil for an imprisoned Guatemalan journalist.[21] She is not always wrong, as when she calls out the study group for not objecting when her purse is searched (for

Annie's missing pen) but backing up Shirley when she objects.[22] She warns Jeff when he is on anti-anxiety medication that over-inflates his ego, and is there for him when he crashes, and reaches out to Abed after Troy is forced to move into the Air Conditioning Repair School, concerned about his mental health in Troy's absence. (Abed, in his "Evil Abed" persona, responds to Britta's attempts to help by undermining her confidence and making her cry.)[23] Even Pierce, despite his ego, bias, and immaturity, manages a few moments of wisdom or thoughtfulness, as when he discovers the troubling circumstances of Annie's living situation (although he later undermines this when he attempts to use the fact he helped her out to get what he wants) or gives up the quest for his father's fortune in favor of his half-brother Gilbert, who he feels deserves it more.[24] While Pierce generally inspires others by embodying what not to do in most situations, he does offer surprising moments of good advice or assistance, including trying to hypnotize Britta to stop smoking or helping a nervous Shirley ace her presentation in business class.[25] Even with his multi-episode descent into villain in the second season, he has enough self-awareness to admit his struggles to keep friends, and thus he tends to sabotage said relationships before he can be rejected.[26] There is even an argument to be made that Ben Chang, the most unhinged character in the series, does get a touch of nuance, as when his struggling marriage makes him (more) of a nightmare professor ("Environmental Science"), and some self-awareness, as when Jeff describes his "season seven" to the group in the final episode, and Chang asks: "Am I on meds in it? I'm mellow and relatable. I like it."[27]

All of these elements, within the main and recurring cast, create a group that may not be considered likable in comparison to their sitcom predecessors, but are certainly more complex. While dramas, starting in the 1990s, tended to focus on heavier story arcs and character growth, sitcoms, by their nature, often "reset" with each episode, minus certain running gags or character catchphrases. This was by design, given that US television, running on the commercial system and reliant on ratings, not only always sought new viewers, but could be canceled at a moment's notice. A show might not know precisely when it will end, so character growth in particular can be stymied so that they don't "grow" out of the series altogether. This would often force series to come up with reasons to keep a character in direct contrast with what's already been established. As per example, Alex P. Keaton, on *Family Ties*, talked of nothing but going to Princeton during the first two seasons of the show. Yet, given Fox's popularity on the series, sending his character to New Jersey (the show is set in Ohio) was never going to happen, leading to an episode in which he tanks his Princeton interview to help his sister over a break-up.[28] He instead gets a scholarship to the local (fictional) Leland College, keeping Fox around until the end of the series. The four central young women on *The Facts of Life* essentially live together for eight years, first at boarding school, before opening a bakery with their housemother, Mrs. Garrett (Charlotte Rae), that later morphs into a notions store. For these earlier series, big changes were limited to cast members electing to leave, or the (planned) end of the series.

Taking a cue from both the arc-based dramas of the era, and other sitcoms that were starting to lean into developing characters and storylines beyond a few episodes, such as *Scrubs*, *Community*'s college setting offered a built-in opportunity for its characters to learn and grow, even if they didn't always take those opportunities. While the show, with its self-awareness and film and television homages, frequently indulges in stylized episodes—the two-episode City College versus Greendale paintball game is Sergio Leone–inspired in the first half before transitioning to a *Star Wars* homage in its second—that doesn't prevent either character or narrative development. "Pillows and Blankets" is presented as a Ken Burns–style documentary (narrated by Keith David, who would later join the cast as Elroy Pasternack), but also represents the first real rupture in Abed and Troy's friendship, building on Abed's reaction to Troy forbidding him from hiring celebrity impersonators.[29] Abed attempts to recreate Louis Malle's *My Dinner with André* (1981), which leads to Jeff opening up about his own insecurities. Even though Jeff is furious when Abed reveals the reenactment, he understands when Abed admits that it was his own way to get closer to Jeff at a time when it felt like they were drifting apart.[30]

Jeff himself acknowledges that he is not the same person who started Greendale with the goal to cheat his way out in the final episode of the third season; his advocating for selflessness in the "court" case between Pierce and Shirley not only pulls Abed out of a spiral, but also convinces Pierce to work with Shirley and fire his barracuda of a lawyer.[31] By the end of the series, Jeff, whose initial goal was to leave Greendale as soon as possible, is one of the ones left behind and imagining ways to maintain this new status quo.

These character complexities—Jeff's selfishness, Annie's drivenness, Shirley's religiosity and anger, Pierce's Pierce-ness—all can be easily perceived as unlikable and un-relatable qualities. While its companions on NBC also featured unlikable and un-relatable characters, they were either intended as caricatures (*30 Rock*), got better (*Parks and Recreation*), or featured an

Community *blends* My Dinner with André *and* Pulp Fiction. NBC/Photofest © NBC.

everyman (or woman) character as a primary point-of-view reacting to the "madness" around them (*The Office*). Other series of the era would blend some of these aspects; *Better Off Ted* featured the eponymous Ted (Jay Harrington) and his attempts to navigate the ethically bankrupt corporation he works for without devolving completely into a soulless corporate puppet, with characters such as his boss Veronica (Portia de Rossi) representing the evil corporate side, and coworker Linda (Andrea Anders), to a limited extent, his conscience. *Community*, I would argue, went on a different route. In this highly self-aware, meta show, Harmon and company are well aware of sitcom tropes both past and present, for both plots and characters, and they frequently embrace, blend, and subvert them. Pierce, as the oldest member of the study group, should theoretically be the "sage," and while he does offer moments of wisdom, this is constantly undermined by his need for attention and his immaturity, lashing out when he thinks he's being ignored or excluded (see most of season two).[32] No *Community* character could be considered conventionally aspirational (aside from looks); as Abed says about Jeff's questionable behavior toward both Britta and Annie, when Jeff lashes out at him for conflating TV with real life: "I can tell life from TV, Jeff. TV makes sense, it has structure, logic, rules, and likable leading men. In life, we have this. We have you."[33] Abed doesn't need to be specific; Jeff understands what he is implying and adjusts his behavior and thinking, but even at the series' conclusion, each character is still a work in progress.

While series like *The Sopranos*, and later, *Breaking Bad* (2008–2013), made space for dramas to build stories around morally questionable—if not outright repugnant—antiheroes, the received wisdom was that such characters had no real place in the sitcom genre. And yet, aside from revisiting series such as *Friends* and questioning the ethics or behavior of its central characters, that particular idea erases pre-2000s shows like *Seinfeld, Married ... with Children*, and *The Simpsons*, all of which featured its characters doing questionable things—at best—and all of which had amazingly lengthy runs on broadcast television: nine seasons for *Seinfeld*, eleven for *Married ... with Children*, and *The Simpsons* debuted its thirty-sixth season in the fall of 2024. Nor did these three series particularly resemble one another, with *Seinfeld* featuring Manhattanites in their thirties, *Married* set in a working-class Chicago suburb and featuring a family frequently fueled by resentment and the wish for a better life, and *The Simpsons* supposedly set in one of the thirty-eight Springfields across the United States, although it does have a distinctly Midwestern vibe.

Community, and the shows that surrounded it on Thursday nights, did represent a departure from NBC's family-friendly, or friends-as-family, warmer comedies of the 1980s and 1990s, whether through satire and parody as a primary distancing tactic, such as *30 Rock*, or its own self-awareness as a created object, figuratively, as *Community* did, or literally, with *The Office* and *Parks and Recreation*'s mockumentary format. None of these series could match the ratings or longevity (except *The Office*) of their predecessors, something frequently attributed to these series' own self-awareness. That is, the distance created by its reflective comedy and knowledge of itself as a fiction makes it hard to care about the Greendale Seven.[34] And yet, as Alan Sepinwall argues: "What Harmon and his 'Community' writers understand ... is that the references can be used for humor, and/or to please audience members who recognize them, but that they have to be tied to honest efforts at characterization to work long-term," using as his example the way that the *GoodFellas* homage in "Contemporary American Poultry" was tied to Abed and Jeff understanding one another on a different level.[35] Its complex characters and pop culture awareness have been blamed, but in fact, the television landscape has changed significantly since the 1980s; even the most popular shows (e.g., *The Big Bang Theory*) couldn't command the kind of audience shares $M^*A^*S^*H$ or *The Cosby Show* did in the 1970s and 1980s.[36] With so many choices—broadcast, cable, and more recently, streaming—likability as a metric for a show's success is outdated.

6

"Some Episodes Too Conceptual to Be Funny"

Community Takes on the Sitcom Genre

In an interview near the end of the first season of *Schitt's Creek* (2015–2020), the Canadian/US coproduced sitcom, creator Dan Levy suggested that he "didn't want it to be a sitcom in a broad sense, in a *2 Broke Girls* sort of way," fully expecting the interview and readers to understand what he meant.[1] That is, a set-bound, multicamera half-hour series with a laugh track, focused on various "situations" mined for their comedic potential. Yet, as Saul Austerlitz argues, these definitions have never fully encompassed what the sitcom is; that is, "there is more to the sitcom than banal familiarity. There was, at times, the sense that within the comforting confines of its well-worn sets and well-worn punchlines, something surprising could happen" that, as reflections of US society, could "warp and bend reality into intriguing new patterns."[2] Moreover, that these "comforting confines" have grown more broad throughout their history, from the "live in front of a studio audience" airings from *I Love Lucy* and the present day, the "theater set" structure of shows such as *All in the Family*, or the blending of studio set and outdoor locations for *M*A*S*H*, which itself shifted from its laugh-tracked early seasons to a more hybridized dramedy sans laugh track as it progressed. While the single-camera, non-laugh-track sitcom dominates the current era, the more traditional models coexist with it.

Community has always been aware of this history. It's no mistake that nearly every article about the series points out how "meta" it is; it is one of the defining features of *Community*. Yet using meta in a series can—and should—go beyond merely glances to the camera or pointed jokes to highlight aspects about the creation of fiction. This chapter will look at the series' mockery of and homages to both film and television, particularly the sitcom genre itself, which not only shows an in-depth knowledge of the sitcom genre but the production of series and the production of humor as knowledge. I'll take a look at some of the episodes that engage with their TV predecessors and contemporaries and what it says about the series itself and the time in which it aired, and the way *Community* as sitcom uses other mediums, such as film, dramas, and cartoons, to comment on its sitcom world.

"I Should Build You a Still for Making Hawkeye Martinis": *Community* and Sitcoms Past

Community, as a series, did not invent taking a metatextual look at sitcom tropes; it wasn't even the only one on NBC in the 2000s to do it. *My Name Is Earl* had a four-episode arc in which its titular character is in a coma and imagines himself in a black-and-white sitcom world, complete with laugh track and featuring sitcom tropes such as the "Cousin Oliver," in which a new, younger child is brought into the story (on shaky grounds) when the regular child cast ages out of their "cute" phase.[3] Teen sitcom *Parker Lewis Can't Lose*, a (relatively) short-lived series that nonetheless had an impact on its descendants (Bill Lawrence cites it as an inspiration for *Scrubs*), an early single-camera/ no laugh track series, also featured a character imagining himself in an early sitcom world.⁴ A later episode, built around a creative writing assignment, has the characters imagining themselves in various other genres, including film noir and teen drama, that end up commenting on the series itself.⁵ *Scrubs* contrasted its usual single-camera aesthetic in "My Life in Four Cameras," with John Dorian (Zach Braff), tasked with treating a (fictional) writer for *Cheers*, Charles James (a combination of *Cheers* creators' names), imagining the hospital as a multicamera sitcom, with high-key lighting, one-liners, and easy resolutions, only for the visual palette to return to normal as James codes and dies.⁶

Community makes this a feature of the series, and does so in two particular ways: direct homage and embracing/subverting tropes. The direct homages were less common; perhaps the first thoroughgoing homage is season one's "Investigative Journalism." While the main plot of the episode is the appearance of Buddy (Jack Black), who tries to push his way into the study group, the B-plot has Jeff named as the editor of the Greendale school paper, a job he does not take seriously. Given that Abed has already dubbed Jeff as "Hawkeye" based on Jeff's new attitude toward making the best of Greendale ("he kept his upbeat humor and charm, even in the eleventh year of the Korean War," as he puts it), that is the persona he adopts as editor, down to the Hawaiian shirts and day drinking, with Abed nominating himself as the Radar O'Reilly to Jeff's Hawkeye. Yet, when he has to step in to expel Buddy in an ugly scene, Jeff worries that he really hasn't grown and matured, nor is he the cool and unruffled Hawkeye. Abed assures him that there were layers to the original Hawkeye, including displaying leadership in difficult situations, and that he has developed as a character too.⁷

While season two's "Competitive Wine Tasting" focuses on Abed taking a class on analyzing 1980s sitcom *Who's the Boss?*, and season three's "Regional Holiday Music" skewers *Glee* (which exists in that gray area between comedy and drama known as "dramedy"), it is only in later seasons that the series offers more direct homages.⁸ The season four premiere—the only season that did not have Dan Harmon at the helm—has Abed dealing with the changes around him and the fear of the study group breaking up by retreating into an imaginary sitcom world he dubs "Abed's Happy Community College Show." While not tied to a specific series, its broad punchlines, laugh track, and lighting suggest the multicamera sitcom more generally, essentially actualizing Jeff's accusation in season one that Abed views everything through the filter of television.[9] The series returns to this conceptual well in the next episode, "Paranormal Parentage," by more successfully parodying *Scooby-Doo, Where Are You?* That is, rather than the more obvious take of "Abed's Happy Community College Show," "Paranormal Parentage" more subtly suggests its source material by first setting it at Pierce's house, the wealthiest of the study group, and then "unmasking" him as the source of most of the uncanny events, as revenge for feeling excluded.[10]

The last direct homages of the series occur in the final episode, when the remaining members of the study group and staff meet at the bar where Britta works to discuss what "season seven" would look like. That this discussion is instigated by Abed is no surprise, although his reason for it is not immediately revealed. Each of these imagined scenarios is preceded by a short version of the *Community* theme song, and range from Britta's drama about fighting government corruption to Chang's take on the study group featuring an animated character named Ice Cube Head. It is Jeff, however, who is given multiple sequences, some of which he shares with the group, and others that are private (including one in which he strangles multiple clones of Abed). Invariably, however, the sitcom that Jeff is paying tribute to is *Community* itself, including one in which the study group is comprised of secondary characters like Garrett, Leonard, and Vicky, as well as Greendale's new owner, Scrunch (Seth Green)—a possible reference to Archie (Zack Pearlman), a wealthy but dim student the dean tried to recruit to Greendale in season four—with Jeff attempting to assert himself as leader again, only to be smacked down by Scrunch, who tells him: "It's your job to work. It is our job to party. And hatch harebrained schemes. And get laid. ... And eventually leave you here as well."¹¹ His next pitch shifts to more of a hangout comedy, in which he's the dean, Annie teaches criminology, Britta is the staff psychologist, and Chang teaches math, although Jeff ends his pitch, oddly, saying "we just might live the good life yet," the final line of the theme song to 1980s sitcom *Mr. Belvedere* (1985–1990). Finally, near the end of the episode, he imagines a study group comprised only of attractive young women, some of whom correspond to the original study group (an idealist, a nerdy one, etc.), which he both proclaims a "community" and recognizes that they too may leave, but "that's something I'm equipped to handle now." What makes this particularly interesting is that each of them, at Abed's suggestion, is imagining a potential season seven, but Abed provides a caveat: "No cutting to any of them. If you cut to them, it won't come true." Yet it does cut to Jeff, calling into question whether that sense of acceptance of being left behind he espouses is actually true.¹²

What the series does more of, however, is take on particular tropes associated with the sitcom genre, rather than tied to individual series. These include

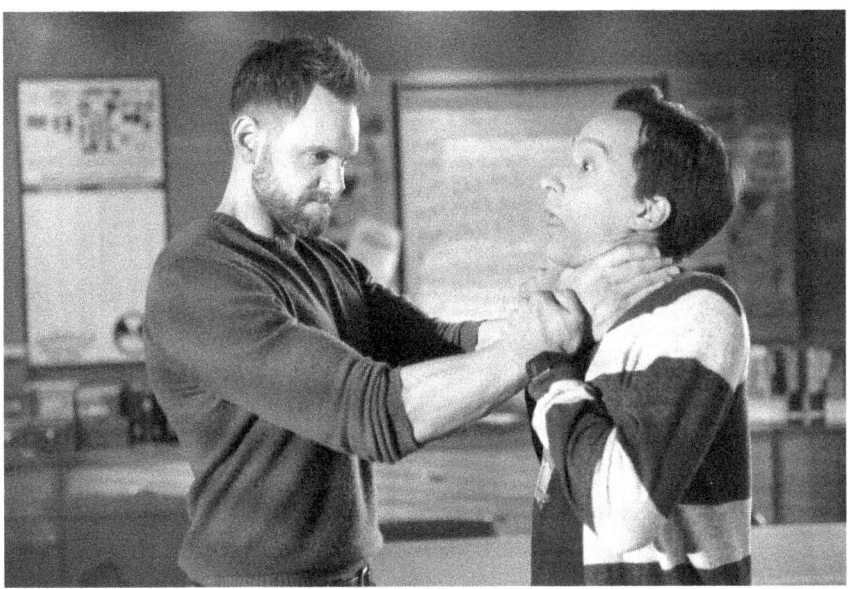

Jeff's fantasy to stop the study group from changing. NBC/Photofest © NBC.

production elements such as bottle episodes and clip shows, and narrative and character tropes, including will-they-won't-they couples, narrative and character resets, and very special episodes, among others. The production trope episodes ended up being some of the most well regarded of the series. Like most sitcoms, locations already tend to be limited, although by the late 1990s or early 2000s, they weren't as set-bound as before. The "bottle episode," however, spanned multiple genres, and was primarily used to save money. (That is, the money saved by setting an episode in a single location could then be used for sweeps or season finale episodes.) The term was coined by Leslie Stevens, who served as executive producer for *The Outer Limits* (1963–1965), as such episodes could be made fast and cheap; that is, making an episode so fast it was like yanking it out of a genie's "bottle."[13] Despite the limited setting, however, these episodes can offer relatively high stakes; *Firefly*'s "Out of Gas" takes place primarily on the ship *Serenity*, featuring flashbacks to how the characters came together, mixed with a ticking clock in the form of an increasing lack of oxygen due to mechanical failure.[14] "The Box" on *Brooklyn Nine-Nine* goes a step further, featuring only two main characters, Captain Raymond Holt (Andre Braugher) and Detective Jake Peralta (Andy Samberg), as they interrogate a suspect to get him to confess before they run out of time and have to let him go.[15] (This episode also serves as a humorous meta-take on Braugher's earlier series, *Homicide: Life on the Street* [1993–1999], whose third episode, "Three Men and Adena," was built on the same premise.)[16] In *Community*'s self-proclaimed bottle episode, "Cooperative Calligraphy," the stakes couldn't possibly be lower. Annie has lost a pen, the latest of many of hers that have gone missing. She refuses to let any of the study group leave the study room until the pen has been recovered. While the pen is not found during the episode, it offers the opportunity for the study group to air out their grievances, issues, and petty squabbles before coming back together and electing to believe Troy's explanation (a ghost took it) rather than continue to turn on one another. It is Abed, of course, who explicitly names it, adding: "I hate bottle episodes. They're wall to wall facial expressions and emotional nuance. I might as well sit in a corner with a bucket on my head."[17] Abed isn't wrong; the lack of outside action does mean that the bulk of these episodes, regardless of genre, is focused on character. Indeed, in his review of the episode, Cory Barker suggests that "Cooperative Calligraphy" is "both the culmination of the last fifteen episodes and the catalyst for a number of surely-awesome plots and episodes to come."[18] That is, the locked-door plot allows the simmering tensions over previous events, including the Halloween party no one can remember, Britta's confession of love at the end of season one and subsequent fallout, as well as the group's differing personalities and life experiences to be aired out and dealt with.[19]

"Cooperative Calligraphy" would not be the only bottle episode of the series, and all shared the element of a focus on the characters, with either the audience or the study group themselves learning more about one another. "Applied Anthropology and Culinary Arts" combines the bottle episode (the episode takes place primarily in the anthropology classroom) with the added trope of giving birth in strange places; TV Tropes refers to this as "Born in an Elevator" based on the sheer volume of series in which women give birth in elevators, including *Night Court*, *Punky Brewster* (1984–1988), *Saved by the Bell*, *Doogie Howser, MD* (1989–1993), and *Early Edition* (1996–2000), among others. In this instance, while an (unseen) riot breaks out at the campus food festival, Shirley goes into labor, with Britta forced to overcome her squeamishness and help her deliver. It's one of the few times in which Britta is forced to live out what she preaches to others, as she'd been advocating quite strongly to Shirley for natural birth, only to be forced to participate in one. Chang also gets a rare moment of (almost) sanity as he helps Shirley through the process before Andre arrives.[20] "Advanced *Dungeons and Dragons*" offers a rare instance of the study group attempting to help someone outside the group; in fact, someone whom Jeff inadvertently had hurt. That person is Neil, known throughout Greendale as Fat Neil. When he gives away his *Dungeons and Dragons* guides to Jeff, who'd noticed that Neil seemed depressed and had thus feigned interest in Neil's favorite role-playing game, Jeff rallies the study group—minus Pierce—to help him out. While this seems out of character for Jeff to randomly reach out to someone like this, it is later revealed why he did so, through an angry Pierce, who feels excluded: Jeff is the one who gave him the nickname Fat Neil as a way to differentiate him from another Neil—a thoughtless moment with lasting ramifications. (Of course, the reason Pierce was excluded was his lack of sensitivity for the emotions or problems of others, which is dialed up when he feels wronged.) One of a handful of episodes that features a narrator, the narrative is built around the study group playing a game of *Dungeons and Dragons* with Neil in order to give him something to live for. When Pierce finds out, he, in the fantasy tradition of the game itself, takes on the role of the villain, targeting Neil in particular because he thinks Neil is his replacement. Yet his egregious behavior throughout the episode actually gives Neil something tangible to fight against; it also suggests that things could be worse: he could be an insecure bully of an old man. The episode never leaves the study room, even to show the narrated action of the game, relying on the narrator, Dungeon Master Abed, and a wordless sequence in which Annie, as Hector the Well-Endowed, seduces elf maiden Abed. It is focused on character, and characters, their personas, as well as the people they would like to be. In that respect, it's significant that Pierce, as villain, does not in fact take on a new identity, and as the narrator indicates at the end of the episode: "And so it was that Pierce Hawthorne saved the life of Fat Neil while learning very, very little."[21]

The most famous and likely best regarded episode of the series, "Remedial Chaos Theory," also qualifies as a bottle episode, as the main action takes place in Troy and Abed's new apartment. In terms of forward plot, the episode offers little. Instead, like the other bottle episodes, it is a character study, although more in terms of the dynamics of the group as a whole. It starts with the study group gathering for Troy and Abed's housewarming party; Shirley has arrived early and started baking—which the rest are attempting to discourage—and they have ordered pizza. Pierce brings a gift for Troy and brags about having hooked up with Eartha Kitt, and Britta attempts to sing along to the iPod playing "Roxanne" by The Police, but Jeff shuts her down. When the buzzer sounds indicating the pizza has arrived, Jeff devises a plan as they sit around the table; he picks up a die and rolls it, and whichever number, from 1 to 6, comes up, that person will go down and get the pizza.

The episode is worth examining at length based on what it says about each character, as well as the narrative moving forward. Abed warns him, before he rolls, that "you are now creating six different timelines" and the viewer is subsequently privy to them all. Jeff first rolls a "2," which is Annie. She leaves her purse on the table, and Troy discovers a gun in it; Annie's neighborhood had previously been established as dangerous. Jeff hits his head on the fan, Pierce laughs and then offers Troy a housewarming gift he doesn't open. Britta takes off to the bathroom; when Abed goes to find her, he says the bathroom "smells weird," to which Britta takes offense until she's distracted by the arrival of the pizza. Shirley offers fresh mini-pies that no one eats. Jeff next rolls a "4," which is Shirley. She departs to get the pizza, but not before reminding everyone to check on her pies in the oven. Annie and Jeff argue about Shirley, Jeff asserting that "we do not enable her baking"; Pierce gives a housewarming gift to Troy, who screams when he opens it. The gift is a Norwegian troll figurine that used to reside outside Troy's bedroom when he lived with Pierce, and clearly freaked him out. Jeff laughs, and Annie admonishes Pierce. When Shirley returns and asks about her pies, she discovers that they forgot and let them burn; Jeff tells her they weren't going to eat them and that she's "not allowed to have baking things as an identity." Shirley is furious, accusing the group of being "horny toads" making "googly eyes" at each other. When Pierce expresses solidarity with her, she storms out crying. A "3" sends Pierce down to get the pizzas, but not before telling his Eartha Kitt story. Annie and Jeff share a look, which makes Shirley roll her eyes. Britta heads off to the bathroom, and Annie tells Troy how much she likes the apartment. Jeff takes this opportunity to rib Troy for being immature; when Annie laughs along with Jeff, Troy leaves, joining Britta in the bathroom. Jeff hits his head on the fan, and Annie treats the wound in the kitchen; both reject Shirley's pies. Britta, now revealed to be smoking pot in the bathroom (the "weird smell" Abed mentions), consoles Troy, suggesting that Jeff's guarded personality is only one way to be a man, and they continue to be on good terms as the scene ends. When Jeff rolls a "6," Britta leaves. When Troy tries to say something nice in the awkward silence following Pierce's sex story, Jeff stands up to get a drink and hits his head on the fan. Both Pierce and Troy laugh, while Annie and Jeff retreat to the bathroom to check his head. When Abed and Troy do their special handshake, Pierce seems jealous, and hands Troy a housewarming gift. Annie and Jeff almost kiss in the bathroom before hearing Troy scream; Pierce is tormenting him with the Norwegian troll doll. Abed correctly identifies Pierce's jealousy; when Pierce accuses Abed of being jealous, Abed asks why he would think that. Pierce's response ends up saying more about himself: "Because you're lonely and crazy." That he is describing himself belatedly dawns on him, only to be interrupted by Britta returning with the pizza guy in tow and informing the group they are getting married. With a "1," Troy leaves, launching a thousand internet references. The slamming door starts the ball rolling on Abed's *Raiders of the Lost Ark* display; the ball lands on the floor unnoticed. Britta heads to the bathroom, and Pierce, looking to start trouble, asks Jeff about his father. Jeff hits his head on the fan, and Annie offers to look at the injury in the bathroom, picking up her purse for the first time. Unfortunately, she trips on the ball, knocks over a table, the rum and Pierce's housewarming gift fall to the floor, and the gun in Annie's purse fires, hitting Pierce in the thigh. Shirley and her pies are doused with blood, Annie and Abed attempt to help Pierce, and Britta runs from the bathroom, cigarette in her mouth. When she sees the chaos, the cigarette falls from her mouth, setting fire to the spilled rum. As they ineffectually try to help Pierce and put out the fire, Troy returns with the pizza, and the last thing he sees is the Norwegian troll doll in a ring of fire; he screams. With "5," Abed leaves, being the only one to ask the group to chip in to pay for the pizzas. Shirley checks on her pies, and Jeff stands to get a drink, hitting his head on the fan. He and Annie head to the kitchen to check the wound. Britta emerges stoned from the bathroom, smells Shirley's pies, and Shirley runs over to give her one. Pierce gives Troy his housewarming gift, but before he opens it, Troy thanks him for letting him live with him the previous year. Shirley admits to Britta that she fears "baking is the only thing I'm good for in the group," suggesting Jeff was right in his concern. The scene cuts to Troy telling Pierce that living with him inspired Troy to attempt to "make it on my own, just like you did." This sincerity gets to Pierce, who tries to take back the gift, and the scene cuts between a fight over the gift, Britta admitting they weren't supposed to enable Shirley's baking, and awkward flirting between Jeff and Annie that leads to a kiss that also ends awkwardly. When Britta tells Shirley she's stoned, Shirley takes back her pies, calling Britta a "godless hippie skank," and Troy and Pierce's tussle over the gift makes the Norwegian troll fly across the room.

Knowing Pierce's reasons for it, Troy is disgusted, telling him "you're a sick, sad, twisted old man." Abed, returning with the pizza, is blissfully unaware of anything that happened, or the bad vibes in the room, saying only that he hopes this is the "real one, because I just found a nickel in the hallway."

In a final turn, Abed finally figures out that, by using a six-sided die and starting to count off to his left, Jeff set things up so he never has to go and get the pizza. He grabs the die before it can fall, saying, "Chaos already dominates enough of our lives" and that the only way to survive is to rely on friends, both in spite and because of their predictability. "Annie will always be driven. Shirley will always be giving. Pierce will never apologize. Britta's sort of a wild card from my perspective. And Jeff will forever remain a conniving son-of-a-bitch." Britta puts on "Roxanne," and Jeff hits his head on the fan. This time everyone laughs; as Annie says, it's "karma" in action. Without Jeff to shut her down, Britta starts to sing along to the music, Shirley and Annie join in, and

Abed invites Annie to move in with them and out of her unsafe neighborhood. Pierce tosses the housewarming gift, and by the time Jeff returns with the pizza, everyone except Pierce is dancing along to the music. Jeff stands to the side and eats a slice of pizza. (There is an end tag, set in the "darkest timeline" with Pierce dead, Shirley drinking, Jeff and Troy maimed, and Abed plotting to return to the best timeline as Evil Abed and take over.)[22]

Abed's analysis of the group in the seventh timeline with the caught die offers a good structure to examine the way this particular bottle episode emphasizes the dynamics of the group as a whole by systematically removing one member. "Annie is driven": when she leaves, everyone else does their own thing and nothing quite gets finished. As per example, Troy doesn't open his gift; Jeff neither gets his drink nor treatment for his head wound. "Shirley is giving": the first thing said when she leaves is Jeff admonishing the group not to eat her offered pies. Pierce offers his housewarming gift and this time Troy opens it and is terrified, which pleases Pierce, the opposite of the right intent in giving a gift. Worse, once she is out of the room, the group forgets the one thing she asks them to do, wrapped up in their own issues. The overall tone in this timeline is angry. "Pierce will never apologize": the connections between Jeff and Pierce, both that which Pierce wants and the actual correspondences between them, are obvious in Pierce's absence. Jeff's ironic detachment and Pierce's mockery are two sides of the same coin. That is, in three of the timelines, Pierce taunts Troy with the troll statue, out of a sense of jealousy that Troy moved out. When Pierce is gone, it is Jeff who teases Troy, making fun of the bunk beds and implying he's a child, while Annie laughs. It's Britta who provides the wisdom, telling Troy that there are other ways to be a man than the ways displayed by Jeff—and, by extension, Pierce. It's a nice moment for Britta that leads into her turn to get the pizza, and underscoring Abed's assertion that she is the "wild card" of the group. In the Britta-less timeline, Annie and Jeff nearly kiss in the bathroom while she treats his head injury; Pierce goes full villain, shoving the troll in Troy's face while screaming at him to "feel the terror"; and Britta returns with the pizza guy—the only timeline in which we meet him—and vows to marry him.

Troy's difference from Jeff and Pierce is made explicit when he is the one to leave. While his qualities aren't listed by Abed, his warmth, openness, and playfulness are almost always on display. In his absence, everything goes to hell. In a "Chekhov's gun" moment, the pistol Troy finds in Annie's purse goes off when she trips, and her nursing skills, talked up in the other timelines, are unequal to the fatal injury Pierce suffers. A stoned Britta only makes things worse by dropping her lit cigarette in the broken bottle of rum. Without Troy to humanize him, Abed only helps Pierce after he rights a fallen figure on his *Raiders* display. When Abed leaves, his own awkwardness in social situations spreads to the rest of the group, with Annie mentioning her dad after she and Jeff kiss, Britta admitting the reason for the group's refusal of Shirley's baking, and Shirley's own confession of feeling out of place among them. The other significant absence occurs when Jeff leaves; in a scenario opposite of what happens when Troy is gone, the group doesn't separate into different areas, but instead sing and dance along with "Roxanne," and Pierce embraces his better instincts and tosses the troll gift in the trash. That Jeff needs the group more than the group needs him is made clear in the final episode of the series; he is undone by the prospect of them moving on and unsure what to do when he is not needed.[23] As bottle episodes go, "Remedial Chaos Theory" packs an enormous amount of character development into its relatively short running time.

The other significant sitcom trope that the series plays with is the now fairly defunct clip show. Clip shows, in which a short framing device would set up clips of previous episodes, was, like the bottle episode, a way to save money. Yet, in the days before TV on DVD and streaming, it was often the only way to revisit older episodes of the series, particularly if they had not yet gone into syndication. Most tended to be fairly perfunctory; the frame device for the episode was usually a relatively new character being "caught up" on what happened before. Some series did have fun with the concept; *Roseanne*'s seventh season featured a two-part clip show episode, one in which a younger Roseanne and her sister visit a fortune teller to see their futures, and the second half featuring the "Sitcom Mom's Welcome Wagon," with guest appearances by Barbara Billingsley (*Leave It to Beaver*), Alley Mills (*The Wonder Years* [1988–1993]), Isabel Sanford (*The Jeffersons* [1975–1985]), June Lockhart (*Lassie* [1954–1973]), and Pat Crowley (*Please Don't Eat the Daisies* [1965–1967]).[24] The curated clips in this half of the episode are focused on the ways in which *Roseanne* as a series differed from its predecessors, including frank talk between mother and daughter about birth control or the then-controversial episode in which Roseanne and another female character share a kiss.[25] While less common in drama series, the series *Dead Like Me* (2003–2004) aired a clip show as its twelfth episode in its first season, following the departure of a main character, and the series *Supernatural* used the concept as a conceit for an episode in which the season's antagonist, Crowley (Mark Sheppard), starts killing people the brothers had saved in earlier episodes.[26] Aside from their place as a cost-saving measure, they also did serve a purpose, through the frame device by which they were presented, in orienting a newer viewer into the character dynamics, as well as reminding longer-term viewers of the plot and character elements they may have forgotten.

Community played with this twice, with "Paradigms of Human Memory" and "Curriculum Unavailable," but each served a slightly different function. While both parodied the clip show, the how and why shifted based on changing plot and character dynamics. "Paradigms" starts with the study group creating a diorama for their anthropology class; the subject of this diorama is the creation of the previous diorama, a subtle reminder of the meta-ness of the series and this episode in particular. It's emblematic of the way the episode both embraces and subverts the clip show structure. From a production standpoint, it is pure subversion; if the point of the clip show is to save money, "Paradigms" fails utterly. Aside from the usual Paramount studios filming set, they also filmed at Universal; Harmon suggests that the film savvy will recognize sets from *Psycho* (1960), *Jaws* (1975), and *War of the Worlds* (2005) among the clips.[27] Indeed, none of the clips shown are from previous episodes, something that is teased at the start when Annie's pens are finally found (they'd been stolen by Troy's missing monkey) and Jeff says: "Do you remember when you got so mad because you thought someone was stealing them?"—a perfect setup to show a clip from "Cooperative Calligraphy." Instead, he picks up a tin star, and the group remembers their trip to an old ghost town, a scene from a nonexistent episode. This is the case for every clip except two: an unseen clip of Britta and Jeff sneaking off into the bathroom during the Halloween party in "Epidemiology," and a non-Claymation scene from "Abed's Uncontrollable Christmas."[28] Like "Cooperative Calligraphy," the episode's focus is on airing out the various grievances, issues, and secrets that the group has experienced over the past year, first by blaming Britta and Jeff's secret hookups before realizing that all of them had a part in the issues they've experienced. Indeed, at the climax of the episode, it layers a clip inside a clip inside a clip, connected by the study group arguing and Troy screaming until it returns to the present day with Troy screaming again. Jeff gives a speech that brings them back together, and the episode ends with an animated tag (in the style of 1980s-era cartoons) of the dean's reaction to Jeff's earlier, mean comments.[29]

What is intriguing about "Paradigms" is not only its parody of the clip show, featuring clips from nonexistent episodes that become increasingly bizarre (e.g., drug runners attempting to execute Pierce; the group in a haunted house) but *Community*'s own tropes, both character and fan-based. There is an extended sequence in which Annie attempts to suggest a connection between herself and Jeff, as Sara Bareilles' "Gravity" plays over a selection of clips; Jeff counters that framing is everything, followed by a succession of clips of Pierce and Abed with the same song playing. This was actually based on a fan-video created following the first season, using that song with clips focused on Annie and Jeff as a potential couple. While it does seem to be a bit of a dig at the show's fans, the series itself plays with the Annie and Jeff dynamic in similar ways throughout the series. Yet they also skewer their own tropes, particularly Jeff's propensity for speechifying. Aside from "Cooperative Calligraphy," Jeff gives speeches in the first episode, as well as "Advanced Criminal Law," when Britta is caught cheating on her Spanish test; in "Anthropology 101," when the group has fractured (again) due to various issues; and in "Early 21st Century Romanticism" over whether to stage an intervention for Pierce, among many others.[30] "Paradigms," however, offers the grandest one of all:

> Look, we've known each other for almost two years now. And yeah, in that time, I've given a lot of speeches. But they all have one thing in common: they're all different. These drug-runners aren't going to execute Pierce because he's racist! It's a locomotive that runs … on us. And the only sharks in that water … are the emotional ghosts that I like to call: fear, anchovies, fear, and the dangers of ingesting mercury. Because the real bugs aren't the ones in those beds. And there's no such thing as a free Caesar salad. And even if there were, *The Cape* still might find a second life on cable. And I'll tell you why: El corazón del agua es verdad. That water … is a lie! Harrison Ford is irradiating our testicles with microwave satellite transmissions! So maybe we are caught in an endless cycle of screw-ups and hurt feelings. But I choose to believe it's just the universe's way of molding us into some kind of supergroup.[31]

Essentially, the speech is a mini–clip show in and of itself, splicing "Winger speeches" across multiple clips to create something that is total nonsense. In that respect, they are parodying their own reliance on such moments to hit the emotional and narrative beats of an episode.

"Curriculum Unavailable," the second clip show episode, comes from a different place. That is, there is no need for the group to air their differences; they are all united in the fact that they have been kicked out of Greendale following a riot they were accused of instigating.[32] The campus has been taken over by Ben Chang, formerly the head of security, and Abed is convinced that Chang has replaced the dean with a "deanalganger" (or "doppeldeaner"), a plot point first suggested in "Contemporary Impressionists." As they are barred from campus, Abed is brought back to the apartment by a police officer, who says that the school is willing to drop any trespassing charges if Abed seeks therapy. To show their support, the entire study group goes with Abed to the school-recommended therapist, Dr. Heidi (John Hodgman). Unlike "Paradigms," the clips in the episode aren't meant to reveal what the group has hidden from one another, but rather converge on what's actually going on with Greendale. The clips originally revolve around proving Abed's not crazy, before Dr. Heidi's reactions lead the group to suggest they are all a little nuts, because Greendale made them that way. These offer a slow build-up that leads them to memories of the ways that the dean always looked out for them, and thus his expulsion of them from Greendale was out of character. Of course, the moment they come to this realization, Dr. Heidi re-contextualizes not only those memories, but also the series as a whole, telling them that they are suffering from a mass delusion: Greendale was never a community college, but a mental hospital in which they were all housed together. The episode cuts to clips of the hospital, with Troy and Jeff jumping on a mattress they think is a trampoline ("Aerodynamics of Gender"), various paintball scenarios, Pierce singing "Baby Boomer Santa" from "Regional Holiday Music," along with characters such as Leonard, Garrett, and the dean as either other patients or staff. The group is briefly rattled by this until they realize it's absurd ("I'm literally wearing a Greendale backpack," Annie says), and it is finally revealed that "Dr. Heidi" was hired by Chang to throw them off his plan.[33]

The subtle differences in the purposes of the clips shown in "Paradigms" versus "Curriculum Unavailable" (one focused on what tears the group apart, the other on their shared experiences and connection to one another and Greendale) actually show the group's growth. Instead of "catching up" the audience on past events, both of *Community*'s clip shows end up serving as

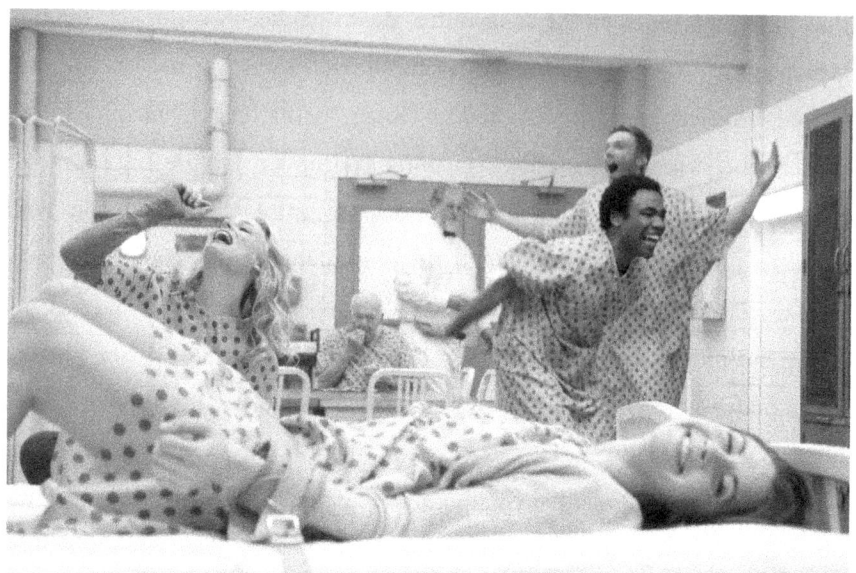

The study group is briefly led to believe everybody had a collective mental breakdown. NBC/Photofest © NBC.

education—not surprising, given the series' setting—on the group's dynamics and connections to one another beyond their meta structure.

"Pick One Reference, Abed": *Community* and the Wider Media Landscape

Community doesn't limit itself to referencing and commenting on the sitcom genre, however; it engages with a broad spectrum of shows, films, and animation. Self-awareness is baked into much of twenty-first-century media; *Community* is not the first, nor will it be the last to do so. Yet the series uses this self-awareness to comment on elements beyond the sitcom genre, incorporating through pastiche elements of other media. This can, although not always, be used to make a broader point about a particular character, plot, or genre. Because this is such a thoroughgoing part of the series, I'll be focusing here on those episodes in which these references and pastiches are an integral part of the plot, and what it says about both the original text and *Community*.

While some of these homages are more amusing than anything else—the first paintball episode, "Modern Warfare," references John Woo films, apocalypse films, and *Die Hard* (1987), among others—they can also be used to deepen characters and relationships. Abed is perhaps the main purveyor of this type of episode, with "Contemporary American Poultry" and "Critical Film Studies" as perhaps the strongest examples of this. "Contemporary American Poultry" seems to focus on the study group's annoyance that the best items the school's cafeteria serves, chicken fingers, always seem to run out before they can get some for themselves. A little sleuthing reveals that the fry cook, Alex, has been appropriating them and giving them to his friends. Jeff suggests they leverage this information to get Alex fired and Abed hired (as he has experience working at his father's falafel restaurant). They do this, only to repeat the same patterns as Alex had: using the chicken fingers to get what they want. While it is originally Jeff's idea, it is Abed's viewpoint that remains primary; he conceives the adventure as a "mafia film" and narrates much of the action in voiceover, casting himself as the Henry Hill (Ray Liotta) within the "gang." In case the *GoodFellas* connection was unclear, the episode also uses "Layla" by Derek and the Dominos as the study group discovers Abed's various retaliations for their greed and disloyalty, as well as using freeze frame in a similar way to Scorsese's film. This homage, however, is actually related to character progress for both Abed and Jeff; Abed uses the film as a way to connect with people, something he struggles with, while Jeff's eventual exclusion shows him the limits of power as well as his own moral limitations.[34]

Surprisingly, "Critical Film Studies" also features Jeff and Abed, suggesting that they are two sides of the same coin. (For all his protestations, Jeff almost always gets the references Abed makes.) The homage here might be less obvious to a broader audience, but is nonetheless used in a similar way to *GoodFellas*. The basic premise is that Abed invites Jeff to have dinner with him, and Jeff goes, knowing it's Abed's birthday. In fact, he has planned an elaborate, *Pulp Fiction*–themed party at the diner where Britta works and gotten Abed what purports to be the famous briefcase from the film as a gift. Abed, however, seems to have no interest in leaving, preferring to stay at the diner and have an in-depth conversation with Jeff. That is, Abed's goal, although never explicitly stated, is to recreate Louis Malle's 1981 film *My Dinner with André*, in which two friends, Wallace Shawn and André Gregory, reconnect after a lengthy separation and discuss the nature of art and life. In this scenario, Jeff is Shawn and Abed Gregory, down to the sweater he wears throughout the meal. Beyond the surface level, however, Abed's conversation with Jeff focuses on the nature of reality through Abed's own particular interests, asking metaphysical questions through his anecdote about appearing as an extra on his favorite series, *Cougar Town* (2009–2015), which ran simultaneously with *Community*. He discusses his invented character, Chad, and the whole backstory and personality he invented for him, and his concern that "Chad" had lived better than he, Abed, had, suggesting Gregory's anecdotes about his time away from acting as a theater director, and the ways in which said experiences taught him what it meant to be human. Abed's seeming openness, and subtle pressure that Jeff applies to give him a "real" conversation without a reliance on popular culture, does lead to Jeff opening up about his own insecurities, including the revelation that he calls phone sex lines posing as an obese man, to prove to himself he'd be lovable even if he wasn't attractive or cool. Thus, when Abed reveals that this was another homage, Jeff initially feels betrayed, only to eventually realize that this is the way that Abed reaches out, and that the homages themselves can actually lead to productive discussion and growth.[35] Other "whole episode" tributes include "Basic Rocket Science," which mixes product placement (KFC) with *Apollo 13* (1995), or "Basic Intergluteal Numismatics" and its stylistic parody of David Fincher's crime oeuvre as the school tries to figure out who is the criminal known as the "Ass Crack Bandit," a mystery that remains unsolved by the end of the episode, suggesting *Zodiac* (2007) as the primary text.[36] "Horror Fiction in Seven Spooky Steps" essentially offers short horror (or horror adjacent) stories: a *Twilight*/Anne Rice–inspired vampire love story between Annie and Jeff, a sci-fi/horror mix (Troy), a cautionary tale about sin (Shirley), and a meta-take on the genre (Abed), among others, all of which reflect the personality of the teller.[37]

The series doesn't limit itself to film, although some homages are a bit wider than others. "Basic Lupine Urology" takes on Dick Wolf's *Law & Order*, changing the opening credits to ones that reflect *Law & Order*: "Greendale Community College is represented by two separate yet equally important types of people: the goofballs who run around stirring up trouble, and the eggheads that make a big deal out of it. These are their stories," and using the still-shot structure of the series' opening. They also cast Leslie Hendrix, who has played medical examiner Dr. Elizabeth Rodgers in the original and also appeared in *SVU* (1999–present) and *Criminal Intent* (2001–2011), and ended the episode with a stinger that recalled an early *Law & Order* episode, "Prince of Darkness." While the character dynamics were not as strong in this episode as in the earlier ones, the interactions between Jeff and Annie suggest his concern that his influence on her has made Annie more cynical; it also subtly suggests her future career path.[38] "Regional Holiday Music" takes aim at the series' competition on the Fox network, *Glee*, dialing up *Glee*'s problematic Glee Club head, Mr. Schuster (Matthew Morrison), into Mr. Radison (Taran Killiam), who admits to massacring the previous Glee Club participants for not listening to him.[39] "Abed's Uncontrollable Christmas," filmed entirely in Claymation, offers insight into Abed's sadness when his mother decides to spend Christmas with her new family, while "G.I. Jeff," in a similar vein, has Jeff deal with turning forty by retreating into 1980s cartoon *G.I. Joe*, where the enemies are always the same and actions have few consequences.[40] It also reinforces his similarity to Abed, suggested throughout the series, in that he finds comfort in retreating into television.[41] Finally, "Pillows and Blankets" brings to a head the simmering tension between Troy and Abed that had been building since "Contemporary Impressionists," using a Ken Burns–style documentary to dramatize their conflict over whether to build a campus-wide blanket fort or pillow fort. (They even cast Keith David, who had at this point done voiceover work for Ken Burns' *Jazz* (2001) as well as a follow-up to Burns' *Baseball* (1994) documentary, as the narrator. David would later join the cast in season six.)[42] Less directly, Abed's (and later Troy's) embrace of the fictional British series *Inspector Spacetime* is a direct play on the BBC's long-running *Doctor Who*, and one that both Abed and Troy (and occasionally Annie) cosplay both in their apartment and, for Abed, out in the world; in "Curriculum Unavailable," he attempts to investigate what's happening at Greendale in his *Inspector Spacetime* persona (and costume). (Indeed, Matt Lucas, who appears in season four as a British *Inspector Spacetime* fan that Abed meets at a fan convention, would later appear on *Doctor Who* as Nardole, a companion of the Twelfth Doctor [Peter Capaldi].)[43] Like the ways in which *Community* interacts with the tropes and plots of the sitcom genre, it also liberally borrows from other media with the same goal: to move beyond simple parody or homage and use these elements to advance both plot and character.

Self-awareness in fiction (books, TV, movies) is often a way to distance the audience from what they are watching/reading so they can more clearly see the elements and tropes that undergird it. Films such as *Popcorn* (1991), *New Nightmare* (1994), *Scream* (1996), and *The Cabin in the Woods* (2011) used their self-reflective turns to comment on particular tropes, whether it was how sexuality and gender operate within the genre, or commentary on spectatorship and violence. *Community* remains an essential part of this tradition, incorporating gimmicks and tropes from sitcoms, films, documentaries, and even animations into its narratives. Yet it is instructive to look at the ways in which *Community* deploys these gimmicks and tropes. That is, rather than simply pointing them out (known as "lampshading"), it uses formats such as the bottle episode and clip show, or tropes such as "will they, won't they" to comment, and occasionally subvert, them as well as advance plot and character in a way that was still new to the sitcom genre when it aired.

PART THREE

"Show May Be Canceled
and Moved to the Internet":
Community's Impact

7

"We're Created by a Joke"
Sony, *Community*, and TV on the Brink

The final episode of *Community* ends with a stinger featuring no members of the central cast, something that the sixth season did more than once. Instead, it features two parents and two kids sitting around a table playing something called "*Community*: The Board Game." Players can insult Leonard, like Jeff "as a friend," drunk dial, or spend time in the Dreamatorium with Troy and Abed. According to the voiceover, the goal is to "collect players' identities and figure out if the game is part of the show," or, as per example, occurring in a snow globe (i.e., the controversial ending to *St. Elsewhere* [1982–1988], which revealed the whole series had taken place inside a young autistic boy's head, known on the internet as the "Tommy Westphall Universe").[1] The boy discovers a script in the box, and thinks he's won the game; unfortunately, it turns out to be a script for this very scene, plunging the entire "family" into an existential crisis regarding their own reality. This moment reaches both back to the past and into the future of television. That is, board games as a cross-promotion for television shows were ubiquitous in the 1960s and 1970s, ranging from the expected (kid-friendly shows such as *The Partridge Family*) to the inexplicable (an *As the World Turns* board game, based on the long-running soap opera), but far less common now, with the exception of themed games, such as *Supernatural* Clue or *The Golden Girls* Monopoly game. Yet this self-aware scene, airing on a streaming service and capped off with a long recap by creator Dan Harmon, including: "Viewers may be measured by a secretive obsolete system based on selected participants keeping handwritten journals of what they watched" (i.e., the Nielsen rating system) versus "Show may be canceled and moved to the internet where it turns out 10s of millions were watching the whole time—may not matter," an early reminder of the challenges of measuring viewership on streaming platforms, serves as a direct representation of *Community*'s position as ahead of its time while honoring its past.[2]

Low-rated but critically lauded, *Community*'s six-year run served as a bellwether for the ongoing shifts in television occurring between its debut in 2009 and its final season in 2015. Surviving casting and showrunning shake-ups, it was one of the first canceled series to find a second life on streaming, something that would become increasingly common as these services proliferated and needed content; shows with a built-in audience/fanbase provided a leg up on new content and could raise the service's profile. Intertwined with this is *Community*'s production company, Sony, one of the only studios without either a dedicated broadcast channel or streaming service, yet responsible for producing mainstays such as *Days of Our Lives*, (1965–present), groundbreakers such as *Soap* and *Designing Women* (1986–1993), and critical darlings *Breaking Bad* and *Hannibal* (2013–2015). This chapter will examine how *Community* embodied the changes and challenges of these shifts, as well as a long-overdue examination of Sony as television producer.

"Millions Were Watching the Whole Time": *Community* and TV's Changing Landscape

Broadcast television has never been the most adept at reacting to certain types of change; that is, the kind that could potentially cut into audience share and advertising rates. This likely stems from the fact that for most of the first thirty years of television broadcasting, few structural changes occurred. The first decade of television featured four networks: NBC, CBS, and ABC, which expanded from radio, and DuMont, which folded in 1956, leaving the Big Three to dominate broadcast television for the next three decades. Lurking in the wings, however, was cable television. Cable actually coexisted with broadcast television throughout most of its history; however, because of a freeze on station licenses and what programs cable could air, as well as the limited channel spectrum, it was primarily used to provide better reception to rural or more remote locations, even as the technology continued to develop and more companies, such as Cox Communications, were investing in cable. In 1972, however, the restrictions were finally lifted, and the first two cable networks, HBO and WTBS, were launched, in 1972 and 1973, respectively. Further deregulation under Reagan's Federal Communications Commission in the 1980s massively expanded cable's reach, and represented the start of cable television as competition with broadcast. It's in the 1980s that HBO starts to air its own original programming, beyond the sports, music, and comedy specials that were already part of its programming. *Not Necessarily the News* (1983–1990), a satirical news show that was the obvious precursor to *The Daily Show*, among others, debuted in 1983, followed by other half-hour comedy series, including *1st & Ten* (1984–1991) and *Dream On* (1990–1996). While these series did garner attention, including from the Emmys, it was the debut of series such as *Oz* (1997–2003) and *The Sopranos*, created by well-regarded television writers and directors such as Tom Fontana (*Homicide: Life on the Street*) and David Chase, who'd written for series such as *The Rockford Files* and *Northern Exposure* (1990–1995), that ushered in what is considered the "prestige TV" era. While the language and the sight of Dennis Franz's naked butt on *NYPD Blue* (1993–2005) ignited a firestorm of controversy (including the formation of the Parents Television Council) in 1993, cable could and did go to narrative and character places not allowed on broadcast.[3] With fewer content restrictions than broadcast, these series could and did take on subjects broadcast television was wary of (such as the gritty and violent world of prisons), and attracted writing and acting talent from multiple mediums that earlier would have considered television a step down. By the 2010s, cable was outstripping broadcast in terms of the amount of original programming, from basic cable networks like TNT, USA, and SyFy to the premium channels, such as HBO and Showtime.[4]

As Michele Hilmes suggests, all of this was already in play by the mid-1980s; she writes that by this time, "the classic network system had not yet died away completely, but it was feeling rather ill."[5] Despite the fact that the great surge of cable programming was still years away, it was still siphoning off broadcast's audience by appealing to smaller, if still significant, audience segments, aka "niche" audiences: MTV for teens; ESPN for sports fans; Lifetime, which billed itself as "television for women"; and Nickelodeon, which focused on children and preteens with animated and live-action series. Broadcast initially responded to this by doubling down on what already worked, with the 1970s and 1980s awash in spin-offs of successful series such as *All in the Family* and *The Mary Tyler Moore Show*. Yet there were glimmers of broadcasting starting to embrace the more niche, and thus more critically lauded, aesthetic of cable, with series such as *Moonlighting* (1985–1989), which blended film, theater, comedy, drama, and noir into a meta package gaining audiences and critical respect, and *thirtysomething* (1987–1991), which didn't make a great splash in the ratings but hit audience demographics (upper middle class) that networks wanted. This accelerated in the 1990s, as the first "fourth" network since DuMont shut down in 1956 gained traction (Fox), followed by the debut of UPN and the WB, which further fragmented audiences by appealing to heretofore undercourted audiences. In the wake of this, some, but not all, of the broadcast networks shifted not only into appealing to niche audiences but also lowering restrictions on content; as per example, the challenges that the

WB threw in the way of showing same-sex kisses—never mind intimacy on par with heterosexual pairings—on *Buffy the Vampire Slayer* and *Dawson's Creek*, were no longer an issue with the CW (the merging of UPN and the WB), with series such as *Crazy Ex-Girlfriend* (2015–2019), *Legends of Tomorrow* (2016–2022), and *Roswell, New Mexico* (2019–2022) featuring a variety of pairings outside of the heteronormative ones of their predecessors. This was evident in basic cable programming as well; while they initially used the same content standards of broadcast (although they were not required to), the 2000s saw a rise in programs that rivaled premium networks in terms of levels of language and action, such as SyFy's *The Magicians* (2015–2020) and USA's *Chucky* (2021–2024).

Despite this, however, network television was in a spiral in terms of viewers that it will likely never recover from. As discussed in Chapter 1, though, that provided an opportunity for broadcast to take a few more risks, and greenlit dramas and sitcoms that might not command big audiences, but appealed to at least a segment of the viewing audience. This is something that NBC, at the bottom of the ratings after two decades of dominance, elected to do, with its Thursday night lineup during that time offering a combo of mockumentary, workplace sitcoms, and backstage/meta series, all sans laugh track and focused primarily on found-family ensembles. This time period (2005–2015), post-*Sopranos*, (mostly) pre-streaming, in many ways represents the end of an era, mixing the quirky ensemble comedy that characterized series from *The Bob Newhart Show* (1972–1978) to *Superstore* with the single-camera aesthetic. While *Parks and Recreation*, *30 Rock*, *The Office*, and *Community* all fit into this structure, it is *Community* that suggests a few elements of what would become standard moving forward. First, of the four series that aired on NBC's iconic Thursday night comedy block, *Community* likely took the most narrative risks, blending, as discussed earlier, any number of mediums, as well as known sitcom tropes, into a character-based metatextual sitcom. In that way, it situated itself quite comfortably as part of the long US TV sitcom history.[6] Yet it also boasted a robust fandom unlike its sitcom predecessors, with an active online community usually reserved for fantasy and sci-fi series such as *Firefly* or *Supernatural*, one that creator Dan Harmon interacted with frequently, and that pushed for the series' continued renewal (e.g., #sixseasonsandamovie). While not the only factor, their vocal response to the series' cancellation by NBC following its fifth season was likely a factor in the newly launched (and quickly shut down) Yahoo! Screen streaming service picking it up for a sixth season.

It should be noted that series being picked up after cancellation by other broadcast networks is not common, but has occurred multiple times throughout TV history, from ABC picking up the final season of *Diff'rent Strokes* after NBC canceled it, to NBC airing three additional seasons of *Brooklyn Nine-Nine* following Fox's cancellation. Yet in 2014, this was not at all common; Netflix, the best-known streaming service at the time,

Community survived despite cast and platform changes, adding Keith David in season 6. NBC/Photofest © NBC.

had only debuted its first original program (*House of Cards*) in 2013, and streaming as an additional place to sell sitcom or drama series for airing was in its infancy. Being a new and untested way of "saving" shows ended with Yahoo! Screen losing money and shutting down within a year after acquiring *Community*.[7] Yet it proved to be a decent test case and way forward for both continuing and new programs. In 2016, Netflix aired a continuation of WB series *Gilmore Girls*, whose initial run had ended without its showrunner and primary writer, Amy Sherman-Palladino. It later picked up *Lucifer* (2016–2021) from Fox after cancellation, airing three additional seasons. The newer streaming service Peacock aired the final two seasons of NBC series *AP Bio* (2018–2021)—a lateral move, as Peacock is under NBC/Universal's corporate umbrella. In a similar lateral move, NBC picked up *Brooklyn Nine-Nine* from Fox on the broadcast side, as *Brooklyn Nine-Nine* was an NBC/Universal production.

This isn't to say that Yahoo picking up *Community* started the trend, only that it suggested a way forward for series that would be considered too niche even for the new standards of broadcast television. Yet it also pointed in another direction: streaming as a supplement to broadcast. *The Good Place*, which debuted in 2016, and *Supernatural*, which first aired in 2005 but also aired its earlier seasons starting in 2011, both benefited from streaming in their continued renewal. These two shows in particular, one that was an arc-based sitcom set in the afterlife and a significant emphasis on moral philosophy, and the other part of the horror genre that has always struggled on broadcast television, were shows with subjects that might not have succeeded in earlier decades.[8] Bill Harvey, a television industry analyst, suggests that "streaming is not competing with linear; it's extending the reach of linear."[9] *Community* may not have benefited from this in its initial streaming stage, but the success of the series when it arrived on Netflix in 2020 was a likely factor in the *Community* movie moving forward.

Mergers, Misfits, and Money: A Brief History of Sony Television

The changes in the Telecommunications Act in 1996, which lifted ownership caps on media companies and eliminated incentives for television stations to license content to other stations, ushered in significant changes in US television that are still playing out in 2025. The lifted caps made it easier for companies to merge or buy out other media companies; as per example, Disney bought ABC in 1996, one of its earlier acquisitions, followed by Marvel Studios, Lucasfilm, and 20th Century Fox over the next twenty years. As for content, the ending of the financial incentives and syndication rule, the purpose of which was to level the playing field between studios and independent producers by not allowing networks to create and air series only developed in their studios, meant that a network would not necessarily have to pay to license other series; they could develop them in-house and air them, and thus retain a greater share of the profits.

Sony started as an electronics shop in Japan in 1946 by Masaru Ibuka. The company's first major success was a transistor radio, which hit big in both Japan and the United States, and they continued to make a name for themselves with electronics throughout the 1950s and 1960s. Yet as they got into subsidiary businesses, such as life insurance, the recession of the 1980s hit electronics sales as well, prompting doom-crying by some in the industry that Sony was on its way out. Despite this, they continued both to develop and diversify, championing the compact disc as a format, debuting the PlayStation game console in the 1990s, and buying up several properties across mediums, including CBS Records and Columbia Pictures. Columbia was initially a film studio started in 1918 by the Cohn brothers, Harry and Jack, with Joe Brandt to produce low-budget short films. They dubbed themselves CBC and had a studio on what was known as Poverty Row (often located on Gower Street in Los Angeles) because of the content they produced (low-cost B-movies).

They produced their first feature-length film in 1922, which did well enough for them to decide to incorporate, and renamed the studio Columbia Pictures. (The name derives from the figure of Columbia, known as the female personification of the United States; a statue of her was part of the studio's logo.) It was their relationship with Frank Capra, however, that really put the studio on the map. They still also created short films, including animated ones like *Silly Symphonies* (1929–1939), and live-action Three Stooges shorts. The animated shorts were developed under what became the Screen Gems division, which was repurposed in 1948 to create commercials and eventually programs for television. Nearly a decade later, they also landed a distribution deal with Hanna-Barbera, which produced series such as *The Flintstones* and *The Jetsons* (1962–1963), among many others. By the mid-1960s, however, with a number of box office failures, Screen Gems' profits in television were the only thing that was keeping the studio afloat, and the two officially merged in 1968. In 1974, they retired the Screen Gems name and became Columbia Pictures Television. Columbia entered into an agreement with HBO and CBS to form Tri-Star Pictures. Columbia also bought up numerous production companies, including Norman Lear's Tandem Productions (later to become Act III Productions), Merv Griffin Enterprises (game shows such as *Jeopardy* [1964–present]), and Danny Arnold Productions, which included series such as *Barney Miller*. They served as distributors to both dramas (*Family* [1976–1980], *Charlie's Angels* [1976–1981], among others) and sitcoms (*Soap, Fish* [1977–1978]), and served as coproducers for shows such as *Fantasy Island* (1977–1984), *T. J. Hooker* (1982–1986), and *What's Happening!!* before being bought out by Coca-Cola in 1982. After acquiring a large library of classic television shows (e.g., *Bewitched*), Columbia revived the Screen Gems name to market them, given its association with classic cinema. They also bought Embassy Communications (co-owned by Norman Lear and Jerry Perenchio), which gave them access to Lear's extensive library of series (*All in the Family, The Jeffersons*, etc.), but executive shake-ups—and the notorious failure of the film *Ishtar* (1987)—led to Columbia and Embassy splitting their television assets, with Columbia focused on drama, and Embassy, unsurprisingly, on comedy. When Columbia merged with Tri-Star Television, Embassy was shunted off as a copyright-holding entity, although by the end of the 1980s, they had formed another partnership with Lear's Act III Communications, which would focus on producing television rather than simply distributing programs. Coca-Cola eventually sold Columbia to Sony in 1989, one of many studio sales and mergers throughout the 1980s.[10] Under their new owners, the studio created talk shows (*Ricki Lake* [1993–2004]), dramas such as *Party of Five* (1994–2000), and sitcoms that either gained critical respect (*News Radio*) if not always ratings, as well as those that became cultural institutions (*Seinfeld*), despite initial struggles to find viewers. By 1994, Columbia and TriStar merged to become Columbia Tristar Television, which lasted until 2002, when it was officially changed to Sony Pictures Television.

While Sony, in historical terms, is thus a relative newcomer to US television, the merging and acquiring done by Columbia before the sale, as well as those acquired by Sony itself, encompass most of the history of television in its back catalogue. Post-1989, however, Sony's production also included both some of the more critically or culturally significant series of the past forty years, as well as some of its most notorious failures. While there were plenty of Sony-produced series that broke no new critical or narrative ground, including sitcoms such as *Mad About You, Just Shoot Me!, The King of Queens* (1998–2007), *Rules of Engagement* (2007–2013), or *The Goldbergs*, there were others, including *Community*, that took risks or upended expectations. *The Larry Sanders Show* used the conceit of the backstage antics of a late-night talk show (as *30 Rock* would a decade later) as satire of both the format and celebrity culture more generally. *The Boondocks* (2005–2014), an adult animated series that aired as part of Cartoon Network's Adult Swim programming block and used anime-style animation, addressed issues of Black identity, politics, and culture that frequently caused controversy and critical acclaim. The antiheroes of series such as *Breaking Bad, Better Call Saul* (2015–2022), and *The Boys* built on the legacy of characters such as Tony Soprano while also highlighting deficits in health care, the legal system, and the darker side of the superhero trend of the 2010s. *The Last of Us* (2023–present), adapted from the video game, is the first of its kind (either in film or television) to receive multiple award nominations.

It should be noted, however, that these acclaimed or genre-busting series all aired on both basic and pay cable, which offers different narrative and content opportunities for programs. Yet several of Sony's broadcast series, in both drama and sitcom, managed to play with the form or break new ground in content. Sometimes their failures were notorious. *Emily's Reasons Why Not* (2006), a sitcom about a self-help writer with a bad dating life, was heavily promoted by Sony and ABC as a possible next big thing, only to be canceled after a single episode had aired. *Viva Laughlin* (2007), an American dramedy based on the BBC series *Blackpool* (2004–2006), starring Hugh Jackman as casino owner Ripley Holden and featuring its cast breaking into contemporary songs at various points, was considered a "train wreck" and canceled after two episodes.[11] Despite these misses, however, they also produced *Hannibal*; its highly cinematic visual style, boundary-pushing content, and re-conception of a familiar villain (Hannibal Lecter) recalled earlier series such as *Twin Peaks* (1990–1991, 2017) while suggesting new ground for broadcast television dramas moving forward. While in most ways a fairly typical teen drama, *Dawson's Creek*'s blend of melodrama and pop culture–savvy teens prone to overthinking everything, set the tone for many teen dramas to follow; it also, along with *Buffy the Vampire Slayer*, featured one of the first same-sex kisses in the teen genre.[12] *Timeless*, with its time travel conceit, offered subtle commentary on the ways in which those in power attempt to rewrite history in their favor. Sitcoms such as *News Radio* and *Parker Lewis Can't Lose* played with the form in a way that *Community* would later perfect. *News Radio*, a workplace sitcom set in a New York City AM radio station, also blended elements of farce, numerous visual gags, and physical comedy, anchored by two actors who'd started in sketch comedy: Dave Foley (*Kids in the Hall* [1988–1995]) and Phil Hartman (*Saturday Night Live*). The episode "Daydream," in which the staff deals with the air conditioning being broken during a heat wave, offers several cutaways and dream sequences to suggest their deteriorating mental states due to the temperature; high-concept episodes, such as "Space," in which the news station becomes a space station, and "Sinking Ship," which satirizes both the then-popular *Titanic* (1997) and the sitcom's constant challenge to stay afloat, could be considered to have set the stage for later series.[13] (This episode took on a darker hue following Phil Hartman's murder two weeks after it aired.) *Parker Lewis Can't Lose* debuted on Fox one year after *The Simpsons*, and stood out not only for its focus on teen protagonists, but also its lack of a laugh track and a visual and aural style that combined cartoons (particularly with its sound effects) with more cinematic effects, a single-camera sitcom more than a decade before *Arrested Development*. This was by design, as the series' creators wanted the visuals to tell as much of a story as the narrative. Director Rob Bowman claimed working on the series was equivalent to attending the "Juilliard school of cinema" for the ways they were encouraged to take risks with both stories and shot composition.[14] For one of the few studios that is not affiliated with a broadcast network (NBC/Universal, CBS and Paramount, the CW with Warner Brothers), Sony has nonetheless managed to create a broad breadth of content for broadcast, cable, and streaming that encompasses both older models (hospital dramas such as *The Good Doctor* [2017–2024]) and, as discussed above, more innovative sitcoms and dramas that pointed to or helped shift television in new and exciting directions.

The idea that broadcast television is dying is one that is resurrected each time a new technology or platform comes to prominence, and yet, as of 2025, it is still holding on. Indeed, more outlets for content have provided more outlets to target traditionally underrepresented stories and creators that struggled to find a foothold on broadcast in earlier eras. This, however, comes with significant caveats, as were brought to the forefront during the Writers Guild of America (WGA) and the Screen Actors Guild (SAG-AFTRA) strikes in 2023, the second longest strike in the unions' history. These included a lack of mentorship for new writers with the shorter episode orders and smaller writing staffs of streaming series, the use of AI for writing and visuals, and the residuals available for both actors and writers outside of broadcast.[15] That being said, with the proliferation of streaming outlets, and the aftereffects of the WGA/SAG strike, production companies, including Sony, seem to be creating a majority of their content for streaming outlets rather than broadcast.[16] Added to this is an overall downturn in scripted content across all platforms, due both to rising costs and the 2023 strikes, and more content being imported from overseas.[17] Indeed, the majority of content Sony has created over the past few years—and those that have been the most successful—appeared on either pay cable or streaming, including *Cobra Kai* (2018–2025), *The Boys*, and *The Last of Us*.

Community, by virtue of timing as well as the narrative and production choices it made, thus becomes, in retrospect, a series that embodies the tensions of the transition from the broadcast/cable to the streaming era. It builds on predecessors such as *Parker Lewis Can't Lose* and *Arrested Development* for its visual language and metatextual structures, as well as the select group of school-based sitcoms of the past through its narrative choices and visual language. While its self-awareness would become a trope of its own in subsequent years, *Community*'s blend of parody and homage in its meta moments moves it beyond merely pointing out the tropes but provides a model for how to use metatext as both commentary and narrative. Like Sony, it blended old and new shows and forms throughout its run.

8

"Six Seasons and a Movie!"
Community's Afterlife

The final episode of *Community*, airing on Yahoo! Screen, featured various "pitches" for what a seventh season of the show would look like. These ranged from a dour environmental drama (Britta) to a reboot featuring only attractive young women (Jeff), most of which had their analogue in other contemporary series (i.e., Jeff's wouldn't have been out of place as a sitcom by Chuck Lorre, a creator Harmon takes a dig at in his final voiceover). Abed eventually reveals he steered the conversation in that direction so that he would have pitches to offer as part of his new job in California working on a TV show he describes as "It's like *30 Rock*, meets *IT Crowd*, meets, well me."[1] While that could vaguely describe *Community*, there's an in-joke buried in Abed's comment: an American version of the British sitcom *The IT Crowd* (2006–2013) almost went to series; the pilot was filmed and the series ordered before NBC pulled the plug. Not only was this version coproduced by Moses Port (who co-show ran season four of *Community*) but Joel McHale was cast in one of the lead roles. Given that this happened a year before the debut of *Community*, had it gone forward, *Community* might have been a very different show without McHale. The last shot of the remaining cast—Jeff, Britta, Chang, Craig, and Frankie—is quiet and understated as they share a drink.

Yet this isn't the final shot. As discussed in the previous chapter, the episode actually ends with an "ad" for *Community: The Board Game*, which, like the show itself, ends up questioning the nature of what we think of as reality, a concept not unfamiliar to many of the series' episodes. The awareness of itself and other media, and playing with that idea, is essential to *Community*. Thus, with its prizing of insider knowledge and improvisational aesthetic, it's no surprise that *Community* garnered a dedicated fanbase, regardless of its low ratings on broadcast television. A documentary, detailing PixelDrip Gallery in Los Angeles and their *Community*-themed art show, came out during the show's third season. That it featured Harmon as well as writers and actors from the series suggested the increased responsiveness of writers, actors, and creators to their fanbase, something that would become far more extreme with Harmon's next project, *Rick and Morty*, as discussed in Chapter 2. This final chapter, however, will focus on the way *Community* and its fandom kept the series alive even after cancellation, including an analysis of the long-awaited "movie" element of the fans' "six seasons and a movie" quest.

"Six Seasons": *Community*'s End and What Happened Next

The rise of TV on DVD in the early 2000s gave new life to older series, as well as a boost to newer ones, although it took some time for the industry to figure that out.[2] In the earlier eras of TV, a viewer could watch series as they aired, or in reruns, and if the series did well enough, in syndication. In this model, though, shows that were offbeat or ahead of their time (or, sometimes, just plain bad) disappeared without a trace. As Derek Johnson wrote, earlier eras of television weren't always considered worthy of rewatching, but also the technology that would make collecting it worthwhile, as most series aired at least twenty-two episodes per season, didn't really exist.[3] That is, VHS tapes could hold, at most, eight hours of content; a box set of a series with 100 episodes (the standard for syndication) would take at least eight tapes. Multiply that by however many series one wanted to revisit, and storage becomes an issue. (One of the few exceptions was the 1993 release of *Twin Peaks* as a ten-tape VHS box set; the original run only aired thirty episodes. This was likely also due to series cocreator David Lynch's association with film, which had a better reputation than television even in the early 1990s.)

In order to avoid a repeat of the format war between VHS and Betamax in the 1980s, the then-president of Warner Home Media, Warren Lieberfarb, was the "most outspoken supporter" of DVD; he brokered compromises between consumer electronic companies to produce a single standard, then "browbeat" studios to back DVDs.[4] That meant that, unlike the VCR/VHS, invented in the early 1970s but not in common use until the 1980s (indeed, it wasn't until 1987 that recent films were priced for consumers rather than rental retailers), DVDs were developed in 1995 and adopted as the preferred format the next year.[5] (Early versions, like the LaserDisc, didn't quite catch on.) Within the media industry, however, releasing TV series on DVD wasn't initially considered. *The X-Files*, which had previously released VHS versions of selected episodes, called "Waves," was an early adopter of DVD, with its first season released in 2000. (The set was initially priced at $149.00.) By 2003, however, this was becoming not only more common—and therefore less expensive—but driving production; canceled after three seasons in 2001, the release of a *Family Guy* DVD set in 2003 sold well enough for Fox to reverse their decision and bring back the series in 2005; it is still running as of 2025.[6] It also gave new life to short-lived series, such as *Wonderfalls* (2004), with perhaps the most famous example being that of *Firefly*; canceled after its first season, a combination of fan pressure and the robust sales of the series on DVD led Universal Studios to greenlight a follow-up movie, *Serenity*, which debuted in 2005.[7] One of the downsides to this, it should be noted, is that because things such as music rights had not been negotiated for the format, certain series were released with either incidental music (*WKRP in Cincinnati*) or not released at all (*Murphy Brown*). The question of residuals on DVD sales for writers was also one of the reasons the Writers Guild went on strike in 2007, as DVD sales topped the $4 billion mark as early as 2005.[8]

By the time *Community* debuted in 2009, however, DVDs were a well-established format for television. By releasing ongoing series' latest season on DVD in late August or early September, it served as a promotion for the upcoming season. While a series like *Community* wasn't an arc-heavy show, the visual gags (like the *Beetlejuice* joke built over three seasons), meta humor, and character development rewarded rewatching, much like earlier series such as *Arrested Development*. While season one was released only two days before the start of season two, the second season's DVD was in the top thirty TV DVD sales for the first three weeks of its release, and season three debuted at number five when it was released in August 2012. The combination of DVDs and the digital video recorder (included in cable and satellite boxes) that allowed viewers to record episodes to watch later made Nielsen ratings for broadcast shows like *Community* (i.e., those that appeal to a smaller audience) more irrelevant. In fact, a study by Nielsen itself found that viewers with DVRs actually watched more television than those who didn't; 26 percent more, according to the study.[9] By the time *Community* debuted in 2009, Nielsen had added time-shifting to their rating numbers (known as "live plus three" or "live plus seven").[10] Combining time-shifting, DVD sales, and a vocal fanbase certainly factored into *Community*'s continued renewal; further, rather than waiting for the expected "100 episode" mark that usually indicated a show could be sold into syndication, the cable channel Comedy Central made a syndication deal following the third season, and older episodes started airing on the network in September 2013, ahead of the debut of season four. It was also syndicated in Canada, and aired on cable in both the UK and India during its original run. Its relatively early syndication was another indicator that the old TV models were on their way out by the time *Community* debuted.

Streaming also proved to be a boon for the series. Aside from the previously discussed sixth season on Yahoo! Screen, *Community* got new life when it was added to Netflix on April 1, 2020. The timing, during the early days of the Covid-19 pandemic, was fortuitous for numerous shows—*Breaking Bad*, *The Office*, and *Friends* saw upswings in streaming viewership—including *Community*. Yet it had been available on Amazon Prime prior to that; it was only when it debuted on Netflix that it became a top-ten show for the streaming service, as well as a trending topic on Twitter, suggesting it had picked up a significant amount of first-time viewers.[11] (There was a small amount of controversy; in June 2020, both Netflix and Hulu—which also had the series available for streaming—pulled "Advanced *Dungeons and Dragons*" due to the intimations of blackface when Chang appears as a "dark elf.")[12] They also did a table read for World Central Kitchen on May 18, 2020, of the season five episode "Cooperative Polygraphy," with Pedro Pascal subbing in for Walton Goggins, who'd played Mr. Stone, the executor of Pierce's estate in the aired episode (Goggins was unavailable). Both its debut on Netflix and the table read fundraiser raised the series' profile five years after the series finale aired. While not necessarily cited as definitive reasons, its success on Netflix, the release of the complete series on DVD in 2019, and the popularity of the table read when it streamed were likely factors in the announcement, in September 2022, that Peacock had ordered a follow-up movie.[13]

"And a Movie": Community and Reboot Culture

In 2011, superhero drama series *The Cape* debuted on NBC, with a two-hour pilot that aired on Sunday, January 9, before subsequent episodes were moved to Mondays at 9 pm Eastern. The series was about a cop, Vince Faraday (David Lyons), who witnesses the murder of his boss by someone known only as Chess and finds himself framed for the crime as well as presumed dead. He allies with circus performers that moonlight as bank robbers, who teach him tricks that make him appear superhuman, and a blogger named Orwell (Summer Glau) who is trying to expose the corrupt CEO of security firm Ark Industries Peter Fleming, aka Chess (James Frain). He is trained by and eventually gifted with a cape that helps maintain this illusion by the head of the circus/bank robbers, Max (Keith David), and vows to fight against Fleming, clear his name, and be reunited with his family. That was all in the first episode; the series would only last for nine more before being canceled.

In what might be the most bizarre—and likely unintentional—cross-promotion, this series was a favorite of Abed's. Abed's obsession with the show is a subthread through "Paradigms of Human Memory": Jeff mentions it could get a "second life" on cable in his final speech, Abed dances in a cape in front of the study group, and in the moment that took on its own life, Abed streaks through the cafeteria at Greendale wearing the cape, using it to knock Jeff's lunch tray off the table. Annoyed, Jeff yells: "Show's gonna last three weeks!" Running out of the cafeteria, Abed yells back: "Six seasons and a movie!"[14] It's a small moment in an episode jam-packed with gags, speeches, and bizarre situations, and yet somehow it became the rallying cry for *Community* fans moving forward. Fan campaigns are nothing new; fans of the original *Star Trek* were quite vocal about their displeasure with its possible cancellation, sending letters to the network throughout all three seasons to express how much they enjoyed the series; these even included the then-governor of New York, Nelson Rockefeller.[15] Fan actions have a mixed history of success; the apocalyptic series *Jericho* (2006–2008) gained a second season after thousands of fans sent bags of peanuts to CBS; fan-funded mobile billboards, however, could not save the WB's *Angel* from cancellation.[16] *Community* fans did take action; in December 2011, they organized a flash mob in December 2011 outside of Rockefeller Center (NBC's headquarters) to protest *Community*'s absence from the spring 2012 TV schedule, with some dressed up in felt goatees (donned by "Evil Troy and Evil Abed" in "Remedial Chaos Theory") or singing "Oh Christmas Troy" from "Comparative Religion," an action praised by Harmon himself via Twitter.[17] On June 24 and 25, 2012, the PixelDrip Gallery held a *Community*-themed art show (funded with a Kickstarter campaign), with pieces solicited from and created by fans, named, not surprisingly, "Six Seasons and a Movie Art Show." These included hand-drawn posters, a series of nesting dolls featuring each cast member nestled inside a giant Pierce, and a version of the video game *Journey to the Center of Hawkthorne* from "Digital Estate Planning," among other things. Dan Harmon played host, and the cast viewed the artwork and mingled with the crowd, despite the fact that Harmon had already been fired from the series and season four's renewal was for a significantly shorter season.

The season six pickup of *Community* by Yahoo! Screen was driven, in many ways, by perceived fan support. The previous seasons were already streaming on Hulu, and according to Harmon, Hulu in fact had made a bid for the sixth season to be produced and air on their streaming service; however, Yahoo outbid them.[18] Hulu, however, was an established streamer, like Netflix, having been launched in 2007 by News Corp and NBC Universal, and already had created original programming by 2012, including variety series, comedies, and dramas. While Yahoo! Screen had also developed original programming, including comedy and drama, many of them were akin to Harmon and Schrab's Channel 101 content; that is, short-form material. Only two of their comedies, *Sin City Saints* (2015) and *Other Space* (2015), followed the standard twenty-plus-minutes sitcom structure. Essentially, Hulu had more experience and a higher profile. What attracted Yahoo to the series, however, is the belief that the arrangement between the series and themselves would represent a mutually beneficial arrangement; that is, *Community* would raise their profile and they would raise *Community*'s. Consequently, they relied on the fans to do much of the promotional heavy lifting.[19] While enlisting fans can work, *Serenity*, based on the series *Firefly*, provided swag for fans to pass out (or keep, in some instances) as well as offered early screenings of the film months before its release to increase word of mouth, which did raise its profile.[20] In that case, however, it was the studio and fans working in tandem, rather than relying solely on the fans. Sadly, this didn't end up working for either Yahoo or *Community*; the sixth season would be the series' last, and Yahoo! Screen shuttered not long afterward.

Yet, as explained above, it wasn't over for *Community*. Its successful release on Netflix and table read fundraiser raised its profile, but there is another, weirder way that *Community* ended up being promoted. In "Remedial Chaos Theory," the timeline in which Troy left to get the pizza and everything fell apart was dubbed by Abed at the end of the episode as the "darkest timeline." In this timeline, Pierce is dead from a gunshot wound, Annie is institutionalized, Jeff lost an arm, Shirley's drinking again, Troy destroyed his voice box trying to eat the Norwegian troll, and Britta has a blue streak in her hair.[21] While *Community* obviously did not invent the concept of multiple, simultaneous realities, the term *darkest timeline* made its way into the pop lexicon, describing everything from bad days to bad relationships. In 2016, however, it took off as a way to describe the events of that year, from the deaths of Prince and David Bowie to the election of Donald Trump. It continued to be used over the next four years; the Covid-19 pandemic only heightened its use. It was quoted and meme-d over and over again, serving, in a strange and dark way (befitting the timeline, so to speak) to raise *Community*'s profile outside of its fans and original viewers.

Taken together, it is perhaps no surprise that Peacock, NBC Universal's streaming service, finally decided to make the "and a movie" part a reality. It was announced on September 29, 2022, and over the coming months, information about who exactly would be involved continued to come out, with Donald Glover as the biggest question mark. While each cast member has continued to work following the series' end, Glover has been one of the series' more high-profile successes, from resuming his music career as Childish Gambino to creating, showrunning, and starring in the acclaimed comedy series *Atlanta*, which won everything from Emmys to Peabodys; Glover was the first African American to win a directing Emmy, for the episode "B.A.N."

Details on the movie remain vague (as of May 2025), and the dual WGA/SAG strike in 2023 also slowed down the film moving forward. According to Glover, the basic plot is, "It's a college reunion, but Abed ... is like this big director now, and basically this is his magnum opus," tying it to episodes like "Intermediate Documentary Filmmaking," where Pierce hires Abed to film the study group's reaction to his "bequeathments"; "Documentary Filmmaking: Redux," in which the dean goes full Coppola filming a new commercial for Greendale; and "Wedding Videography," with Abed filming Garrett's marriage proposal, and the study group's wedding prep and behavior at the ceremony and reception.[22] Tying it to a concept used on the series (but not paintball) and focusing on character could work well for the film, making it feel like a part of the series without either undermining the original character and story dynamics or becoming a saccharine love fest that would not work well with the series' original tone.

There is no denying that the current era seems to have gone all in on reboots, both in film and television. Part of this is due to the quick multiplying of streaming services hungry for content mixed with rising costs that make taking a chance on a new, untested series more of a risk. Some of it is due to nostalgia, or revisiting series whose endings were either premature, disliked, or nonexistent because they were canceled. The CW rebooted two of the WB's 1990s-era series, *Charmed* and *Roswell*: both reboots featured more ethnically and sexually diverse casts than their earlier iterations; this was particularly egregious for the original *Roswell*, set in New Mexico but only featuring a single Latine (recurring) character despite the fact that the state's population is more than 50 percent Latine, and one episode with an Indigenous character who never reappeared. *One Day at a Time* (2017–2020) came back as a multicamera sitcom about a single mom, with Norman Lear as executive producer, just as with the 1975 original, but making the family Cuban American—as well as airing at a time when a single parent was no longer a rarity on television—opened up new story avenues. Shows like *Bel-Air*

(2022–present) and *Chilling Adventures of Sabrina* (2018–2020) turned their sitcom predecessors into dramas, and existing storylines (Will's relationship with his father; the use and misuse of magic) into darker directions. *Bel-Air* may be the first series ever created out of a parody; independent director and writer Morgan Cooper made a mock trailer for a gritty reboot of *The Fresh Prince of Bel-Air*; it was seen by Will Smith, who thought it was "brilliant," and the series ended up being picked up by and airing on Peacock.[23] (Its fourth and final season will debut sometime in 2025.)

Perhaps what makes some reboots work, while others don't, is a compelling reason to exist. That is, revisiting stories that never got to be completed, or those that perhaps couldn't reach their full potential in the climate in which they aired. The 1994 adaptation of Anne Rice's *Interview with the Vampire* certainly included the homoerotic subtext of the novel, but the queer nature of the central relationship between Louis (Brad Pitt) and Lestat (Tom Cruise) stayed on that subtextual level. The television series, however, despite changing certain facets of the novel (shifting the time period from antebellum New Orleans to the early twentieth century) leaned into that relationship in all its complexity; the Louis (Jacob Anderson) and Lestat (Sam Reid) are most definitely "out." Fans of the 2000s series *Gilmore Girls* were thrilled when a limited series was commissioned by Netflix, which would allow series creator Amy Sherman-Palladino to complete the series as she'd intended; she had frequently said that she'd written the "final four words" of the series when it started. Set ten years after the original finale, however, the characters had made little progress, and the long-awaited reveal of the final four words disappointed fans by suggesting that children are doomed to repeat their parents' poor choices. Others seem to be driven by the actors themselves; Kelsey Grammer pushed for, and eventually got, a reboot of his series *Frasier*, but absent the family dynamic of the posh intellectual sons Frasier and Niles (David Hyde Pierce, who turned down a role in the reboot) and their blue-collar, cynical father, Martin (John Mahoney, who died), it lasted only two seasons before being canceled. *Fuller House* (2016–2020), a continuation of the multicamera saccharine Friday night staple, simply rebooted the premise (widowed parent whose family and friends move in to help care for the kids) to the next generation, breaking no new narrative or comedy ground in the process; nostalgia was clearly the primary driver, but the series still managed to run for five seasons on Netflix.

So what will it be for *Community*? By the end of the series, original study group members Abed and Annie had moved away from Colorado to pursue their respective careers, Shirley to care for her father, Troy to sail around the world, and Pierce died. This left Britta and Jeff still associated with Greendale, surrounded by a slightly different iteration of friends than they started with but still somewhat stagnant. Britta was still working at a bar and attending Greendale, Jeff was engaged in some low-effort teaching, despite his avowed desire to leave Greendale as soon as possible. The series finale aired a decade ago, and there's no denying nostalgia has a role to play in revisiting these characters, and yet there are, if not loose ends, character and plot threads that could be picked up and examined in the *Community* movie: what happened on Troy's around the world journey, whether Jeff and Britta ever leave Greendale, Abed and Annie's careers, and the state of Shirley's tumultuous personal and professional lives a decade later.

There are other elements that might set *Community* apart from the glut of reboots of the past few years. *Community*'s inherent meta-ness is one; it was always aware of itself as a sitcom, as well as the shows that came before it and those it aired against (see "Regional Holiday Music" for its takedown of *Glee*, a show that kept beating it in the ratings). Further, the writers, and Harmon in particular, are well-versed in the tropes of sitcom, film, and drama more generally; that Harmon would have opinions and ideas about reboots is likely. See, as per example, Annie and Jeff's conversation about the "bland" Marvel films, spoken in whispers to one another, in the final episode; the subtext, for fans of the show, is Joe and Anthony Russos' involvement in the Marvel

Cinematic Universe taking them away from *Community* in the first place. *Community* the film, as both a continuation of the story and part of the culture of reboots, could be brilliant, like "Remedial Chaos Theory" and its perfectly character-calibrated alternate timelines. Or it could be like the "Jesus" movie that Abed makes at Shirley's behest, that he suggests be a "post-post-modern" take in which he is Jesus and the camera is God, but becomes an embarrassing mess of faux-meta profundity.[24] Yet the balance, and the risk, are part of what has always made *Community* worth watching.

APPENDIX

A Highly Subjective List of Twenty-Five Must-See *Community* Episodes (in No Particular Order)

1. Season 1, Episode 1: "Pilot" (September 17, 2009)

An effective pilot should not only introduce the main characters, but sow the seeds of how they'll develop throughout the series. We get our first glimpse of Greendale through Jeff's eyes (although we don't know that at first), including the dean making an announcement in the quad that essentially introduces four of the main characters, as Troy, Britta, Shirley, and Pierce react to the dean's description of the typical community college student. It finally cuts to Jeff with Abed, a pairing that seems unlikely and yet reveals that the two understand each other in a way Jeff won't acknowledge initially. Jeff notices Britta; Abed fills him in on what he knows about her, which is fairly extensive; and Jeff tells him, "I see your value now." Abed is touched, responding with, "That's the nicest thing anyone's ever said to me." Jeff invites Britta to join his nonexistent study group, telling her he's a "board-certified Spanish tutor" taking the class for an easy A. He then goes to see Professor Ian Duncan, whom he got off a drunk-driving charge by invoking September 11, a moment that suggests Jeff's amorality even before he asks Duncan for cheat sheets so he can get his credits and return to his life before he was disbarred for faking his credentials. The episode flips back and forth between the ever-growing study group (Britta invites Abed, who invites Troy, Shirley, Pierce, and Annie) and Jeff stalking Duncan for the test answers. Duncan finally gives in—in exchange for Jeff's Lexus. Having gotten what he wanted, he returns to the group, which has already devolved into chaos and argument that he instigated; he makes an inspirational speech (which will become a Winger specialty), but Britta calls him out for being disingenuous, and suggests the group doesn't really need him. He claims he doesn't need them either, as he's already got the test answers, and leaves. Duncan, however, has screwed him over; the "test answers" are blank pages. Pierce, finding Jeff sitting outside, tells him how much he reminds him of himself, a statement that combines both truth and wish-fulfillment. While the group decides to let him back in, what the pilot does so well is not only quickly set up (most) of the individual characters but their dynamics with one another. For Jeff, who is the central focus of the episode, he gets paralleled with two characters who are nothing alike—Pierce and Abed—representing what Jeff might become if he doesn't mature and Jeff's nerdier side, respectively. Jeff gets every one of Abed's references, from the relatively easy (comparing the study group to *The Breakfast Club*) to the less obvious, comparing Jeff first to early career Bill Murray before switching to Michael Douglas, both of which Jeff comprehends. In case this wasn't entirely clear, the final lines of the episode mirror Abed and Jeff's first conversation, with the roles reversed; Abed tells Jeff "I see your value now," and Jeff responds with, "That's the nicest thing anyone's ever said to me."

2. Season 1, Episode 9: "Debate 109" (November 12, 2009)

Putting aside the slight in-joke of the title (109 is the production code for the episode), "Debate 109" shows that the series has settled into itself while still setting up particular plot and character beats that will become more important as the show progresses. The main plot of the episode revolves around the dean and Annie trying to convince Jeff to join the debate team in order to beat City College, with the topic being whether humanity is good or evil. Jeff, seeming to prove the point before the debate even begins, only agrees when the dean offers him a better parking space, and he goes into the debate thinking he can charm the judges without making much of an effort. This doesn't work, and Jeff's ego is bruised enough to make an actual effort, prepping with Annie one-on-one in a way that soon becomes uncomfortable. (There's also a subplot in which Abed's short films seem to predict the future; his reasoning is that people are predictable, although when even his more outré predictions come true, he becomes concerned.) While a relatively quiet episode, with no high-concept parody or homage, it sets up certain elements that will continue through most of the series, particularly the ongoing rivalry with City College and the weirdness that is the Jeff/Annie dynamic.

3. Season 1, Episode 12: "Comparative Religion" (December 10, 2009)

While not the first episode to focus more particularly on Shirley ("Social Psychology" had Shirley and Jeff bonding over their mutual dislike of Britta's boyfriend Vaughn), "Comparative Religion" goes deeper into her character. That her religion was important to her in the wake of her husband's infidelity and their subsequent divorce was clear in previous episodes, "Comparative Religion" makes it explicit, as well as the fact that the study group itself serves as a replacement for the family bonds that have grown tenuous. Yet Shirley struggles not to control … everything, dismissing the other beliefs of the study group in passive-aggressive ways (Annie's Jewish, Troy's a Jehovah's Witness, Abed is Muslim, Britta's an atheist, Pierce is in a strange cult, and Jeff, to the mockery of the rest of the group, declares himself agnostic). Paired with this is Abed and then Jeff being menaced by a bully, Mike (Anthony Michael Hall), and Shirley making Jeff choose between attending her party or fighting Mike. (In a meta moment that almost goes unnoticed, Pierce posits that Mike was probably a skinny nerd as a kid: "He used to be a nerd, now he's a meathead"; Hall specialized in playing skinny nerd kids in *Sixteen Candles*, *Weird Science* (1985), *The Breakfast Club*, and *Vacation* (1983), with Chase himself.) Britta gets a great moment as she stands up to Shirley about supporting one's friends rather than controlling them, followed by another where her assertions that guys fight to exorcise any latent homosexual impulses is followed by Mike's crew whipping their shirts off; "Come on, I'm being punk'd, right?" is her response. In the end, the study group as a whole, including Shirley, jump into the fight, followed by Shirley singing an inclusive carol at their holiday party. It's a step forward for her that isn't entirely permanent (she's still apt to judge based on what she considers violations of her Christian beliefs), but it's a great ensemble piece just in time for Christmas, the first of many excellent holiday episodes.

4. Season 1, Episode 21: "Contemporary American Poultry" (April 22, 2010)

The first major high-concept episode, in which the concept is the primary driver, sees the study group take over the cooking and distribution of chicken fingers in the cafeteria. Frustrated by the fact that the best food in the cafeteria always runs out before they can get some, and catching cafeteria fry cook Star-Burns giving them to his friends, Jeff concocts a plan to put them in charge, starting with Abed being hired as Star-Burns's replacement. Abed immediately views this as a chance to envision the entire scenario as a mafia movie, with *GoodFellas* as the primary text used throughout and Abed as the Henry Hill narrator. While a gimmick, the episode doesn't feel gimmicky—it actually ends up being a solid character study of Abed, who finds it easier to relate to people through his newly powerful position; Jeff, rendered powerless through Abed's ascension; and the slow corruption of the study group, made all the worse given the ridiculousness of chicken fingers as contraband.

5. Season 1, Episode 23: "Modern Warfare" (May 6, 2010)

In his book *Sitcom*, tracing the history of the sitcom, Saul Austerlitz suggests that "Modern Warfare" set the model for what *Community* would become; that is, with "pastiche and parody as its preferred mode of attack," and his point is valid. Blending action films, from *Die Hard* to *The Warriors* (1979), with post-apocalyptic visuals (the deserted campus, the half-destroyed school), it embraces the faux combat trappings of paintball by having the campus devolve into chaos in the hour it took for Jeff to take a nap in his car, all based on the announcement of the prize for last person standing: priority registration. After Jeff barely escapes a paintbomb attack by Chang—registered briefly as a student to take out the competition, with the dean's complicity—it's eventually resolved by Jeff going full John McClane on the dean, who finally reveals that he can't actually offer the promised prize. The episode is perfectly paced and balances between parody and homage so well that the fact that Jeff and Britta finally consummate their "relationship" is almost a footnote.

6. Season 2, Episode 1: "Anthropology 101" (September 23, 2010)

I'd be happy to include this episode merely for the existence of the final scene, in which Troy and Abed, along with Betty White's June Bauer—their new, and short-lived, anthropology professor—rap about anthropological classification followed by an impromptu rendition of Toto's "Africa." Yet it does much more than that. Dealing immediately with the fallout from the first season finale, when Britta declared she was in love with Jeff at the final dance of the year, and Jeff ran out, eventually kissing Annie, the episode opens with a great shot of each member of the study group waking up on the first day of school, in bedrooms that reflect their personalities (e.g., Pierce sleeps on a waterbed with a giant picture of his younger self above him that strongly resembles *Caddyshack*-era Chevy Chase), Britta is the only one not excited, thinking that everyone is laughing at her after her big confession and rejection. In a fun turnabout, Britta finds that she is actually considered the underdog and Jeff the bad guy, and the two engage in a horrifying one-upmanship that devolves into arguments and recriminations at the impromptu wedding Abed has set up (looking for new storylines and adventures in the new year, of course). In the context of an anthropology assignment, in which Bauer asks them to identify which tool of several is the most important, Jeff's answer, after everything, is respect for one another, something that doesn't come naturally to humans. As a counterpoint, Bauer assembles the tools into a powerful weapon, using it to attack Jeff (she's suspended from teaching after that). In that respect, it offers two competing views: a group of friends who strive to respect one another, or a group that, once assembled, is deadly. That'll be the question that haunts the series going forward.

7. Season 2, Episode 6: "Epidemiology" (October 28, 2010)

"Epidemiology" isn't the first Halloween episode (that would be season one's "Introduction to Statistics"), but perhaps it's the most fun. Leaving realism behind, the episode takes place at a Halloween party that goes sideways when the supposed "taco meat" the dean bought at an army–navy surplus store causes a zombie breakout among the students, all set to the tunes of ABBA. The episode mixes old-school 1950s sci-fi and modern zombie movies to great effect, with each member of the study group acting within character despite the extraordinary circumstances, such as Jeff putting himself in danger rather than dirty his expensive suit and Abed's relative calm and knowledge of how to survive the situation. In many ways, however, this is Troy's episode, as he makes a last-ditch effort to maintain his cool jock persona before realizing that the geeky and nerdy friendship he's built with Abed is better for him and those around him. (Also, the whole bit with the random cat is worth the price of admission.)

8. Season 2, Episode 10: "Mixology Certification" (December 2, 2010)

There's no great premise or homage here; this is a quiet episode built around Troy's discovery he's actually turning twenty-one on his birthday (his mom lied to him about his age when he failed a grade). The group decides to take him out for a drink, scoring Annie (who's nineteen) a fake ID so she can join them. After Jeff and Britta argue endlessly about the best bar to go to (L Street or the Red Door), they settle on a place only Shirley objects to, the reasons why revealed when the bouncer recognizes her, and pictures of her drunk are shown on the walls. Rather than being an episode about Troy drinking too much and learning a lesson about responsible consumption, Troy actually stays sober while Jeff, Britta, Annie, and Abed get drunk (Pierce refused help to get in and ended up getting stuck; Shirley left after she was outed and teased by Jeff, Britta, and Troy when they discovered one of the pictures). Troy's disillusionment with the so-called "adults" around him reaches its apex when he realizes the bar Jeff and Britta were arguing about is the same bar. While alcohol is the catalyst through which Troy realizes the frailties of those around him, the episode seems to suggest that it allows Troy the freedom to define what kind of adult he wants to be.

9. Season 2, Episode 11: "Abed's Uncontrollable Christmas" (December 9, 2010)

Surprisingly, "Abed's Uncontrollable Christmas" is not actually the first live-action series to use Claymation in an episode; *Moonlighting* did it first in the episode "Come Back, Little Shiksa" back in 1987. Like the best high-concept episodes of the series, though, the concept itself illuminates a greater point. While Abed convinces himself, and tries to convince the study group, that his seeing everything around him through Claymation is part of his search for the meaning of Christmas, Britta, trying to help him, tricks him into a group therapy session with Professor Duncan, one that ends up illuminating more of Duncan's issues than Abed's. While the Claymation can be viewed as Abed's retreating into a childhood where his family was together (he suffers this particular break with reality when his mom cancels their usual Christmas plans), the use of Claymation also leans into the inherent melancholy of not just the holiday, but the Christmas specials so much of the audience grew up with. Like "Mixology," it also offers a moment of growth for both Abed and the study group.

10. Season 2, Episode 14: "Advanced *Dungeons and Dragons*" (February 3, 2011)

Aside from the later controversy around Ken Jeong's Chang appearing as a "dark elf" serving as blackface (something the episode calls out itself),

"Advanced *Dungeons and Dragons*" offers a rare glimpse into the way the study group's actions affect others. Indeed, the episode starts by telling the story of Neil, a character who has appeared in other episodes, either in a minor role or in the background. The narrator tells the story of his difficult high school years as an overweight kid who escaped into fantasy, such as *Dungeons and Dragons*. His hope that college would be different was dashed when he was dubbed by a then-unseen fellow as "Fat Neil." When Jeff notices Neil seems to be struggling, he reaches out to him, feigning enough of an interest in *Dungeons and Dragons* that Neil gifts him with all of his *D & D* books, saying he doesn't need them anymore. Realizing this is a bad sign, the study group assembles a quick game with Abed as Dungeon Master, but minus Pierce. This omission seems to activate all of Pierce's not-so-latent insecurities, and he hijacks the game, targeting Neil in particular. This ends up being the nadir of Pierce's arc in season two; his injury followed by pill addiction exacerbates all of his worst qualities, but actually ends up bringing out the best in the rest of the study group, and showing Neil that things could be worse: he could be Pierce.

11. Season 2, Episode 19: "Critical Film Studies" (March 24, 2011)

Showing that the series could approach texts that were not necessarily the most popular of popular culture, "Critical Film Studies" uses *My Dinner with André*, the 1981 Louis Malle film featuring Wallace Shawn and André Gregory discussing aspects of art, life, and spirituality over dinner, as its primary source. This is obvious if you've seen the film, from Jeff's voiceover outside the restaurant to Abed's outfit mirroring that of André Gregory's in the film, but even without the context, it's a nice character study of two characters who have more in common than at least one of them (Jeff) is willing to admit, with both of them using pop culture, and film in particular, to connect with the others, even when they aren't aware of it.

12. Season 2, Episode 21: "Paradigms of Human Memory" (May 6, 2010)

The show's first parody of a clip show actually goes beyond its central joke to close certain plot doors and even poke fun at its fans. The meta nature of the episode is front and center from the beginning, with the study group tasked with making a diorama of their previous diorama, before Troy's monkey (gone since "Contemporary American Poultry") reappears and steals a paintbrush from the table. That discovery leads to a treasure trove of various items the monkey absconded with, all of which have some particular memory attached. Of course, none of these "clips" have ever been seen before, unlike the traditional clip show. Further, while the premise of most clips in the past has been characters "catching up" newer ones on their "history"—that is, making them a part of the group—the memories of "Paradigms" tend to drive the group (temporarily) apart. The show also makes a bit of fun of Jeff/Annie shippers, alluding to a fandom-famous Jeff/Annie fanvid set to Sara Bareilles' "Gravity," turning ordinary moments between both Jeff and Annie, and later Pierce and Abed, into a symphony of longing looks and significant interactions.

13. Season 3, Episode 4: "Remedial Chaos Theory" (October 13, 2011)

Possibly the series' best episode, "Remedial Chaos Theory" offers seven character-centered timelines, asking the question of how things would change when you remove one element. Summing it all up is pointless; seriously, just watch it. You won't be sorry.

14. Season 3, Episode 5: "Horror Fiction in Seven Spooky Steps" (October 27, 2011)

Britta, having administered psychological evaluations to the study group as part of her newly declared psych major, reveals that the results suggest that one of the study group is a possible psychopath. In order to determine which one it is (the tests are anonymous), Britta asks each of them to tell a scary story. Each story illuminates each character—Abed's is logical and concerned with the violence and death being earned; Pierce's reveals his own fantasies, insecurities, and racism; Shirley's is a sermon that shows her feelings of persecution—while also being a collection of fun short stories on their own.

15. Season 3, Episode 8: "Documentary Filmmaking: Redux" (November 17, 2011)

The fact that the episode is an homage to *Hearts of Darkness: A Filmmaker's Apocalypse* is immediately stated by Abed, but what really makes this work is the delightfully low stakes of what is happening. Dean Pelton gets $2,000 to update Greendale's commercial for television, but when Greendale alum Luis Guzman agrees to appear, the dean spirals into auteurist madness, dragging everyone in his orbit down with him. Add in some wisdom from Guzman himself that brings the dean back to earth and a subplot with Pierce demanding a trailer and it is a joy to watch.

16. Season 3, Episode 9: "Foosball and Nocturnal Vigilantism" (December 1, 2011)

Of all the characters on *Community*, Shirley was the least well-served. Indeed, she didn't even get a proper send-off episode like Troy or Pierce when Yvette

Nicole-Brown left after season five. "Foosball and Nocturnal Vigilantism" finally offers a showcase for Shirley that doesn't revolve around her Christianity or her family. Annoyed with a group of German students who loudly dominate the foosball table in the student lounge, and surprised by her proficiency, Jeff asks Shirley to teach him to be a better player, as he'd given it up after a traumatic foosball incident when he was a kid. Shirley warns him that the game brings out her dark side, but Jeff indicates that that's his favorite side of her. They bond over the game, going out for drinks afterward, but when Jeff asks her why she gave up something she was so good at, she reveals that she humiliated a kid at foosball when she was young, topping off winning the game by jabbing him with the foosball bar hard enough to make him pee his pants. Surprise: that kid was Jeff. While the trope of adult characters discovering they knew each other as children is not at all new, the episode actually offers good insight as to how both of them ended up as adults as affected by this interaction. That they work out their issues via an anime foosball sequence is just icing.

17. Season 3, Episode 10, "Regional Holiday Music" (December 8, 2011)

Less of a parody and more of a slam, "Regional Holiday Music" takes on *Glee* with, well, glee. Keeping with *Community*'s own darker-tinged holiday episodes, the series' first full-on musical episode ("Abed's Uncontrollable Christmas" featured a few songs, but mostly sung by Abed only) starts with Jeff "ASCAP"-ing (American Society of Composers, Authors and Publishers) the current glee club, who suffer a collective nervous breakdown. Corey Radison, aka "Mr. Rad," the glee club instructor, asks the study group to take over, citing how well they did last time (seen in "Paradigms of Human Memory"), or else the holiday pageant will be canceled. They refuse, with Jeff suggesting they keep their guard up, as Mr. Rad comes off as "equal parts Hanson and Manson," but Abed is swept into the moment, being the first recruited by Rad via song. Abed then recruits Troy and so on, until Britta is the last hold-out. (*Invasion of the Body Snatchers* is also referenced, as Jeff sings and points at Britta in a call-out to Donald Sutherland in the 1978 film.) How each of them targets the other is a testament to how well they know each other at this point, with Troy and Abed appealing to Pierce's generational narcissism with "Baby Boomer Santa," or Pierce recruiting Shirley using a choir of children lamenting that they can't say "Merry Christmas" in their public schools. The original songs, scored by series composer Ludwig Göransson, with the writing staff taking lyrics duty, are sometimes hit and miss, but for all the purported "darkness" in the episode, it ends on a touching moment of togetherness.

18. Season 3, Episode 14: "Pillows and Blankets" (April 5, 2012)

Paying off the seemingly subtle rift between Troy and Abed during "Contemporary Impressionists," Greendale erupts into a full-scale pillow fight war when Abed and Troy fall out over whether to make that year's blanket fort out of blankets and pillows, spurred on by the potential to be in the *Guinness Book of World Records*. Shot and narrated in the style of Ken Burns, including casting Keith David, who had already narrated four of Burns' documentaries, as the narrator, the inherent silliness of the conflict is given the needed gravitas, considering that, despite the ridiculousness of the argument, the show's real central relationship is at risk.

19. Season 3, Episode 17: "Basic Lupine Urology" (April 26, 2012)

Somewhere between parody and homage, "Basic Lupine Urology" nails the tropes of the ubiquitous *Law & Order (L&O)*. This stretches from the discovery of the "body"—a smashed yam in the study group's biology class—to the blending of the *L & O* theme song and credits with *Community*'s; Troy and Abed and Annie and Jeff cosplaying as the series' cops and lawyers; the casting of Leslie Hendrix, who has played medical examiner Elizabeth Rodgers on four series in *the L & O* franchise; and the final twist at the end. Playing it completely straight highlights how easily the *L & O* formula translates into other shows, but it's also fun to watch the way the cast plays with these particular roles. (Also to catch the last appearance of the late Michael K. Williams on the series, a stand out in a pretty stand-out season.)

20. Season 3, Episode 19: "Curriculum Unavailable" (May 10, 2012)

The second of the "clip show" episodes, "Curriculum Unavailable" takes it a step farther by better incorporating the premise of the clips into the storyline. Having been kicked out of Greendale after being accused of starting a riot, the group strives to stay together regardless, while Abed appears to have gone off the rails, convinced that the dean has been replaced by a doppelganger. When he sneaks onto Greendale's campus—they've been banned—the "dean" agrees not to press charges as long as Abed seeks help. This turns into a group therapy session, as the entire study group joins them, sharing memories first of Abed, then of themselves, the dean, and finally Chang's increasingly erratic behavior. Unlike "Paradigms," each of these clusters of fake clips builds its own narrative, helping the study group realize what's really happening at Greendale and setting things in motion for the finale.

21. Season 3, Episode 20: "Digital Estate Planning" (May 17, 2012)

Primarily presented as an 8-bit video game, the filming of the episode ended up being something of a nightmare, with the ending changed due to conflict between Harmon and Chase, but it actually ends up being a nice character study of the series' most problematic character. Set up by his even-worse father, Cornelius, Pierce and his friends have to play an old-school video game Cornelius had developed in order to win his inheritance, as explained by Gilbert Lawson, Cornelius's longtime assistant. That there is more to this is obvious when Gilbert joins the game, not only revealing the depths of Cornelius's racism, but that Pierce and Gilbert have a closer connection than Pierce ever knew. Plus, watching the group take down a MeccaCornelius with bombs, helicopters, and tiny Abed babies is extremely satisfying.

22. Season 5, Episode 4: "Cooperative Polygraphy" (January 16, 2014)

Despite not appearing in the episode at all, "Cooperative Polygraphy" accurately captures the outsized presence of both Pierce and Chase himself. Chase's time on the series had been fraught, between the long hours and clashes with Harmon, with Chase appearing only as a hologram in "Repilot" before the announcement of his death at the end of "Basic Intergluteal Numismatics." Having just returned from Pierce's funeral, the study group is informed by Mr. Stone, the executor of Pierce's estate, that Pierce requested members undergo a polygraph examination to, at first, determine whether any of them were responsible for his death; Mr. Stone then reveals that successful completion makes them eligible for what Pierce has bequeathed them in his will, a call-back to season two's "Intermediate Documentary Filmmaking" in more ways than one. Even in death, Pierce retains the ability to get under everyone's skin and honing in on their weak spots, before a surprisingly touching conclusion.

23. Season 5, Episode 5: "Geothermal Escapism" (January 23, 2014)

The proper send-off for a character who became the surprising heart of the series: Troy Barnes. Driven by Glover's burgeoning career outside of *Community*, the episode deals with the fall-out from Troy's decision to accept Pierce's challenge to sail around the world (as Pierce never did) and thereby inherit Pierce's fortune. Nobody takes this harder, however, than Abed, who hides his pain and inability to let go of his best friend through a game of *The Floor Is Lava*, a nice switch from paintball. Not surprisingly, the school soon goes apocalyptic (the prize is a near-mint comic worth $50,000), but the real apocalypse is Abed's processing of Troy leaving him behind. The silliness and pathos are perfectly balanced in this episode, and it makes a great send-off for Troy/Glover.

24. Season 6, Episode 12: "Wedding Videography" (May 26, 2015)

While I know this episode, part of the lengthier Yahoo! Screen–era episodes, isn't going on anyone's "best of" lists, it is a late reminder of the ways the study group, despite losing some members and adding some new ones, are great for one another (Frankie's advice to Annie to "embrace" her dragon) and kind of terrible for everyone else (most of their actions at Garrett's wedding). Yet the great part about the episode is that it isn't just a jab at the codependence of the study group; it also shows that everyone has their own terribleness, and carries on in spite of it.

25. Season 6, Episode 13: "Emotional Consequences of Broadcast Television" (June 2, 2015)

The final episode is a quiet one, as Greendale is declared "saved" from its various issues (technical, scholastic, financial), leaving the group temporarily at loose ends. Over drinks, each of them floats ideas of how they could continue; or, in their own words, what "season seven" would look like. Like with "Horror Fiction," each scenario says something about the teller, whether it's Chang's ridiculous "Ice Cube Head" added character, or Britta's self-serious drama. It's Jeff's stories, however, that we spend the most time with, bringing both the series and Jeff himself full circle: the man who wanted out of Greendale as fast as he could now struggles to leave it, and the friends he made there, behind. And, of course, it ends with one more meta scene that questions the series' reality; an excellent ending to the show.

NOTES

Introduction

1   *Community*, season 3, episode 17, "Basic Lupine Urology," directed by Rob Schrab, written by Megan Ganz, featuring Joel McHale, Alison Brie, Donald Glover, Danny Pudi, and Yvette Nicole Brown, aired April 26, 2012, on NBC, Sony, 2020, DVD.

2   *Community*, season 4, episode 9, "Intro to Felt Surrogacy," directed by Tristram Shapeero, written by Gene Hong, featuring Joel McHale, Alison Brie, Donald Glover, Danny Pudi, and Yvette Nicole Brown, aired April 11, 2013, on NBC, Sony, 2020, DVD.

3   *Community*, season 5, episode 1, "Repilot," directed by Tristram Shapeero, written by Dan Harmon and Chris McKenna, featuring Joel McHale, Alison Brie, Donald Glover, Danny Pudi, and Yvette Nicole Brown, aired January 2, 2014, on NBC, Sony, 2020, DVD.

4   *Community*, season 6, episode 13, "Emotional Consequences of Broadcast Television," directed by Rob Schrab, written by Dan Harmon and Chris McKenna, featuring Joel McHale, Alison Brie, Danny Pudi, Gillian Jacobs, and Keith David, aired June 2, 2015, on Yahoo! Screen, Sony, 2020, DVD.

5   Priya Sridhar, "The Good Parts of Community, Season Four," *Medium*, February 4, 2021, https://medium.com/permanent-nerd-network/the-good-parts-of-community-season-four-ff8455d00014

6   *Community*, season 4, episode 10, "Intro to Knots," directed by Tristram Shapeero, written by Andy Bobrow, featuring Joel McHale, Alison Brie, Donald Glover, Danny Pudi, and Yvette Nicole Brown, aired April 18, 2013, on NBC, Sony, 2020, DVD.

7   *Community*, season 1, episode 13, "Investigative Journalism," directed by Joe Russo, written by Jon Pollack and Tim Hobert, featuring Joel McHale, Alison Brie, Donald Glover, Danny Pudi, and Yvette Nicole Brown, aired January 14, 2010, on NBC, Sony, 2020, DVD.

8   *Community*, season 4, episode 7, "Economics of Marine Biology," directed by Tricia Brock, written by Tim Saccardo, featuring Joel McHale, Alison Brie, Donald Glover, Danny Pudi, and Chevy Chase, aired March 21, 2013, on NBC, Sony, 2020, DVD.

Chapter 1

1. David Marc, "Origins of the Genre: In Search of the Radio Sitcom," in *The Sitcom Reader: America Re-viewed, Still Skewed*, 2nd ed., edited by Mary M. Dalton and Laura R. Linder (Albany: SUNY Press, 2016), 1.

2. Sam Chase, "Mary Kay and Johnny," *The Billboard*, March 6, 1948, 38.

3. The first show to use a laugh track was called *The Hank McCune Show*, airing on NBC in 1950. McCune plays himself as the host of a variety show, and the short-lived series focused on the backstage hijinks of the cast and crew, a sort of early version of series like *The Larry Sanders Show* (1992–1998).

4. Marc, "Origins of the Genre," 19.

5. Paul Lomartire, "Have I Got News for You about Molly," *The Palm Beach Post*, June 18, 1994, 1D.

6. Carol A. Stabile, *The Broadcast 41: Women and the Anti-Communist Blacklist* (London: Goldsmiths Press, 2018).

7. Noel Holston, "Hooterville's Head Hillbilly Henning Put Rural Life on a Television Pedestal," *Orlando Sentinel*, August 3, 1986.

8. *The Munsters*, season 1, episode 1, "Munster Masquerade," directed by Lawrence Dobkin, written by Joe Connelly and Bob Mosher, featuring Fred Gywnne, Beverely Owen, and Al Lewis, aired September 24, 1964, on CBS, Universal, 2008, DVD; *The Munsters*, season 1, episode 2, "My Fair Munster," directed by David Alexander, written by Norm Liebmann and Ed Haas, featuring Fred Gywnne, Beverely Owen, and Al Lewis, aired October 1, 1964, on CBS, Universal, 2008, DVD.

9. *The Addams Family*, season 1, episode 2, "Morticia and the Psychiatrist," directed by Jean Yarbrough, written by Hannibal Coons and Harry Winkler, featuring John Astin, Carolyn Jones, and Ken Weatherwax, aired September 25, 1964, on ABC, MGM, 2007, DVD.

10. Lorna Jowett and Stacey Abbott, *TV Horror: Investigating the Dark Side of the Small Screen* (London: IB Tauris, 2013), 24; 11.

11. *I Dream of Jeannie*, season 1, episode 1, "The Lady in the Bottle," directed by Gene Nelson, written by Sidney Sheldon, featuring Barbara Eden and Larry Hagman, aired September 18, 1965, on NBC, Sony, 2006, DVD.

12. Sarah K. Eskridge, *Rube Tube: CBS and the Rural Comedy in the Sixties* (Columbia: University of Missouri Press, 2018), 172.

13. *The Mary Tyler Moore Show*, season 3, episode 11, "You've Got a Friend," directed by Jerry Belson, written by Steve Pritzker, featuring Mary Tyler Moore, Ed Asner, and Valerie Harper, aired November 25, 1972, on CBS, 20th Century Fox, 2006, DVD.

14. *Day by Day*, season 2, episode 11, "A Very Brady Episode," directed by Asaad Kelada, written by Andy Borowitz, featuring Christopher Barnes, Ann B. Davis, Florence Henderson, and Robert Reed, aired February 5, 1989, on NBC.

15. Following his ouster in 2018, Bloodworth-Thomason, who'd been given a $50 million contract to develop a series for CBS, revealed that CBS president Les Moonves, who took over the network in 1995, intentionally derailed her career, not picking up a single pilot she was offered, regardless of the stars or writers attached. (The nature of her contract meant exclusivity to CBS, so she could not shop them elsewhere.) Moonves was eventually forced out in 2018 following numerous allegations of harassment throughout his career at the network. Linda Bloodworth-Thomason, "'Designing Women' Creator Goes Public With Les Moonves War: Not All Harassment Is Sexual [Guest Column]," *The Hollywood Reporter*, September 12, 2008, https://www.hollywoodreporter.com/news/general-news/designing-women-creator-les-moonves-not-all-harassment-is-sexual-1142448/

16. *The Cosby Show*, season 5, episode 15, "The Lost Weekend," directed by Tony Singletary, written by John Markus, Carmen Finestra, and Gary Kott, featuring Bill Cosby, Phylicia Rashad, and Malcolm Jamal-Warner, aired February 2, 1989, on NBC, Mill Creek, 2008, DVD.

17. *The Cosby Show*, season 3, episode 6, "The March," directed by Tony Singletary, written by Gary Kott, featuring Bill Cosby, Phylicia Rashad, and Malcolm Jamal-Warner, aired October 30, 1986, on NBC, Mill Creek, 2008, DVD.

18. *A Different World*, season 5, episode 11, "Mammy Dearest," directed by Debbie Allen, written by Glenn Berenbeim, featuring Jasmine Guy, Kadeem Hardison, Dawnn Lewis, and Jada Pinkett Smith, aired December 5, 1991, on NBC.

19. Shelby Abayie, "How 'Living Single' Was the Blueprint for Friends: The Impact of Living Single Can't Be Understated or Ignored," *34th Street Magazine*, November 22, 2021, https://www.34st.com/article/2021/11/livingsingle-friends-black-television-creators-tv-ratings

20. Jess Cagle and Joe Flint, "As Gay As It Gets," *Entertainment Weekly*, May 8, 1998.

21. EW Staff, "'Will and Grace': In the Pink," *Entertainment Weekly*, September 10, 1999, https://ew.com/article/1999/09/10/will-and-grace-pink/

22. *Will & Grace*, season 2, episode 14, "Acting Out," directed by James Burrows, written by David Kohan and Max Mutchnick, featuring Debra Messing, Eric McCormack, Sean Hayes, and Megan Mullaly, aired February 22, 2000, on NBC, Lions Gate, 2004, DVD.

23. Wendall Wittler, "Television Grapples With a Weighty Matter," *Today*, October 5, 2004, https://www.today.com/popculture/television-grapples-weighty-matter-wbna5991977

Chapter 2

1. Andy Downing, "Dan in Real Life: 'Community' Creator Talks about Creativity on the Show and After," *The Cap Times*, January 17, 2013, https://captimes.com/entertainment/television/dan-in-real-life-community-creator-talks-about-creativity-on-the-show-and-after/article_4f602721-e5e5-5bf9-b64b-c3e58975fc34.htm

2. David Maddox, "A Conversation With Rob Schrab," *SF Site*, March 2008, https://www.sfsite.com/05a/rs271.htm

3. Nick Carter, "Alewives to Alewives, Dust to Dust, Their Comedy Act Soon Will Be Nevermore," *Milwaukee Journal Sentinel*, January 5, 2001.

4. *Community*, season 2, episode 14, "Advanced *Dungeons and Dragons*," directed by Joe Russo, written by Andrew Guest, featuring Joel McHale, Alison Brie, Donald Glover, Danny Pudi, Chevy Chase, and Yvette Nicole Brown, aired February 3, 2011, on NBC, Sony, 2020, DVD; *Community*, season 5, episode 10, "Advanced Advanced *Dungeons and Dragons*," directed by Joe Russo, written by Matt Roller, featuring Joel McHale, Alison Brie, Danny Pudi, Jonathan Banks, and Yvette Nicole Brown, aired March 20, 2014, on NBC, Sony, 2020, DVD.

5. Daniel Robert Epstein, "Channel 101 Co-Creator Rob Schrab," *Suicide Girls*, June 30, 2005, https://www.suicidegirls.com/girls/anderswolleck/blog/2679269/channel-101-co-creator-rob-schrab/

6. "About," Channel 101, accessed December 31, 2024, https://channel101.org/about/

7. Ibid.

8. David Itzkoff, "'Community' Creator Writes to Child, Disses Spielberg and Wins Our Hearts," *New York Times*, March 29, 2010, https://archive.nytimes.com/artsbeat.blogs.nytimes.com/2010/03/29/community-creator-writes-to-child-disses-spielberg-and-wins-our-hearts/

9. *Paste* Staff, "Catching Up With … *Community* Creator Dan Harmon," *Paste Magazine*, May 5, 2010, https://www.pastemagazine.com/tv/dan-harmon/catching-up-with-communitys-creator-dan-harmon

10. Steven Hyden, "Interview: How Dan Harmon Went From Doing Comedy Sportz in Milwaukee to Creating NBC's *Community*," *The AV Club*, October 19, 2009, https://web.archive.org/web/20091023172513/http://www.avclub.com/milwaukee/articles/how-dan-harmon-went-from-doing-comedysportz-in-mil,34126/

11. Megan O'Neil, "Dan Harmon Screens 'Community' at GCC," *Los Angeles Times*, November 5, 2010, https://www.latimes.com/socal/glendale-news-press/news/tn-gnp-screening-20101105-story.html

12 Brian Raftery, "How Dan Harmon Drives Himself Crazy Making *Community*," *Wired*, September 22, 2011, https://www.wired.com/2011/09/mf-harmon/

13 Ibid.

14 *Community*, season 1, episode 1, "Pilot," directed by Anthony and Joe Russo, written by Dan Harmon, featuring Joel McHale, Alison Brie, Donald Glover, Danny Pudi, and Yvette Nicole Brown, aired September 17, 2009, on NBC, Sony, 2020, DVD.

15 *Community*, season 2, episode 24, "For a Few Paintballs More," directed by Joe Russo, written by Hilary Winston, featuring Joel McHale, Alison Brie, Donald Glover, Danny Pudi, Chevy Chase, and Yvette Nicole Brown, aired May 12, 2011, on NBC, Sony, 2020, DVD.

16 *Community*, season 2, episode 14, "Advanced *Dungeons and Dragons*," directed by Joe Russo, written by Andrew Guest, featuring Joel McHale, Alison Brie, Donald Glover, Danny Pudi, Chevy Chase, and Yvette Nicole Brown, aired February 3, 2011, on NBC, Sony, 2020, DVD.

17 Lacey Rose, "'Community's' Dan Harmon Reveals the Wild Story Behind His Firing and Rehiring," *The Hollywood Reporter*, July 17, 2013, https://www.hollywoodreporter.com/news/general-news/communitys-dan-harmon-reveals-wild-586084/

18 Ibid.

19 Ibid.

20 Simon Bland, "'We Were Around Each Other More than Our Family': An Oral History of *Community*," *The Independent*, September 18, 2024, https://www.independent.co.uk/arts-entertainment/tv/features/community-movie-netflix-tv-series-cast-b2614804.html

21 Peter Biskind, *Easy Riders, Raging Bulls: How the Sex-Drugs-and-Rock-'n'-Roll Generation Saved Hollywood* (New York: Simon & Schuster, 1998), 401–403.

22 Jim Emerson, "Hot Pick—Life of Peter Bogdanovich Told in Satire," *Orange County Register*, November 13, 1992, P41.

23 Alonso Duralde, "Polly Platt: Accomplished and Forthcoming—Even About 'Irreconcilable Differences,'" *Reuters*, July 27, 2011.

24 Julia Sweeten, "'Gilmore Girls': Dragonfly Inn and Scenes From Stars Hollow," *Hooked on Houses*, May 16, 2010, https://hookedonhouses.net/2010/05/16/gilmore-girls-dragonfly-inn-and-scenes-from-stars-hollow/

25 Michele Hilmes, *Only Connect: A Cultural History of Broadcasting in the United States*, 3rd ed. (Boston: Wadsworth Cengage Learning, 2011), 265.

26 "The X-Files," Fanlore, accessed December 31, 2024, https://fanlore.org/wiki/The_X-Files

27. Randi Richardson, "'Living Single' Fans React to Jennifer Aniston Downplaying 'Friends' Being Offensive: 'Living Single' Was a Trending Topic on Twitter March 30," *Today*, March 31, 2023, https://www.today.com/popculture/tv/living-single-fans-react-jennifer-aniston-downplaying-friends-offensiv-rcna77434

28. Emily Nussbaum, "Cahiers Du Buffy," *The New Yorker*, March 28, 2014, https://www.newyorker.com/culture/culture-desk/cahiers-du-buffy

29. Michael Z. Newman and Elana Levine, *Legitimating Television: Media Convergence and Cultural Status* (New York: Routledge, 2012), 48.

30. Downing, "Dan in Real Life," 2013.

31. Sean O'Neal, "The Tortured Mind of Dan Harmon," *GQ*, May 30, 2018, https://www.gq.com/story/dan-harmon-rick-and-morty-profile

32. Polygon Staff, "How a *Rick and Morty* Joke Led to a McDonald's Szechuan Sauce Controversy," *Polygon*, February 21, 2018, https://www.polygon.com/2017/10/12/16464374/rick-and-morty-mcdonalds-szechuan-sauce

33. Maureen Ryan, *Burn It Down: Power, Complicity, and a Call for Change in Hollywood* (New York: HarperCollins, 2023), 196.

34. Bland, "'We Were Around Each Other More than Our Family,'" 2024.

35. Rose, "'Community's' Dan Harmon," 2013.

36. O'Neal, "The Tortured Mind," 2018.

37. Annemarie Navar-Gill, "The Fan/Creator Alliance: Social Media, Audience Mandates, and the Rebalancing of Power in Studio-Showrunner Disputes," *Media Industries* 5, no. 2 (2018), accessed December 1, 2024, https://quod.lib.umich.edu/m/mij/15031809.0005.202/–fan-creator-alliance-social-media-audience-mandates?rgn=main;view=fulltext#N35-ptr1

Chapter 3

1. Richard Zoglin, "Late-Night Mugging," *Time*, September 20, 1993, https://web.archive.org/web/20101028054014/http://www.time.com/time/magazine/article/0,9171,979242,00.html; Ken Tucker, "The Chevy Chase Show," *Entertainment Weekly*, October 8, 1993, https://ew.com/article/1993/10/08/chevy-chase-show/

2. Carolyn Sayre, "10 Questions for Chevy Chase," *Time*, April 11, 2007, https://content.time.com/time/subscriber/article/0,33009,1609793,00.html

3   "Fine Writing Spurs Chevy to Move to 'Community,'" *Omaha World-Herald*, October 22, 2009, https://archive.ph/20130104083338/http://www.omaha.com/article/20091022/ENTERTAINMENT/710229873#selection-1949.0-1949.209

4   "I Am Dan Harmon, Creator of Community, Writer of Monster House, and Executive Producer of the Upcoming Charlie Kaufman Stop Motion Animated Feature Anomalisa, Ask Me Anything!" r/IAmA, Reddit, August 22, 2012, https://www.reddit.com/r/IAmA/comments/yne9x/i_am_dan_harmon_creator_of_community_writer_of/

5   Ibid.

6   *Community*, season 1, episode 1, "Pilot," directed by Anthony and Joe Russo, written by Dan Harmon, featuring Joel McHale, Alison Brie, Donald Glover, Danny Pudi, and Yvette Nicole Brown, aired September 17, 2009, on NBC, Sony, 2020, DVD.

7   *Community*, season 2, episode 2, "Accounting for Lawyers," directed by Joe Russo, written by Emily Cutler, featuring Joel McHale, Alison Brie, Donald Glover, Danny Pudi, and Yvette Nicole Brown, aired September 30, 2010, on NBC, Sony, 2020, DVD.

8   *Community*, season 3, episode 22, "Introduction to Finality," directed by Tristram Shapeero, written by Steve Basilone and Annie Mebane, featuring Joel McHale, Alison Brie, Donald Glover, Danny Pudi, Chevy Chase, and Yvette Nicole Brown, aired May 17, 2012, on NBC, Sony, 2020, DVD.

9   *Community*, season 1, episode 21, "Contemporary American Poultry," directed by Tristram Shapeero, written by Emily Cutler and Karey Dornetto, featuring Joel McHale, Alison Brie, Donald Glover, Danny Pudi, and Yvette Nicole Brown, aired April 22, 2010, on NBC, Sony, 2020, DVD.

10 *Community*, season 3, episode 1, "Biology 101," directed by Anthony Russo, written by Garrett Donovan and Neil Goldman, featuring Joel McHale, Alison Brie, Donald Glover, Danny Pudi, Chevy Chase, and Yvette Nicole Brown, aired September 22, 2011, on NBC, Sony, 2020, DVD.

11 *Community*, season 4, episode 1, "Advanced Introduction to Finality," directed by Tristram Shapeero, written by Megan Ganz, featuring Joel McHale, Alison Brie, Donald Glover, Danny Pudi, and Yvette Nicole Brown, aired May 9, 2013, on NBC, Sony, 2020, DVD.

12 *Community*, season 5, episode 1, "Repilot," directed by Tristram Shapeero, written by Dan Harmon and Chris McKenna, featuring Joel McHale, Alison Brie, Donald Glover, Danny Pudi, and Yvette Nicole Brown, aired January 2, 2014, on NBC, Sony, 2020, DVD.

13 *Community*, season 5, episode 11, "G. I. Jeff," directed by Rob Schrab, written by Dino Stamatopoulos, featuring Joel McHale, Alison Brie, Donald Glover, Danny Pudi, and Yvette Nicole Brown, aired April 3, 2014, on NBC, Sony, 2020, DVD.

14 *Community*, season 6, episode 13, "Emotional Consequences of Broadcast Television," directed by Rob Schrab, written by Dan Harmon and Chris McKenna, featuring Joel McHale, Alison Brie, Danny Pudi, Gillian Jacobs, and Keith David, aired June 2, 2014, on Yahoo! Screen, Sony, 2020, DVD.

15 *Community*, season 1, episode 6, "Football, Feminism and You," directed by Joe Russo, written by Hilary Winston, featuring Joel McHale, Alison Brie, Donald Glover, Danny Pudi, and Yvette Nicole Brown, aired October 22, 2009, on NBC, Sony, 2020, DVD.

16 *Community*, season 1, episode 4, "Social Psychology," directed by Anthony Russo, written by Liz Cackowski, featuring Joel McHale, Alison Brie, Donald Glover, Danny Pudi, and Yvette Nicole Brown, aired October 8, 2009, on NBC, Sony, 2020, DVD.

17 *Community*, season 1, episode 5, "Advanced Criminal Law," directed by Joe Russo, written by Andrew Guest, featuring Joel McHale, Alison Brie, Donald Glover, Danny Pudi, and Yvette Nicole Brown, aired October 15, 2009, on NBC, Sony, 2020, DVD.

18 *Community*, season 2, episode 6, "Epidemiology," directed by Anthony Hemingway, written by Karey Dornetto, featuring Joel McHale, Alison Brie, Donald Glover, Danny Pudi, and Yvette Nicole Brown, aired October 28, 2010, on NBC, Sony, 2020, DVD.

19 *Community*, season 2, episode 10, "Mixology Certification," directed by Jay Chandrasekhar, written by Andy Bobrow, featuring Joel McHale, Alison Brie, Donald Glover, Danny Pudi, and Yvette Nicole Brown, aired December 2, 2010, on NBC, Sony, 2020, DVD.

20 *Community*, season 2, episode 24, "For a Few Paintballs More," directed by Joe Russo, written by Hilary Winston, featuring Joel McHale, Alison Brie, Donald Glover, Danny Pudi, and Yvette Nicole Brown, aired May 12, 2011, on NBC, Sony, 2020, DVD.

21 *Community*, season 3, episode 21, "The First Chang Dynasty," directed by Jay Chandrasekhar, written by Matt Fusfeld and Alex Cuthbertson, featuring Joel McHale, Alison Brie, Donald Glover, Danny Pudi, and Yvette Nicole Brown, aired May 17, 2012, on NBC, Sony, 2020, DVD.

22 *Community*, season 4, episode 11, "Basic Human Anatomy," directed by Beth McCarthy-Miller, written by Jim Rash, featuring Joel McHale, Alison Brie, Donald Glover, Danny Pudi, and Yvette Nicole Brown, aired April 25, 2013, on NBC, Sony, 2020, DVD.

23 *Community*, season 5, episode 5, "Geothermal Escapism," directed by Joe Russo, written by Tim Saccardo, featuring Joel McHale, Alison Brie, Donald Glover, Danny Pudi, and Yvette Nicole Brown, aired January 23, 2014, on NBC, Sony, 2020, DVD.

24 *Community*, season 2, episode 16, "Intermediate Documentary Filmmaking," directed by Joe Russo, written by Megan Ganz, featuring Joel McHale, Alison Brie,

Donald Glover, Danny Pudi, Chevy Chase, and Yvette Nicole Brown, aired February 17, 2011, on NBC, Sony, 2020, DVD.

25 *Community*, season 2, episode 13, "Celebrity Pharmacology," directed by Fred Goss, written by Hilary Winston, featuring Joel McHale, Alison Brie, Donald Glover, Danny Pudi, Chevy Chase, and Yvette Nicole Brown, aired January 27, 2011, on NBC, Sony, 2020, DVD.

26 *Community*, season 3, episode 4, "Remedial Chaos Theory," directed by Jeff Melman, written by Chris McKenna, featuring Joel McHale, Alison Brie, Donald Glover, Danny Pudi, Chevy Chase, and Yvette Nicole Brown, aired October 13, 2011, on NBC, Sony, 2020, DVD.

27 *Community*, season 3, episode 7, "Studies in Modern Movement," directed by Tristram Shapeero, written by Adam Countee, featuring Joel McHale, Alison Brie, Donald Glover, Danny Pudi, Chevy Chase, and Yvette Nicole Brown, aired November 10, 2011, on NBC, Sony, 2020, DVD.

28 *Community*, season 3, episode 2, "Geography of Global Conflict," directed by Joe Russo, written by Andy Bobrow, featuring Joel McHale, Alison Brie, Donald Glover, Danny Pudi, and Yvette Nicole Brown, aired September 29, 2011, on NBC, Sony, 2020, DVD.

29 *Community*, season 1, episode 15, "Romantic Expressionism," directed by Joe Russo, written by Andrew Guest, featuring Joel McHale, Alison Brie, Donald Glover, Danny Pudi, Chevy Chase, and Yvette Nicole Brown, aired February 4, 2010, on NBC, Sony, 2020, DVD.

30 *Community*, season 3, episode 17, "Basic Lupine Urology," directed by Rob Schrab, written by Megan Ganz, featuring Joel McHale, Alison Brie, Donald Glover, Danny Pudi, Chevy Chase, and Yvette Nicole Brown, aired April 26, 2012, on NBC, Sony, 2020, DVD.

31 *Law & Order*, season 17, episode 7, "In Vino Veritas," directed by Tim Hunter, written by David Wilcox, featuring Sam Waterston, Jesse L. Martin, Milena Govich, Alana de la Garza, and Chevy Chase, aired November 3, 2006, on NBC, Universal, 2011, DVD.

32 *Community*, season 1, episode 18, "Basic Genealogy," directed by Ken Whittingham, written by Karey Dornetto, featuring Joel McHale, Alison Brie, Donald Glover, Danny Pudi, Chevy Chase, and Yvette Nicole Brown, aired March 11, 2010, on NBC, Sony, 2020, DVD.

33 *Community*, season 1, episode 22, "The Art of Discourse," directed by Adam Davidson, written by Chris McKenna, featuring Joel McHale, Alison Brie, Donald Glover, Danny Pudi, Chevy Chase, and Yvette Nicole Brown, aired April 29, 2010, on NBC, Sony, 2020, DVD.

34 *Community*, season 2, episode 7, "Aerodynamics of Gender," directed by Tristram Shapeero, written by Adam Countee, featuring Joel McHale, Alison Brie, Donald

Glover, Danny Pudi, Chevy Chase, and Yvette Nicole Brown, aired November 4, 2010, on NBC, Sony, 2020, DVD.

35   *Community*, season 2, episode 11, "Abed's Uncontrollable Christmas," directed by Duke Johnson, written by Dino Stamatopoulos and Dan Harmon, featuring Joel McHale, Alison Brie, Donald Glover, Danny Pudi, Chevy Chase, and Yvette Nicole Brown, aired December 9, 2010, on NBC, Sony, 2020, DVD.

36   *Community*, season 2, episode 14, "Advanced *Dungeons and Dragons*," directed by Joe Russo, written by Andrew Guest, featuring Joel McHale, Alison Brie, Donald Glover, Danny Pudi, Chevy Chase, and Yvette Nicole Brown, aired February 3, 2011, on NBC, Sony, 2020, DVD.

37   *Community*, season 2, episode 16, "Intermediate Documentary Filmmaking," aired February 17, 2011.

38   *Community*, season 2, episode 24, "For a Few Paintballs More," aired May 12, 2011, on NBC.

39   *Community*, season 3, episode 6, "Advanced Gay," directed by Joe Russo, written by Matt Murray, featuring Joel McHale, Alison Brie, Donald Glover, Chevy Chase, and Yvette Nicole Brown, aired November 3, 2011, on NBC, Sony, 2020, DVD.

40   *Community*, season 3, episode 20, "Digital Estate Planning," directed by Adam Davidson, written by Matt Warburton, featuring Joel McHale, Alison Brie, Donald Glover, Chevy Chase, Danny Pudi, and Yvette Nicole Brown, aired May 17, 2012, on NBC, Sony, 2020, DVD.

41   Jenny Nelson, "Talking to Broken Lizard's Jay Chandrasekhar about 'Freeloaders' and the Chevy Chase *N*-Word Thing," *Vulture*, May 16, 2013, https://www.vulture.com/2013/05/talking-to-broken-lizards-jay-chandrasekhar-about-freeloaders-and-the-chevy-chase-n-word-thing.html; *Community*, season 5, episode 1, "Repilot," aired January 2, 2014; *Community*, season 5, episode 4, "Cooperative Polygraphy," directed by Tristram Shapeero, written by Alex Rubens, featuring Joel McHale, Alison Brie, Donald Glover, Danny Pudi, and Yvette Nicole Brown, aired January 16, 2014, on NBC, Sony, 2020, DVD.

42   *Community*, season 1, episode 2, "Spanish 101," directed by Joe Russo, written by Dan Harmon, featuring Joel McHale, Alison Brie, Donald Glover, Gillian Jacobs, Danny Pudi, and Yvette Nicole Brown, aired September 24, 2009, on NBC, Sony, 2020, DVD.

43   *Community*, season 2, episode 8, "Cooperative Calligraphy," directed by Joe Russo, written by Megan Ganz, featuring Joel McHale, Alison Brie, Donald Glover, Danny Pudi, and Yvette Nicole Brown, aired November 11, 2010, on NBC, Sony, 2020, DVD.

44   *Community*, season 1, episode 14, "Interpretive Dance," directed by Justin Lin, written by Lauren Pomerantz, featuring Joel McHale, Alison Brie, Gillian Jacobs, Donald Glover, Danny Pudi, and Yvette Nicole Brown, aired January 21, 2010, on NBC, Sony, 2020, DVD

45 *Community*, season 1, episode 5, "Advanced Criminal Law," directed by Joe Russo, written by Andrew Guest, featuring Joel McHale, Alison Brie, Gillian Jacobs, Donald Glover, Danny Pudi, and Yvette Nicole Brown, aired October 14, 2009, on NBC, Sony, 2020, DVD.

46 *Community*, season 2, episode 11, "Abed's Uncontrollable Christmas," aired December 9, 2010.

47 *Community*, season 1, episode 23, "Modern Warfare," directed by Justin Lin, written by Emily Cutler, featuring Joel McHale, Alison Brie, Donald Glover, Danny Pudi, Gillian Jacobs, and Yvette Nicole Brown, aired May 6, 2010, on NBC, Sony, 2020, DVD.

48 *Community*, season 1, episode 25, "Pascal's Triangle Revisited," directed by Joe Russo, written by Hilary Winston, featuring Joel McHale, Alison Brie, Donald Glover, Danny Pudi, Gillian Jacobs, and Yvette Nicole Brown, aired May 20, 2010, on NBC, Sony, 2020, DVD.

49 *Community*, season 2, episode 1, "Anthropology 101," directed by Joe Russo, written by Chris McKenna, featuring Joel McHale, Alison Brie, Donald Glover, Danny Pudi, Gillian Jacobs, Chevy Chase, and Yvette Nicole Brown, aired September 23, 2010, on NBC, Sony, 2020, DVD.

50 *Community*, season 2, episode 18, "Custody Law and Eastern European Diplomacy," directed by Anthony Russo, written by Chris McKenna, featuring Joel McHale, Alison Brie, Donald Glover, Danny Pudi, Gillian Jacobs, Chevy Chase, and Yvette Nicole Brown, aired September 23, 2010, on NBC, Sony, 2020, DVD.

51 *Community*, season 3, episode 2, "Geography of Global Conflict," aired September 29, 2011.

52 *Community*, season 3, episode 5, "Horror Fiction in Seven Spooky Steps," directed by Tristram Shapeero, written by Dan Harmon, featuring Joel McHale, Alison Brie, Donald Glover, Danny Pudi, and Yvette Nicole Brown, aired October 27, 2011, on NBC, Sony, 2020, DVD; *Community*, season 3, episode 22, "Introduction to Finality," aired May 17, 2012.

53 *Community*, season 6, episode 2, "Lawnmower Maintenance and Postnatal Care," directed by Jim Rash and Nat Faxon, written by Alex Rubens, featuring Joel McHale, Alison Brie, Danny Pudi, Gillian Jacobs, and Keith David, aired March 17, 2015, on Yahoo! Screen, Sony, 2020, DVD.

54 "I Am Dan Harmon," 2012.

55 *Community*, season 3, episode 10, "Regional Holiday Music," directed by Tristram Shapeero, written by Steve Basilone and Annie Mebane, featuring Joel McHale, Alison Brie, Donald Glover, Danny Pudi, and Yvette Nicole Brown, aired December 8, 2011, on NBC, Sony, 2020, DVD.

56 *Community*, season 2, episode 1, "Anthropology 101," aired September 23, 2010.

57 *Community*, season 5, episode 7, "Bondage and Beta Male Sexuality," directed by Tristram Shapeero, written by Dan Guterman, featuring Joel McHale, Alison Brie, Donald Glover, Danny Pudi, Gillian Jacobs, and Yvette Nicole Brown, aired February 27, 2014, on NBC, Sony, 2020, DVD; *Community*, season 5, episode 10, "Advanced Advanced *Dungeons and Dragons*," directed by Joe Russo, written by Matt Roller, featuring Joel McHale, Alison Brie, Donald Glover, Danny Pudi, and Yvette Nicole Brown, aired March 20, 2014, on NBC, Sony, 2020, DVD.

58 *Community*, season 2, episode 24, "For a Few Paintballs More," aired May 12, 2011.

59 *Community*, season 1, episode 13, "Investigative Journalism," directed by Joe Russo, written by Jim Pollack and Tim Hobert, featuring Joel McHale, Alison Brie, Donald Glover, Danny Pudi, and Yvette Nicole Brown, aired January 4, 2010, on NBC, Sony, 2020, DVD.

60 *Community*, season 2, episode 19, "Critical Film Studies," directed by Richard Ayoade, written by Sona Panos, featuring Joel McHale, Alison Brie, Donald Glover, Danny Pudi, and Yvette Nicole Brown, aired March 24, 2011, on NBC, Sony, 2020, DVD.

61 *Community*, season 3, episode 19, "Curriculum Unavailable," directed by Adam Davidson, written by Adam Countee, featuring Joel McHale, Alison Brie, Donald Glover, Danny Pudi, and Yvette Nicole Brown, aired May 10, 2012, on NBC, Sony, 2020, DVD.

62 *Community*, season 3, episode 22, "Introduction to Finality," aired May 17, 2012.

63 *Community*, season 3, episode 16, "Virtual Systems Analysis," directed by Tristram Shapeero, written by Matt Murray, featuring Joel McHale, Alison Brie, Donald Glover, Danny Pudi, and Yvette Nicole Brown, aired April 19, 2012, on NBC, Sony, 2020, DVD.

64 *Community*, season 1, episode 3, "Introduction to Film," directed by Anthony Russo, written by Tim Hobert and Jon Pollack, featuring Joel McHale, Alison Brie, Donald Glover, Danny Pudi, and Yvette Nicole Brown, aired October 1, 2009, on NBC, Sony, 2020, DVD.

65 *Community*, season 1, episode 9, "Debate 109," directed by Joe Russo, written by Tim Hobert, featuring Joel McHale, Alison Brie, Donald Glover, Danny Pudi, and Yvette Nicole Brown, aired November 12, 2009, on NBC, Sony, 2020, DVD.

66 *Community*, season 6, episode 13, "Emotional Consequences of Broadcast Television," aired June 2, 2014.

67 *Community*, season 2, episode 10, "Mixology Certification," aired December 2, 2010; *Community*, season 1, episode 10, "Environmental Science," directed by Seth Gordon, written by Zack Paez, featuring Joel McHale, Alison Brie, Donald Glover, Danny Pudi, and Yvette Nicole Brown, aired November 19, 2009, on NBC, Sony, 2020, DVD.

68 *Community*, season 2, episode 6, "Epidemiology," aired October 28, 2010.

69 *Community*, season 2, episode 12, "Asian Population Studies," directed by Anthony Russo, written by Emily Cutler, featuring Joel McHale, Alison Brie, Donald Glover, Danny Pudi, and Yvette Nicole Brown, aired January 20, 2011, on NBC, Sony, 2020, DVD.

70 *Community*, season 3, episode 11, "Urban Matrimony and the Sandwich Arts," directed by Kyle Newacheck, written by Vera Santamaria, featuring Joel McHale, Alison Brie, Donald Glover, Danny Pudi, and Yvette Nicole Brown, aired March 15, 2012, on NBC, Sony, 2020, DVD.

71 *Community*, season 5, episode 1, "Repilot," aired January 2, 2014; *Community*, season 5, episode 4, "Cooperative Polygraphy," aired January 16, 2014.

72 *Community*, season 6, episode 1, "Ladders," directed by Rob Schrab, written by Dan Harmon and Chris McKenna, featuring Joel McHale, Alison Brie, Donald Glover, Danny Pudi, and Yvette Nicole Brown, aired March 17, 2015, on Yahoo! Screen, Sony, 2020, DVD.

73 *Community*, season 4, episode 12, "Heroic Origins," directed by Vince Nelli Jr., written by Steve Basilone, Annie Mebane, and Maggie Bandur, featuring Joel McHale, Alison Brie, Donald Glover, Danny Pudi, and Yvette Nicole Brown, aired May 2, 2013, on NBC, Sony, 2020, DVD.

74 *Community*, season 3, episode 9, "Foosball and Nocturnal Vigilantism," directed by Anthony Russo, written by Chris Kula, featuring Joel McHale, Alison Brie, Donald Glover, Danny Pudi, and Yvette Nicole Brown, aired December 1, 2011, on NBC, Sony, 2020, DVD.

75 *Community*, season 4, episode 5, "Cooperative Escapism in Familial Relations," directed by Tristram Shapeero, written by Steve Basilone and Annie Mebane, featuring Joel McHale, Alison Brie, Donald Glover, Danny Pudi, and Yvette Nicole Brown, aired March 7, 2013, on NBC, Sony, 2020, DVD.

Chapter 4

1 "About the BBC: Mission, Values and Public Purpose," BBC, accessed November 5, 2024, https://www.bbc.com/aboutthebbc/governance/mission

2 *Growing Pains*, season 4, episode 20, "Second Chance," directed by John Tracy, written by David Kendall, featuring Tracey Gold, Kirk Cameron, Alan Thicke, and Matthew Perry, aired April 12, 1989, on ABC, Warner, 2015, DVD; *Diff'rent Strokes*, season 5, episodes 16–17, "The Bicycle Man, Parts 1 and 2," directed by Gerren Keith, written by Blake Hunter, featuring Gary Coleman, Conrad Bain, Shavar Ross, and Gordon Jump, aired February 5 and 12, 1983, on NBC, Shout! Factory, 2017, DVD.

3   Erin Giannini, "'And Was There a Lesson in All This?': Weaponizing—and Subverting—the Very Special Episode," in *Very Special Episodes: Televising Industrial and Social Change*, edited by Jonathan Cohn and Jennifer Porst (New Brunswick: Rutgers, 2021), 145–158.

4   *Head of the Class*, season 3, episodes 3–4, "Mission to Moscow," directed by Eric Laneuville, written by Michael Elias and Rich Eustis, featuring Howard Hesseman, Robin Givens, Rain Pryor, and William G. Schilling, aired November 2, 1988, on ABC, Warner, 2021, DVD.

5   *Boston Public*, season 1, episode 18, "Chapter Eighteen," directed by Elodie Keene, written by David E. Kelley, featuring Chi McBride, Anthony Heald, Jessalyn Gilsig, and Nicky Katt, aired April 23, 2001, on Fox.

6   *Abbott Elementary*, season 1, episode 3, "Wishlist," directed by Randall Einhorn, written by Morgan Murphy, featuring Quinta Brunson, Tyler James Williams, Janelle James, and Sheryl Lee Ralph, aired January 11, 2022, on ABC, Warner, 2022, DVD; *Abbott Elementary*, season 1, episode 1, "Pilot," directed by Randall Einhorn, written by Quinta Brunson, featuring Quinta Brunson, Tyler James Williams, Janelle James, and Sheryl Lee Ralph, aired December 7, 2021, on ABC, Warner, 2022, DVD; *Abbott Elementary*, season 2, episode 19, "Festival," directed by Randall Einhorn, written by Brian Rubenstein, featuring Quinta Brunson, Tyler James Williams, Janelle James, and Sheryl Lee Ralph, aired March 15, 2023, on ABC, Warner, 2023, DVD.

7   *Abbott Elementary*, season 3, episode 9, "Alex," directed by Randall Einhorn, written by Justin Tan, featuring Quinta Brunson, Tyler James Williams, Janelle James, and Sheryl Lee Ralph, aired April 10, 2024, on ABC, Warner, 2025, DVD.

8   *The Many Loves of Dobie Gillis*, season 2, episode 20, "The Second Childhood of Herbert T. Gillis," directed by Robert Gordon, written by Joel Kane, featuring Dwayne Hickman, Frank Faylen, Florida Friebus, and Bob Denver, aired March 7, 1961, on CBS, Shout! Factory, 2013, DVD.

9   Mark Voger, "'Dobie Gillis': The Complete Series on DVD," *NJ.com*, July 5, 2013, https://www.nj.com/entertainment/2013/07/dobie_gillis.html; Brian Cronin, "Jinkies! The Mysterious Origins of 'Scooby-Doo,'" *Comic Book Resources*, September 25, 2013, https://www.cbr.com/tv-legends-revealed-jinkies-the-mysterious-origins-of-scooby-doo/

10 *Square Pegs*, season 1, episode 9, "Muffy's Bat Mitzvah," directed by Kim Friedman, written by Margaret Oberman and Rosie Shuster, featuring Sarah Jessica Parker, Amy Linker, Jami Gertz, and Tracy Nelson, aired November 29, 1982, on CBS, Sony, 2008, DVD; *Square Pegs*, season 1, episode 1, "Pilot," directed by Kim Friedman, written by Anne Beatts, featuring Sarah Jessica Parker, Amy Linker, Jami Gertz, and Tracy Nelson, aired September 27, 1982, on CBS, Sony, 2008, DVD.

11 *It's Your Move*, season 1, episodes 12–13, "The Dregs of Humanity, Parts 1 and 2," directed by Jim Drake, written by Ron Leavitt and Michael G. Moye, featuring Jason

Bateman, Caren Kaye, Adam Sadowsky, and David Garrison, aired January 2 and 9, 1985, on NBC.

12 *Sabrina the Teenage Witch*, season 1, episode 1, "Pilot," directed by Robby Benson, written by Nell Scovell, featuring Melissa Joan Hart, Jason Bateman, Caroline Rhea, Beth Broderick, and Soleil Moon Frye, aired September 27, 1996, on ABC, CBS Home Media, 2007, DVD.

13 *Everybody Hates Chris*, season 1, episode 3, "Everybody Hates Basketball," directed by Lev L. Spiro, written by Aron Abrams and Gregory Thompson, featuring Tyler James Williams, Terry Crews, Tichina Arnold, and Vincent Martella, aired October 6, 2005, on UPN, CBS Home Media, 2009, DVD.

14 *Ferris Bueller*, season 1, episode 1, "Pilot," directed by Jonathan Lynn, written by John Masius, featuring Charlie Schlatter, Richard Riehl, Jennifer Aniston, and Ami Dolenz, aired August 23, 1990, on NBC.

15 Keegan Kelly, "The Awful 'Ferris Beuller' Show Opened With the New Ferris Chainsawing Matthew Broderick in Half," *Cracked*, June 17, 2024, https://www.cracked.com/article_42529_the-awful-ferris-bueller-tv-show-opened-with-the-new-ferris-chainsawing-matthew-brodericks-likeness-in-half.html

16 *Parker Lewis Can't Lose*, season 1, episode 15, "Heather the Class," directed by Max Tash, written by Alan Cross and Tom Spezialy, featuring Corin Nemec, Billy Jayne, Troy Slaten, and Melanie Chartoff, aired January 13, 1991, on Fox, Shout! Factory, 2009, DVD; *Parker Lewis Can't Lose*, season 3, episode 7, "Beauty and the Kube," directed by Mike Finney, written by Adam Barr and Peter Ocko, featuring Corin Nemec, Billy Jayne, Troy Slaten, and Melanie Chartoff, aired September 6, 1992, on Fox, Turbine Medien, 2015, DVD; *Parker Lewis Can't Lose*, season 3, episode 15, "Write or Die," directed by Larry Shaw, written by Clyde Phillips, featuring Corin Nemec, Billy Jayne, Troy Slaten, and Melanie Chartoff, aired April 18, 1993, on Fox, Turbine Medien, 2015, DVD.

17 *Parker Lewis Can't Lose*, season 2, episode 22, "Geek Tragedy," directed by Larry Shaw, written by Peter Ocko and Adam Barr, featuring Corin Nemec, Billy Jayne, Troy Slaten, and Melanie Chartoff, aired April 18, 1993, on Fox, Shout! Factory, 2015, DVD.

18 *Daria*, season 5, episode 1, "Fizz Ed," directed by Karen Disher, written by Glenn Eichler, featuring Tracy Grandstaff, Wendy Hoopes, and Julian Rebolledo, aired February 19, 2001, on MTV, Paramount 2010, DVD.

19 *Freaks and Geeks*, season 1, episode 17, "The Little Things," directed by Jake Kasdan, written by Jon Kasdan, featuring Linda Cardellini, Seth Rogan, John Francis Daley, Busy Phillips, and Jason Segel, aired July 8, 2000, on NBC, Shout! Factory, 2004, DVD; *Freaks and Geeks*, season 1, episode 18, "Discos and Dragons," directed by Paul Feig, written by Paul Feig, featuring Linda Cardellini, Seth Rogan, John Francis Daley, Busy Phillips, and Jason Segel, aired July 8, 2000, on NBC, Shout! Factory, 2004, DVD.

20. Tim Stack, "Ryan Murphy Says the WB Was Homophobic during *Popular*: The Creator of the Teen Comedy Reveals the Network Would Give Him Notes to Make the Series 'Less Gay,'" *Entertainment Weekly*, September 26, 2016, https://ew.com/article/2016/09/26/ryan-murphy-wb-popular-homophobic/

21. *Grosse Pointe*, season 1, episode 16, "Passion Fish," directed by Pail Feig, written by Paul Feig, featuring Irene Molloy, William Ragsdale, Lindsay Sloane, and Bonnie Somerville, aired February 16, 2001, on the WB, Sony, 2007, DVD.

22. Henry Louis Gates Jr., "Did Black People Own Slaves?," *The Root*, March 4, 2013, https://web.archive.org/web/20130308014646/http://www.theroot.com/views/did-black-people-own-slaves; Mary Elliot and Jazmine Hughes, "Four Hundred Years after Enslaved Africans Were First Brought to Virginia, Most Americans Don't Know the Full Story of Slavery," *New York Times Magazine*, August 19, 2019, https://www.nytimes.com/interactive/2019/08/19/magazine/history-slavery-smithsonian.html

Chapter 5

1. Tom Shales, "NBCees Paul Klein to the Door: NBC's Paul Klein: Out in the Shuffle," *Washington Post*, March 5, 1979, https://www.washingtonpost.com/archive/lifestyle/1979/03/06/nbcees-paul-klein-to-the-door/998c31db-7e66-4bc0-bbd3-b3090f0b97d1; Paul Klein, "Why You Watch What You Watch When You Watch," *TV Guide*, July 24, 1971, 6–9.

2. *Night Court*, season 3, episode 12, "Dan's Escort," directed by Jeff Melman, written by Bob Stevens, featuring Harry Anderson, Markie Post, Charles Robinson, John Larroquette, and Richard Moll, aired January 9, 1986, on NBC, Warner Brothers, 2023, DVD.

3. *It's Your Move*, season 1, episodes 12–13, "The Dregs of Humanity, Parts 1 and 2," directed by Jim Drake, written by Ron Leavitt and Michael G. Moye, featuring Jason Bateman, Caren Kaye, Adam Sadowsky, and David Garrison, aired January 2 and 9, 1985, on NBC.

4. Nick Griffiths, "America's First Family," *The Times Magazine*, April 15, 2000, 25, 27–28.

5. John Consoli, "Analysis: Is Reilly a Scapegoat for NBC's Failures?" *Mediaweek*, May 28, 2007, https://web.archive.org/web/20071008103640/http://www.mediaweek.com/mw/news/networktv/article_display.jsp?vnu_content_id=1003591026

6. *My Name Is Earl*, season 1, episode 1, "Pilot," directed by Marc Buckland, written by Greg Garcia, featuring Jason Lee, Ethan Suplee, Jaime Pressley, and Eddie Steeples, aired September 20, 2005, on NBC, Fox, 2006, DVD.

7   Will Leitch, "The Poehler Effect: Can Amy Poehler's *Parks and Recreation* Resurrect NBC? No Pressure or Anything ... " *New York Magazine*, April 5, 2009, https://web.archive.org/web/20120413052905/; http://nymag.com/arts/tv/features/55851/

8   Saul Austerlitz, *Sitcom: A History in 24 Episodes from* I Love Lucy *to* Community (Chicago: Chicago Review Press, 2014), 356.

9   *Arrested Development*, season 3, episode 9, "S.O.B.s," directed by Robert Berlinger, written by Richard Day and Jim Vallely, featuring Jason Bateman, Jessica Walters, Portia de Rossi, and Will Arnett, aired January 2, 2006, on NBC, Fox, 2006, DVD.

10 Maureen Ryan, "'Parks and Recreation': Less Funny than 'Joey'?" *Chicago Tribune*, May 13, 2009, http://featuresblogs.chicagotribune.com/entertainment_tv/2009/05/parks-recreation-amy-poehler-nbc.html; Rob Owen, "Comedy in 'Parks' Gets Lost in Translation," *Pittsburgh Post-Gazette*, April 9, 2009, http://www.post-gazette.com/pg/09099/961595-67.stm

11 Alan Sepinwall, "Parks and Recreation: Interviewing Co-creator Mike Schur," *New Jersey Star-Ledger*, September 17, 2009, http://www.nj.com/entertainment/tv/index.ssf/2009/09/parks_and_recreation_interview.html

12 *Community*, season 4, episode 12, "Heroic Origins," directed by Vince Nelli Jr., written by Steve Basilone, Annie Mebane, and Maggie Bandur, featuring Joel McHale, Alison Brie, Donald Glover, Danny Pudi, and Yvette Nicole Brown, aired May 2, 2013, on NBC, Sony, 2020, DVD; *Community*, season 6, episode 1, "Ladders," directed by Rob Schrab, written by Dan Harmon and Chris McKenna, featuring Joel McHale, Alison Brie, Danny Pudi, Keith David, and Yvette Nicole Brown, aired March 17, 2015, on NBC, Sony, 2020, DVD.

13 *Community*, season 1, episode 1, "Pilot," directed by Anthony and Joe Russo, written by Dan Harmon, featuring Joel McHale, Alison Brie, Donald Glover, Danny Pudi, and Yvette Nicole Brown, aired September 17, 2009, on NBC, Sony, 2020, DVD.

14 *Community*, season 1, episode 21, "Contemporary American Poultry," directed by Tristram Shapeero, written by Emily Cutler and Karey Dornetto, featuring Joel McHale, Alison Brie, Donald Glover, Danny Pudi, and Yvette Nicole Brown, aired April 22, 2010, on NBC, Sony, 2020, DVD; *Community*, season 3, episode 1, "Biology 101," directed by Anthony Russo, written by Garrett Donovan and Neil Goldman, featuring Joel McHale, Alison Brie, Donald Glover, Danny Pudi, and Yvette Nicole Brown, aired September 22, 2011, on NBC, Sony, 2020, DVD.

15 *Community*, season 1, episode 9, "Debate 109," directed by Joe Russo, written by Tim Hobert, featuring Joel McHale, Alison Brie, Donald Glover, Danny Pudi, and Yvette Nicole Brown, aired November 12, 2009, on NBC, Sony, 2020, DVD; *Community*, season 2, episode 8, "Cooperative Calligraphy," directed by Joe Russo, written by Megan Ganz, featuring Joel McHale, Alison Brie, Donald Glover, Danny Pudi, and Yvette Nicole Brown, aired November 11, 2010, on NBC, Sony, 2020, DVD.

16. *Community*, season 1, episode 12, "Comparative Religion," directed by Adam Davidson, written by Liz Cackowski, featuring Joel McHale, Alison Brie, Donald Glover, Danny Pudi, and Yvette Nicole Brown, aired December 10, 2009, on NBC, Sony, 2020, DVD; *Community*, season 3, episode 5, "Horror Fiction in Seven Spooky Steps," directed by Tristram Shapeero, written by Dan Harmon, featuring Joel McHale, Alison Brie, Donald Glover, Danny Pudi, and Yvette Nicole Brown, aired October 27, 2011, on NBC, Sony, 2020, DVD.

17. *Community*, season 2, episode 10, "Mixology Certification," directed by Jay Chandrasekhar, written by Andy Bobrow, featuring Joel McHale, Alison Brie, Donald Glover, Danny Pudi, and Yvette Nicole Brown, aired December 2, 2010, on NBC, Sony, 2020, DVD.

18. *Community*, season 5, episode 7, "Bondage and Beta Male Sexuality," directed by Tristram Shapeero, written by Dan Guterman, featuring Joel McHale, Alison Brie, Gillian Jacobs, Danny Pudi, and Yvette Nicole Brown, aired February 27, 2014, on NBC, Sony, 2020, DVD; *Community*, season 3, episode 12, "Contemporary Impressionists," directed by Kyle Newacheck, written by Alex Cooley, featuring Joel McHale, Alison Brie, Gillian Jacobs, Danny Pudi, and Yvette Nicole Brown, aired March 22, 2012, on NBC, Sony, 2020, DVD.

19. *Community*, season 2, episode 1, "Anthropology 101," directed by Joe Russo, written by Chris McKenna, featuring Joel McHale, Alison Brie, Gillian Jacobs, Danny Pudi, and Yvette Nicole Brown, aired September 23, 2010, on NBC, Sony, 2020, DVD.

20. *Community*, season 3, episode 21, "The First Chang Dynasty," directed by Jay Chandrasekhar, written by Matt Fusfeld and Alex Cuthbertson, featuring Joel McHale, Alison Brie, Donald Glover, Gillian Jacobs, Danny Pudi, and Yvette Nicole Brown, aired May 17, 2012, on NBC, Sony, 2020, DVD.

21. *Community*, season 1, episode 2, "Spanish 101," directed by Joe Russo, written by Dan Harmon, featuring Joel McHale, Alison Brie, Donald Glover, Gillian Jacobs, Danny Pudi, and Yvette Nicole Brown, aired September 24, 2009, on NBC, Sony, 2020, DVD.

22. *Community*, season 2, episode 8, "Cooperative Calligraphy," aired November 11, 2010.

23. *Community*, season 3, episode 12, "Contemporary Impressionists," aired March 22, 2012; *Community*, season 3, episode 22, "Introduction to Finality," directed by Tristram Shapeero, written by Steve Basilone and Annie Mebane, featuring Joel McHale, Alison Brie, Gillian Jacobs, Danny Pudi, and Yvette Nicole Brown, aired May 17, 2012, on NBC, Sony, 2020, DVD.

24. *Community*, season 2, episode 13, "Celebrity Pharmacology," directed by Fred Goss, written by Hillary Winston, featuring Joel McHale, Alison Brie, Chevy Chase, Danny Pudi, and Yvette Nicole Brown, aired January 27, 2011, on NBC, Sony, 2020, DVD; *Community*, season 3, episode 20, "Digital Estate Planning," directed by Adam Davidson, written by Matt Warburton, featuring Joel McHale, Alison Brie, Chevy

Chase, Danny Pudi, and Yvette Nicole Brown, aired May 17, 2012, on NBC, Sony, 2020, DVD.

25. *Community*, season 1, episode 9, "Debate 109," aired November 12, 2009; *Community*, season 1, episode 10, "Environmental Science," directed by Seth Gordon, written by Zack Paez, featuring Joel McHale, Alison Brie, Donald Glover, Danny Pudi, and Yvette Nicole Brown, aired November 19, 2009, on NBC, Sony, 2020, DVD.

26. *Community*, season 2, episode 24, "For a Few Paintballs More," directed by Joe Russo, written by Hilary Winston, featuring Joel McHale, Alison Brie, Donald Glover, Danny Pudi, and Yvette Nicole Brown, aired May 12, 2011, on NBC, Sony, 2020, DVD.

27. *Community*, season 6, episode 13, "Emotional Consequences of Broadcast Television," directed by Rob Schrab, written by Dan Harmon and Chris McKenna, featuring Joel McHale, Alison Brie, Gillian Jacobs, Danny Pudi, and Keith David, aired June 2, 2015, on Yahoo! Screen, Sony, 2020, DVD.

28. *Family Ties*, season 2, episode 12, "Go Tigers," directed by Will Mackenzie, written by Michael J. Weithorn, featuring Michael J. Fox, Meredith Baxter, Justine Bateman, and Michael Gross, aired January 12, 1984, on NBC, Paramount, 2007, DVD.

29. *Community*, season 2, episode 23, "A Fistful of Paintballs," directed by Joe Russo, written by Andrew Guest, featuring Joel McHale, Alison Brie, Donald Glover, Danny Pudi, and Yvette Nicole Brown, aired May 5, 2011, on NBC, Sony, 2020, DVD; *Community*, season 2, episode 24, "For a Few Paintballs More," aired May 12, 2011; *Community*, season 3, episode 14, "Pillows and Blankets," directed by Tristram Shapeero, written by Andy Bobrow, featuring Joel McHale, Alison Brie, Donald Glover, Danny Pudi, and Yvette Nicole Brown, aired April 5, 2012, on NBC, Sony, 2020, DVD; *Community*, season 3, episode 12, "Contemporary Impressionists," aired March 22, 2012.

30. *Community*, season 2, episode 19, "Critical Film Studies," directed by Richard Ayoade, written by Sona Pados, featuring Joel McHale, Alison Brie, Donald Glover, Danny Pudi, and Yvette Nicole Brown, aired March 24, 2011, on NBC, Sony, 2020, DVD.

31. *Community*, season 3, episode 22, "Introduction to Finality," aired May 17, 2012.

32. "Sitcom Character Archetypes," *TV Tropes*, accessed October 14, 2024, https://tvtropes.org/pmwiki/pmwiki.php/Main/SitcomCharacterArchetypes

33. *Community*, season 2, episode 1, "Anthropology 101," aired September 23, 2010.

34. Hampton Stevens, "The Meta, Innovative Genius of *Community*: It's One of the Most Innovative Shows in Sitcom History. But Can It Make Us Care about the Characters?" *The Atlantic*, May 12, 2011, https://www.theatlantic.com/entertainment/archive/2011/05/the-meta-innovative-genius-of-community/238740/

35 Alan Sepinwall, "For 'Community', How Much Meta Is Too Much?," *Uproxx*, May 5, 2010, https://uproxx.com/sepinwall/for-community-how-much-meta-is-too-much/

36 Tim Molloy, "'Community' Canceled by NBC After 5 Seasons of Critical Acclaim, Low Ratings: Goodbye, Paintball, Animation and Tributes," *The Wrap*, May 9, 2014, https://www.thewrap.com/community-canceled-nbc-5-seasons-critical-acclaim-low-ratings/

Chapter 6

1 Michael Martin, "Dan Levy Discusses *Schitt's Creek*, His Eyebrows and Being a Sex Object: When You're Born into Comedy Royalty, Just Grab the Crown and Run with It," *Out Magazine*, March 9, 2015, https://www.out.com/television/2015/3/09/dan-levy-discusses-schitts-creek-his-eyebrows-being-sex-object#toggle-gdpr

2 Saul Austerlitz, *Sitcom: A History in 24 Episodes From I Love Lucy to Community* (Chicago: Chicago Review Press, 2014), 2.

3 *My Name Is Earl*, season 3, episode 16, "Stole a Motorcycle," directed by Eyal Gordin, written by Kat Likkel and John Hoberg, featuring Jason Lee, Ethan Suplee, Jaime Pressley, and Eddie Steeples, aired April 10, 2008, on NBC, Fox, 2008, DVD.

4 Pete Keeley, "'Parker Lewis Can't Lose' at 25: Like 'Going to the Juilliard School of Cinema,'" *Hollywood Reporter*, June 14, 2018, https://www.hollywoodreporter.com/tv/tv-news/parker-lewis-cant-lose-directors-talk-shooting-innovative-series-1120072/; *Parker Lewis Can't Lose*, season 3, episode 7, "Beauty and the Kube," directed by Mike Finney, written by Adam Barr and Peter Ocko, featuring Corin Nemec, Billy Jayne, Troy Slaten, and Melanie Chartoff, aired September 6, 1992, on Fox, Turbine Medien, 2015, DVD.

5 *Parker Lewis Can't Lose*, season 3, episode 15, "Write or Die," directed by Larry Shaw, written by Clyde Phillips, featuring Corin Nemec, Billy Jayne, Troy Slaten, and Melanie Chartoff, aired April 18, 1993, on Fox, Turbine Medien, 2015, DVD.

6 *Scrubs*, season 4, episode 17, "My Life in Four Cameras," directed by Adam Bernstein, written by Debra Fordham, featuring Zach Braff, Donald Faison, Sarah Chalke, Judy Reyes, and John C. McGinley, aired February 15, 2005, on NBC, Buena Vista, 2006, DVD.

7 *Community*, season 1, episode 13, "Investigative Journalism," directed by Joe Russo, written by Jon Pollack and Tim Hobert, featuring Joel McHale, Alison Brie, Donald Glover, Danny Pudi, and Yvette Nicole Brown, aired January 14, 2010, on NBC, Sony, 2020, DVD.

8   *Community*, season 2, episode 20, "Competitive Wine Tasting," directed by Joe Russo, written by Emily Cutler, featuring Joel McHale, Alison Brie, Donald Glover, Danny Pudi, and Yvette Nicole Brown, aired April 14, 2011, on NBC, Sony, 2020, DVD; *Community*, season 3, episode 10, "Regional Holiday Music," directed by Tristram Shapeero, written by Steve Basilone and Annie Mebane, featuring Joel McHale, Alison Brie, Donald Glover, Danny Pudi, and Yvette Nicole Brown, aired December 8, 2011, on NBC, Sony, 2020, DVD.

9   *Community*, season 4, episode 1, "History 101," directed by Tristram Shapeero, written by Andy Bobrow, featuring Joel McHale, Alison Brie, Donald Glover, Danny Pudi, and Yvette Nicole Brown, aired February 7, 2013, on NBC, Sony, 2020, DVD.

10 *Community*, season 4, episode 2, "Paranormal Parentage," directed by Tristram Shapeero, written by Megan Ganz, featuring Joel McHale, Alison Brie, Donald Glover, Danny Pudi, and Yvette Nicole Brown, aired February 14, 2013, on NBC, Sony, 2020, DVD.

11 *Community*, season 4, episode 7, "Economics of Marine Biology," directed by Tricia Brock, written by Tim Saccardo, featuring Joel McHale, Alison Brie, Donald Glover, Danny Pudi, and Yvette Nicole Brown, aired March 21, 2013, on NBC, Sony, 2020, DVD.

12 *Community*, season 6, episode 13, "Emotional Consequences of Broadcast Television," directed by Rob Schrab, written by Dan Harmon and Chris McKenna, featuring Joel McHale, Alison Brie, Gillian Jacobs, Danny Pudi, and Keith David, aired June 2, 2015, on Yahoo! Screen, Sony, 2020, DVD.

13 Kathryn VanArendonk, "What Is a Bottle Episode? The People on the Internet Are Wrong. Or Are They?" *Vulture*, February 7, 2025, https://www.vulture.com/article/what-is-a-bottle-episode-meaning.html

14 *Firefly*, season 1, episode 8, "Out of Gas," directed by David Solomon, written by Tim Minear, featuring Nathan Fillion, Gina Torres, Alan Tudyk, Ron Glass, and Summer Glau, aired October 25, 2002, on Fox, Fox, 2003, DVD.

15 *Brooklyn Nine-Nine*, season 5, episode 14, "The Box," directed by Claire Scanlon, written by Luke Del Tredici, featuring Andre Braugher, Andy Samberg, Melissa Fumero, Terry Crews, and Chelsea Peretti, aired April 1, 2018, on Fox, Universal, 2022, DVD.

16 *Homicide: Life on the Street*, season 1, episode 6, "Three Men and Adena," directed by Martin Campbell, written by Tom Fontana, featuring Andre Braugher, Kyle Secor, Yaphet Kotto, and Melissa Leo, aired March 3, 1993, on NBC, Shout! Factory, 2017, DVD.

17 *Community*, season 2, episode 8, "Cooperative Calligraphy," directed by Joe Russo, written by Megan Ganz, featuring Joel McHale, Alison Brie, Donald Glover, Danny Pudi, and Yvette Nicole Brown, aired November 11, 2010, on NBC, Sony, 2020, DVD.

18 Cory Barker, "Community, 'Cooperative Calligraphy,'" *TV Surveillance*, November 13, 2010, http://web.archive.org/web/20120322133135/http://tvsurveillance.com/2010/11/13/community-cooperative-calligraphy/

19 *Community*, season 2, episode 6, "Epidemiology," directed by Anthony Hemingway, written by Karey Dornetto, featuring Joel McHale, Alison Brie, Donald Glover, Danny Pudi, and Yvette Nicole Brown, aired October 28, 2010, on NBC, Sony, 2020, DVD; *Community*, season 1, episode 25, "Pascal's Triangle Revisited," directed by Joe Russo, written by Hilary Winston, featuring Joel McHale, Alison Brie, Donald Glover, Danny Pudi, and Yvette Nicole Brown, aired May 20, 2010, on NBC, Sony, 2020, DVD; *Community*, season 2, episode 1, "Anthropology 101," directed by Joe Russo, written by Chris McKenna, featuring Joel McHale, Alison Brie, Donald Glover, Danny Pudi, and Yvette Nicole Brown, aired September 23, 2010, on NBC, Sony, 2020, DVD.

20 *Community*, season 2, episode 22, "Applied Anthropology and Culinary Arts," directed by Jay Chandrasekhar, written by Karey Dornetto, featuring Joel McHale, Alison Brie, Donald Glover, Danny Pudi, and Yvette Nicole Brown, aired April 28, 2011, on NBC, Sony, 2020, DVD.

21 *Community*, season 2, episode 14, "Advanced *Dungeons and Dragons*," directed by Joe Russo, written by Andrew Guest, featuring Joel McHale, Alison Brie, Donald Glover, Danny Pudi, and Yvette Nicole Brown, aired February 3, 2011, on NBC, Sony, 2020, DVD.

22 *Community*, season 3, episode 4, "Remedial Chaos Theory," directed by Jeff Melman, written by Chris McKenna, featuring Joel McHale, Alison Brie, Donald Glover, Danny Pudi, Chevy Chase, Gillian Jacobs, and Yvette Nicole Brown, aired October 13, 2011, on NBC, Sony, 2020, DVD.

23 *Community*, season 6, episode 13, "Emotional Consequences of Broadcast Television," aired June 2, 2015.

24 *Roseanne*, season 7, episode 19, "All About Rosey, Part 1," directed by Gail Mancuso, written by Rob Ulin and Perry Dance, featuring Roseanne Barr, John Goodman, Sarah Chalke, and Sara Gilbert, aired March 1, 1995, on ABC, Mill Creek, 2013, DVD; *Roseanne*, season 7, episode 20, "All About Rosey, Part 2," directed by Gail Mancuso, written by Rob Ulin and Perry Dance, featuring Roseanne Barr, John Goodman, Sarah Chalke, and Sara Gilbert, aired March 1, 1995, on ABC, Mill Creek, 2013, DVD.

25 *Roseanne*, season 4, episode 1, "A Bitter Pill to Swallow," directed by Andrew D. Weyman, written by Amy Sherman and Jennifer Heath, featuring Roseanne Barr, John Goodman, Lecy Goranson, and Sara Gilbert, aired March 1, 1995, on ABC, Mill Creek, 2013, DVD; *Roseanne*, season 6, episode 18, "Don't Ask, Don't Tell," directed by Philip Charles MacKenzie, written by James Berg and Stan Zimmerman, featuring Roseanne Barr, John Goodman, Sarah Chalke, and Sara Gilbert, aired March 1, 1994, on ABC, Mill Creek, 2013, DVD.

26 *Supernatural*, season 8, episode 22, "Clip Show," directed by Thomas J. Wright, written by Andrew Dabb, featuring Jensen Ackles, Jared Padalecki, Misha Collins, and Mark Sheppard, aired May 8, 2013, on the CW, Warner Brothers, 2013, DVD.

27 Sandra Gonzalez, "'Community' Creator Dan Harmon on a Clip Show Like No Other," *Entertainment Weekly*, December 16, 2011, https://ew.com/article/2011/12/16/community-creator-dan-harmon-clip-show-best-of-behind-the-scenes/

28 *Community*, season 2, episode 6, "Epidemiology," aired October 28, 2010; *Community*, season 2, episode 10, "Abed's Uncontrollable Christmas," directed by Duke Johnson, written by Dino Stamatopoulos and Dan Harmon, featuring Joel McHale, Alison Brie, Donald Glover, Danny Pudi, and Yvette Nicole Brown, aired December 9, 2010, on NBC, Sony, 2020, DVD.

29 *Community*, season 2, episode 21, "Paradigms of Human Memory," directed by Tristram Shapeero, written by Chris McKenna, featuring Joel McHale, Alison Brie, Donald Glover, Danny Pudi, and Yvette Nicole Brown, aired April 21, 2011, on NBC, Sony, 2020, DVD.

30 *Community*, season 1, episode 5, "Advanced Criminal Law," directed by Joe Russo, written by Andrew Guest, featuring Joel McHale, Alison Brie, Donald Glover, Danny Pudi, and Yvette Nicole Brown, aired October 15, 2009, on NBC, Sony, 2020, DVD; *Community*, season 2, episode 1, "Anthropology 101," aired September 23, 2010, on NBC; *Community*, season 2, episode 15, "Early 21st Century Romanticism," directed by Steven Sprung, written by Karey Dornetto, featuring Joel McHale, Alison Brie, Donald Glover, Danny Pudi, and Yvette Nicole Brown, aired February 10, 2011, on NBC, Sony, 2020, DVD.

31 *Community*, season 2, episode 21, "Paradigms of Human Memory," aired April 21, 2011.

32 *Community*, season 3, episode 18, "Course Listing Unavailable," directed by Tristram Shapeero, written by Tim Saccardo, featuring Joel McHale, Alison Brie, Donald Glover, Danny Pudi, and Yvette Nicole Brown, aired May 3, 2012, on NBC, Sony, 2020, DVD.

33 *Community*, season 3, episode 19, "Curriculum Unavailable," directed by Adam Davidson, written by Adam Countee, featuring Joel McHale, Alison Brie, Donald Glover, Danny Pudi, and Yvette Nicole Brown, aired May 10, 2012, on NBC, Sony, 2020, DVD.

34 *Community*, season 1, episode 21, "Contemporary American Poultry," directed by Tristram Shapeero, written by Emily Cutler and Karey Dornetto, featuring Joel McHale, Alison Brie, Donald Glover, Danny Pudi, and Yvette Nicole Brown, aired April 22, 2010, on NBC, Sony, 2020, DVD.

35 *Community*, season 2, episode 19, "Critical Film Studies," directed by Richard Ayoade, written by Sona Panos, featuring Joel McHale, Alison Brie, Donald Glover,

Danny Pudi, and Yvette Nicole Brown, aired March 24, 2011, on NBC, Sony, 2020, DVD.

36. *Community*, season 2, episode 4, "Basic Rocket Science," directed by Anthony Russo, written by Andy Bobrow, featuring Joel McHale, Alison Brie, Donald Glover, Danny Pudi, and Yvette Nicole Brown, aired October 14, 2010, on NBC, Sony, 2020, DVD; *Community*, season 5, episode 3, "Basic Intergluteal Numismatics," directed by Tristram Shapeero, written by Erik Sommers, featuring Joel McHale, Alison Brie, Donald Glover, Danny Pudi, and Yvette Nicole Brown, aired January 9, 2014, on NBC, Sony, 2020, DVD.

37. *Community*, season 3, episode 5, "Horror Fiction in Seven Spooky Steps," directed by Tristram Shapeero, written by Dan Harmon, featuring Joel McHale, Alison Brie, Donald Glover, Danny Pudi, and Yvette Nicole Brown, aired October 27, 2011, on NBC, Sony, 2020, DVD.

38. *Community*, season 3, episode 17, "Basic Lupine Urology," directed by Rob Schrab, written by Megan Ganz, featuring Joel McHale, Alison Brie, Donald Glover, Danny Pudi, and Yvette Nicole Brown, aired April 26, 2012, on NBC, Sony, 2020, DVD.

39. *Community*, season 3, episode 10, "Regional Holiday Music," aired December 8, 2011.

40. *Community*, season 2, episode 10, "Abed's Uncontrollable Christmas," aired December 9, 2010.

41. *Community*, season 5, episode 11, "G.I. Jeff," directed by Rob Schrab, written by Dino Stamatopoulos, featuring Joel McHale, Alison Brie, Jonathan Banks, Danny Pudi, and Yvette Nicole Brown, aired April 3, 2014, on NBC, Sony, 2020, DVD.

42. *Community*, season 3, episode 14, "Pillows and Blankets," directed by Tristram Shapeero, written by Andy Bobrow, featuring Joel McHale, Alison Brie, Jonathan Banks, Danny Pudi, and Yvette Nicole Brown, aired April 5, 2012, on NBC, Sony, 2020, DVD.

43. *Community*, season 4, episode 3, "Conventions of Space and Time," directed by Michael Patrick Jann, written by Maggie Bandur, featuring Joel McHale, Alison Brie, Jonathan Banks, Danny Pudi, and Yvette Nicole Brown, aired February 21, 2013, on NBC, Sony, 2020, DVD.

Chapter 7

1. Jake Rossen, "The Tommy Westphall Theory of a Unified TV Universe, Explained," *Mental Floss*, January 21, 2024, https://www.mentalfloss.com/article/500756/tommy-westphall-theory-unified-tv-universe-explained

NOTES

2   *Community*, season 6, episode 13, "Emotional Consequences of Broadcast Television," directed by Rob Schrab, written by Dan Harmon and Chris McKenna, featuring Joel McHale, Alison Brie, Gillian Jacobs, Danny Pudi, and Keith David, aired June 2, 2015, on Yahoo! Screen, Sony, 2020, DVD.

3   James Poniewozik, "The Decency Police," *Time*, March 20, 2005, https://time.com/archive/6671688/the-decency-police/

4   Brad Adgate, "The Rise and Fall of Cable Television," *Forbes*, November 3, 2020, https://www.forbes.com/sites/bradadgate/2020/11/02/the-rise-and-fall-of-cable-television

5   Michele Hilmes, *Only Connect: A Cultural History of Broadcasting in the United States*, 3rd ed. (Boston: Wadsworth Cengage Learning, 2011), 296.

6   Saul Austerlitz, *Sitcom: A History in 24 Episodes From I Love Lucy to Community* (Chicago: Chicago Review Press, 2014), 369–83.

7   Andrew Wallenstein, "Yahoo Shutters Video Service Yahoo Screen," *Variety*, January 4, 2016, https://variety.com/2016/digital/news/yahoo-shutters-video-service-yahoo-screen-exclusive-1201671374/

8   Matthew Hills, *The Pleasures of Horror* (London: Continuum, 2005); Lorna Jowett and Stacey Abbott, *TV Horror: Investigating the Dark Side of the Small Screen* (London: IB Tauris, 2013): Stephen King, *Danse Macabre* (New York: Scribner, 2010).

9   Brad Adgate, "The Future of Television Is Broadcast & Streaming: Here's Why," *Forbes*, August 8, 2024, https://www.forbes.com/sites/bradadgate/2024/08/08/the-future-of-television-is-broadcast--streaming-heres-why

10 Paul Richter, "Sony to Buy Columbia, Says Americans Will Run Studio: 1st Sale of Film Maker to Japanese," *Los Angeles Times*, September 27, 1989, https://www.latimes.com/archives/la-xpm-1989-09-27-mn-335-story.html

11 Diane Werts, "Review: CBS' 'Viva Laughlin' a Train Wreck," *Newsday*, October 18, 2007, https://web.archive.org/web/20071020034800/http://www.newsday.com/entertainment/tv/ny-ettell5415699oct18,0,5351094.story

12 *Dawson's Creek*, season 3, episode 23, "True Love," directed by James Whitmore Jr., written by Tom Kapinos and Gina Fattore, featuring James Van Der Beek, Katie Holmes, Michelle Williams, and Joshua Jackson, aired May 24, 2000, on the WB, Sony, 2004, DVD.

13 *News Radio*, season 3, episode 7, "Daydream," directed by Tom Cherones, written by Paul Simms, featuring Dave Foley, Phil Hartman, Maura Tierney, Steven Root, and Vicky Lewis, aired November 13, 1996, on NBC, Sony, 2008, DVD; *News Radio*, season 3, episode 24, "Space," directed by Tom Cherones, written by Joe Furey, Josh Lieb, and Paul Simms, featuring Dave Foley, Phil Hartman, Maura Tierney, Steven Root, and Vicky Lewis, aired May 21, 1997, on NBC, Sony, 2008, DVD; *News Radio*,

season 4, episode 22, "Sinking Ship," directed by Tom Cherones, written by Joe Furey, Brian Kelley, Josh Lieb, and Sam Johnson, featuring Dave Foley, Phil Hartman, Maura Tierney, Steven Root, and Vicky Lewis, aired May 12, 1998, on NBC, Sony, 2008, DVD.

14 Pete Keeley, "'Parker Lewis Can't Lose' at 25: Like 'Going to the Juilliard School of Cinema,'" *Hollywood Reporter*, June 14, 2018, https://www.hollywoodreporter.com/tv/tv-news/parker-lewis-cant-lose-directors-talk-shooting-innovative-series-1120072/.

15 Katie Kilkenny, "Writers Guide Calls First Strike in 15 Years: Picketing by Hollywood Scribes Is Slated to Begin at 1 pm PT in Los Angeles at Production Sites across the City with Simultaneous Demonstrations Occurring in New York," *The Hollywood Reporter*, May 1, 2023, https://www.hollywoodreporter.com/business/business-news/wga-writers-strike-moves-forward-contract-negotiations-1235404087/.

16 Julie Hinds, "Broadcast vs. Cable vs. Streaming: The Future of Television Is a Confusing Maze for Viewers," *Detroit Free Press*, March 4, 2024, https://www.freep.com/story/entertainment/television/2024/03/04/the-future-of-tv-chaos-confusion-and-a-war-for-eyeballs/72805782007/.

17 Todd Spangler, "Off-Peak TV: Number of Scripted Shows Fell 24% in 2023, Study Finds," *Variety*, January 19, 2024, https://variety.com/2024/tv/news/us-scripted-tv-shows-2023-peak-tv-study-1235877669/.

Chapter 8

1 *Community*, season 6, episode 13, "Emotional Consequences of Broadcast Television," directed by Rob Schrab, written by Dan Harmon and Chris McKenna, featuring Joel McHale, Alison Brie, Danny Pudi, Gillian Jacobs, and Keith David, aired June 2, 2014, on Yahoo! Screen, Sony, 2020, DVD.

2 Tim Gray, "At One with the Cult of the DVD," *Variety*, January 6–12, 2003, 52; Scott Hettrick, "So They Just Discovered DVD? Studio Data Suggest No Clear Consumer Switch," *Variety* (Special section: DVD Exclusive), July 2005, 1; Paul Sweeting, "PCs, Vidgames Give DVD Plenty of Drive in Rental," *Variety*, October 2–8, 2000, 12.

3 Derek Johnson, "Inviting Audiences In: The Spatial Reorganization of Production and Consumption in 'TVIII,'" *New Review of Film and Television Studies* 5, no. 1 (2007): 61–80.

4 Paul Sweeting, "DVD Warrior Makes the Case for VOD," *Variety*, March 25–April 1, 2001, 26.

5   Dave Farquhar, "How Much Did VHS Tapes Cost in the 80s?" *The Silicon Underground*, March 8, 2022, https://dfarq.homeip.net/how-much-did-vhs-tapes-cost-in-the-80s/#ixzz8xkpnTcSG

6   Entertainment Editors, "*Family Guy* Returns to Production with an Initial Order of 22 New Episodes to Premiere in Early 2005," *Business Wire*, March 26, 2004, https://web.archive.org/web/20090717064830/http://www.allbusiness.com/media-telecommunications/information-services/5639961-1.html

7   M. E. Russell, "The Browncoats Rise Again: The Best Sci-Fi Series You've Never Seen Has Gone from Cancellation to the Big Screen. Will a Never-Tried Marketing Strategy Work for 'Serenity'?" *The Weekly Standard*, June 25, 2005, http://www.weeklystandard.com/Content/Public/Articles/000/000/005/757fhfxg.asp; Neva Chonin, "When Fox Canceled *Firefly*, It Ignited an Internet Fan Base Whose Burning Desire for More Led to 'Serenity,'" *San Francisco Chronicle*, June 8, 2005, E1, https://www.sfgate.com/entertainment/article/when-fox-canceled-firefly-it-ignited-an-2628890.php

8   Isaac Pollock, "Fifteen Years Later: A Retrospective on the '07 Writers Guild Strike," *34th Street*, June 16, 2023, https://www.34st.com/article/2023/06/writers-guild-strike-chat-gpt-friday-night-lights-reality-tv-equal-pay; Ben Fritz, "TV Traumatized by Tech Turmoil: Nets Enthused but Confused by Digital Shifts," *Variety*, November 14–20, 2005,18, https://variety.com/2005/digital/features/tv-traumatized-by-tech-turmoil-1117932834/

9   *Nielsen Media*, "Nielsen Reports DVR Playback Is Adding to TV Viewing Levels" [press release], February 14, 2008.

10 Marisa Guthrie, "'Live-Plus-Three' Wins Upfront Fans," *Broadcasting and Cable*, June 18, 2007, 26.

11 Nick Venable, "*Community* Is Everyone's Latest Netflix Obsession, and Fans Can't Get Enough," *Cinema Blend*, April 12, 2020, https://www.cinemablend.com/television/2494328/community-is-everyones-latest-netflix-obsession-and-fans-cant-get-enough

12 Denise Petski, "Netflix & Hulu Pull Episode of 'Community' Due to Blackface Scene," *Deadline*, June 26, 2020, https://deadline.com/2020/06/netflix-hulu-pull-episode-community-due-to-blackface-scene-1202971493/

13 Michael Schneider, "'Community' Movie Is Finally Happening, at Peacock, Fulfilling the Show's Prophesy," *Variety*, September 30, 2022, https://variety.com/2022/tv/news/community-movie-peacock-dan-harmon-joel-mchale-1235389233/

14 *Community*, season 2, episode 21, "Paradigms of Human Memory," directed by Tristram Shapeero, written by Chris McKenna, featuring Joel McHale, Alison Brie, Donald Glover, Danny Pudi, and Yvette Nicole Brown, aired April 21, 2011, on NBC, Sony, 2020, DVD.

15 Benjamin Svetkey, "The 'Enterprise' Turns 25: A Look Back at *Star Trek*'s history," *Entertainment Weekly*, September 27, 2001, https://ew.com/article/1991/09/27/enterprise-turns-25/

16 Maria Elena Fernandez, "'Jericho' Can Thank the Peanut Gallery," *Los Angeles Times*, February 10, 2008, https://www.latimes.com/archives/la-xpm-2008-feb-10-ca-jericho10-story.html; Tamara Jude, "9 Craziest Fan Campaigns That Actually Worked (And 6 That Failed)," *Screen Rant*, July 30, 2017, https://screenrant.com/9-craziest-fan-campaigns-that-actually-worked-and-6-that-failed/

17 *Community*, season 3, episode 4, "Remedial Chaos Theory," directed by Jeff Melman, written by Chris McKenna, featuring Joel McHale, Alison Brie, Donald Glover, Danny Pudi, Chevy Chase, Gillian Jacobs, and Yvette Nicole Brown, aired October 13, 2011, on NBC, Sony, 2020, DVD; *Community*, season 1, episode 12, "Comparative Religion," directed by Adam Davidson, written by Liz Cackowski, featuring Joel McHale, Alison Brie, Donald Glover, Danny Pudi, Chevy Chase, Gillian Jacobs, and Yvette Nicole Brown, aired December 10, 2009, on NBC, Sony, 2020, DVD; Sarah Anne Hughes, "'Community' Fans Hold Protest outside Rockefeller Center [video]," *Washington Post*, December 23, 2011, https://www.washingtonpost.com/blogs/celebritology/post/community-fans-hold-protest-outside-of-rockefeller-plaza-video/2011/12/23/gIQAaqRgDP_blog.html

18 Liz Shannon Miller, "'Community' Creator Dan Harmon Is Not Ashamed, and Yahoo Doesn't Mind," *IndieWire*, October 2, 2014, https://www.indiewire.com/features/general/community-creator-dan-harmon-is-not-ashamed-and-yahoo-doesnt-mind-69471/

19 Todd Spangler, "Why Yahoo's Foray Into Original TV Series Failed," *Variety*, October 27, 2015, https://variety.com/2015/digital/news/yahoo-community-other-space-money-loss-1201627039/

20 M. E. Russell, "The Browncoats Rise Again," June 25, 2005.

21 *Community*, season 3, episode 4, "Remedial Chaos Theory," aired October 13, 2011.

22 Lacey Rose, "Donald Glover and Maya Erskine on Real-Life Marriage, Professional Divorce and When to Walk Away," *Hollywood Reporter*, February 7, 2024, https://www.hollywoodreporter.com/tv/tv-features/donald-glover-maya-erskine-interview-marriage-mr-and-mrs-smith-1235817327/; *Community*, season 2, episode 16, "Intermediate Documentary Filmmaking," directed by Joe Russo, written by Megan Ganz, featuring Joel McHale, Alison Brie, Donald Glover, Danny Pudi, Chevy Chase, Gillian Jacobs, and Yvette Nicole Brown, aired February 17, 2011, on NBC, Sony, 2020, DVD; *Community*, season 3, episode 8, "Documentary Filmmaking: Redux," directed by Joe Russo, written by Megan Ganz, featuring Joel McHale, Alison Brie, Donald Glover, Danny Pudi, Chevy Chase, Gillian Jacobs, and Yvette Nicole Brown, aired November 17, 2011, on NBC, Sony, 2020, DVD; *Community*, season 6, episode 12, "Wedding Videography," directed by Adam Davidson, written by Briggs Hatton, featuring Joel McHale, Alison Brie, Danny Pudi, Gillian Jacobs, and Keith David, aired May 26, 2015, on Yahoo! Screen, Sony, 2020, DVD.

23 Ryan Parker, "Will Smith Calls Dramatic Fan-Made 'Bel-Air' Trailer 'Brilliant,'" *The Hollywood Reporter*, April 26, 2019, https://www.hollywoodreporter.com/lifestyle/lifestyle-news/will-smith-calls-fan-made-bel-air-trailer-brilliant-1205187/

24 *Community*, season 2, episode 5, "Messianic Myths and Ancient Peoples," directed by Tristram Shapeero, written by Andrew Guest, featuring Joel McHale, Alison Brie, Donald Glover, Danny Pudi, Chevy Chase, Gillian Jacobs, and Yvette Nicole Brown, aired October 21, 2010, on NBC, Sony, 2020, DVD.

BIBLIOGRAPHY

Abayie, Shelby. "How 'Living Single' Was the Blueprint for 'Friends': The Impact of 'Living Single' Can't Be Understated or Ignored." *34th Street Magazine*, November 22, 2021. https://www.34st.com/article/2021/11/livingsingle-friends-black-television-creators-tv-ratings

Abbott, Stacey, and Lorna Jowett. *TV Horror: Investigating the Dark Side of the Small Screen*. London: IB Tauris, 2013.

"About." Channel 101. Accessed December 31, 2024. https://channel101.org/about/

"About the BBC: Mission, Values and Public Purpose." BBC. Accessed November 5, 2024. https://www.bbc.com/aboutthebbc/governance/mission

Abram, Aron, and Gregory Thompson, writers. *Everybody Hates Chris*. Season 1, episode 3, "Everybody Hates Basketball." Directed by Lev L. Spiro, featuring Tyler James Williams, Terry Crews, Tichina Arnold, and Vincent Martella. Aired October 6, 2005, on UPN, CBS Home Media, 2009, DVD.

Adgate, Brad. "The Future of Television Is Broadcast & Streaming: Here's Why." *Forbes*, August 8, 2024. https://www.forbes.com/sites/bradadgate/2024/08/08/the-future-of-television-is-broadcast--streaming-heres-why

Adgate, Brad. "The Rise and Fall of Cable Television." *Forbes*, November 3, 2020. https://www.forbes.com/sites/bradadgate/2020/11/02/the-rise-and-fall-of-cable-television/

Austerlitz, Saul. *Sitcom: A History in 24 Episodes from* I Love Lucy *to* Community (Chicago: Chicago Review Press, 2014).

Bandur, Maggie, writer. *Community*. Season 4, episode 3, "Conventions of Space and Time." Directed by Michael Patrick Jann, featuring Joel McHale, Alison Brie, Jonathan Banks, Danny Pudi, and Yvette Nicole Brown. Aired February 21, 2013, on NBC, Sony, 2020, DVD.

Barker, Cory. "Community, 'Cooperative Calligraphy.'" *TV Surveillance*, November 13, 2010. http://web.archive.org/web/20120322133135/http://tvsurveillance.com/2010/11/13/community-cooperative-calligraphy/

Barr, Adam, and Peter Ocko, writers. *Parker Lewis Can't Lose*. Season 3, episode 7, "Beauty and the Kube." Directed by Mike Finney, featuring Corin Nemec, Billy Jayne, Troy Slaten, and Melanie Chartoff. Aired September 6, 1992, on Fox, Turbine Medien, 2015, DVD.

Basilone, Steve, and Annie Mebane, writers. *Community*. Season 3, episode 10, "Regional Holiday Music." Directed by Tristram Shapeero, featuring Joel McHale, Alison Brie, Donald Glover, Danny Pudi, and Yvette Nicole Brown. Aired December 8, 2011, on NBC, Sony, 2020, DVD.

Basilone, Steve, and Annie Mebane, writers. *Community*. Season 3, episode 22, "Introduction to Finality." Directed by Tristram Shapeero, featuring Joel McHale,

Alison Brie, Gillian Jacobs, Danny Pudi, and Yvette Nicole Brown. Aired May 17, 2012, on NBC, Sony, 2020, DVD.

Basilone, Steve, and Annie Mebane, writers. *Community*. Season 4, episode 5, "Cooperative Escapism in Family Relations." Directed by Tristram Shapeero, featuring Joel McHale, Alison Brie, Donald Glover, Danny Pudi, and Yvette Nicole Brown. Aired March 7, 2013, on NBC, Sony, 2020, DVD.

Basilone, Steve, Annie Mebane, and Maggie Bandur, writers. *Community*. Season 4, episode 12, "Heroic Origins." Directed by Vince Nelli Jr., featuring Joel McHale, Alison Brie, Donald Glover, Danny Pudi, and Yvette Nicole Brown. Aired May 2, 2013, on NBC, Sony, 2020, DVD.

Beatts, Anne, writer. *Square Pegs*. Season 1, episode 1, "Pilot." Directed by Kim Friedman, featuring Sarah Jessica Parker, Amy Linker, Jami Gertz, and Tracy Nelson. Aired September 27, 1982, on CBS, Sony, 2008, DVD.

Berenbeim, Glenn, writer. *A Different World*. Season 5, episode 11, "Mammy Dearest." Directed by Debbie Allen, featuring Jasmine Guy, Kadeem Hardison, Dawnn Lewis, and Jada Pinkett Smith. Aired December 5, 1991, on NBC.

Berg, James, and Stand Zimmerman, writers. *Roseanne*. Season 6, episode 18, "Don't Ask, Don't Tell." Directed by Philip Charles MacKenzie, featuring Roseanne Barr, John Goodman, Sarah Chalke, and Sara Gilbert. Aired March 1, 1994, on ABC, Mill Creek, 2013, DVD.

Bland, Simon. "'We Were Around Each Other More than Our Family': An Oral History of *Community*." *The Independent*, September 18, 2024. https://www.independent.co.uk/arts-entertainment/tv/features/community-movie-netflix-tv-series-cast-b2614804.html

Bloodworth-Thomason, Linda. "'Designing Women' Creator Goes Public With Les Moonves War: Not All Harassment Is Sexual [Guest Column]." *The Hollywood Reporter*, September 12, 2008. https://www.hollywoodreporter.com/news/general-news/designing-women-creator-les-moonves-not-all-harassment-is-sexual-1142448/

Bobrow, Andy, writer. *Community*. Season 2, episode 4, "Basic Rocket Science." Directed by Anthony Russo, featuring Joel McHale, Alison Brie, Donald Glover, Danny Pudi, and Yvette Nicole Brown. Aired October 14, 2010, on NBC, Sony, 2020, DVD.

Bobrow, Andy, writer. *Community*. Season 2, episode 10, "Mixology Certification." Directed by Jay Chandrasekhar, featuring Joel McHale, Alison Brie, Donald Glover, Danny Pudi, and Yvette Nicole Brown. Aired December 2, 2010, on NBC, Sony, 2020, DVD.

Bobrow, Andy, writer. *Community*. Season 2, episode 18, "Custody Law and Eastern European Diplomacy." Directed by Anthony Russo, featuring Joel McHale, Alison Brie, Donald Glover, Danny Pudi, and Yvette Nicole Brown. Aired March 17, 2011, on NBC, Sony, 2020, DVD.

Bobrow, Andy, writer. *Community*. Season 3, episode 2, "Geography of Global Conflict." Directed by Joe Russo, featuring Joel McHale, Alison Brie, Donald Glover, Danny Pudi, and Yvette Nicole Brown. Aired September 29, 2011, on NBC, Sony, 2020, DVD.

Bobrow, Andy, writer. *Community*. Season 3, episode 14, "Pillows and Blankets." Directed by Tristram Shapeero, featuring Joel McHale, Alison Brie, Jonathan Banks, Danny Pudi, and Yvette Nicole Brown. Aired April 5, 2012, on NBC, Sony, 2020, DVD.

Bobrow, Andy, writer. *Community*. Season 4, episode 1, "History 101." Directed by Tristram Shapeero, featuring Joel McHale, Alison Brie, Donald Glover, Danny Pudi, and Yvette Nicole Brown. Aired February 7, 2013, on NBC, Sony, 2020, DVD.

Bobrow, Andy, writer. *Community*. Season 4, episode 10, "Intro to Knots." Directed by Tristram Shapeero, featuring Joel McHale, Alison Brie, Donald Glover, Danny Pudi, and Yvette Nicole Brown. Aired April 18, 2013, on NBC, Sony, 2020, DVD.

Borowitz, Andy, writer. *Day by Day*. Season 2, episode 11, "A Very Brady Episode." Directed by Asaad Kelada, featuring Christopher Barnes, Ann B. Davis, Florence Henderson, and Robert Reed. Aired February 5, 1989, on NBC.

Brunson, Quinta, writer. *Abbott Elementary*. Season 1, episode 1, "Pilot." Directed by Randall Einhorn, featuring Quinta Brunson, Tyler James Williams, Janelle James, and Sheryl Lee Ralph. Aired December 7, 2021, on ABC, Warner, 2022, DVD.

Cackowski, Liz, writer. *Community*. Season 1, episode 4, "Social Psychology." Directed by Anthony Russo, featuring Joel McHale, Alison Brie, Donald Glover, Danny Pudi, and Yvette Nicole Brown. Aired October 8, 2009, on NBC, Sony, 2020, DVD.

Cackowski, Liz, writer. *Community*. Season 1, episode 12, "Comparative Religion." Directed by Adam Davidson, featuring Joel McHale, Alison Brie, Donald Glover, Danny Pudi, Gillian Jacobs, and Yvette Nicole Brown. Aired December 10, 2009, on NBC, Sony, 2020, DVD.

Cagle, Jess, and Joe Flint. "As Gay As It Gets." *Entertainment Weekly*, May 8, 1998.

Carter, Nick. "Alewives to Alewives, Dust to Dust, Their Comedy Act Soon Will Be Nevermore." *Milwaukee Journal Sentinel*, January 5, 2001.

Chase, Sam. "Mary Kay and Johnny." *The Billboard*, March 6, 1948: 38.

Chonin, Neva. "When Fox Canceled *Firefly*, It Ignited an Internet Fan Base Whose Burning Desire for More Led to 'Serenity.'" *San Francisco Chronicle*, June 8, 2005, E1. https://www.sfgate.com/entertainment/article/when-fox-canceled-firefly-it-ignited-an-2628890.php

Connelly, Joe, and Bob Mosher, writers. *The Munsters*. Season 1, episode 1. "Munster Masquerade." Directed by Lawrence Dobkin, featuring Fred Gywnne, Beverely Owen, and Al Lewis. Aired September 24, 1964, on CBS, Universal, 2008, DVD.

Consoli, John. "Analysis: Is Reilly a Scapegoat for NBC's Failures?" *Mediaweek*, May 28, 2007. https://web.archive.org/web/20071008103640/http://www.mediaweek.com/mw/news/networktv/article_display.jsp?vnu_content_id=1003591026

Cooley, Alex, writer. *Community*. Season 3, episode 12, "Contemporary Impressionists." Directed by Kyle Newacheck, featuring Joel McHale, Alison Brie, Gillian Jacobs, Danny Pudi, and Yvette Nicole Brown. Aired March 22, 2012, on NBC, Sony, 2020, DVD.

Coons, Hannibal, and Harry Winkler, writers. *The Addams Family*. Season 1, episode 2, "Morticia and the Psychiatrist." Directed by Jean Yarbrough, featuring John Astin, Carolyn Jones, and Ken Weatherwax. Aired September 25, 1964, on ABC, MGM, 2007, DVD.

Countee, Adam, writer. *Community*. Season 2, episode 7, "Aerodynamics of Gender." Directed by Tristram Shapeero, featuring Joel McHale, Alison Brie, Donald Glover, Danny Pudi, and Yvette Nicole Brown. Aired November 4, 2010, on NBC, Sony, 2020, DVD.

Countee, Adam, writer. *Community*. Season 3, episode 7, "Studies in Modern Movement." Directed by Tristram Shapeero, featuring Joel McHale, Alison Brie, Donald Glover, Danny Pudi, and Yvette Nicole Brown. Aired November 10, 2011, on NBC, Sony, 2020, DVD.

Countee, Adam, writer. *Community*. Season 3, episode 19, "Curriculum Unavailable." Directed by Adam Davidson, featuring Joel McHale, Alison Brie, Donald Glover, Danny Pudi, and Yvette Nicole Brown. Aired May 10, 2012, on NBC, Sony, 2020, DVD.

Cronin, Brian. "Jinkies! The Mysterious Origins of 'Scooby-Doo.'" Comic Book Resources, September 25, 2013. https://www.cbr.com/tv-legends-revealed-jinkies-the-mysterious-origins-of-scooby-doo/

Cross, Alan, and Tom Spezialy, writers. *Parker Lewis Can't Lose*. Season 1, episode 15, "Heather the Class." Directed by Max Tash, featuring Corin Nemec, Billy Jayne, Troy Slaten, and Melanie Chartoff. Aired January 13, 1991, on Fox, Shout! Factory, 2009, DVD.

Cutler, Emily, writer. *Community*. Season 1, episode 23, "Modern Warfare." Directed by Justin Lin, featuring Joel McHale, Alison Brie, Donald Glover, Danny Pudi, and Yvette Nicole Brown. Aired May 6, 2010, on NBC, Sony, 2020, DVD.

Cutler, Emily, writer. *Community*. Season 2, episode 12, "Asian Population Studies." Directed by Anthony Russo, featuring Joel McHale, Alison Brie, Donald Glover, Danny Pudi, and Yvette Nicole Brown. Aired January 20, 2011, on NBC, Sony, 2020, DVD.

Cutler, Emily, writer. *Community*. Season 2, episode 20, "Competitive Wine Tasting." Directed by Joe Russo, featuring Joel McHale, Alison Brie, Donald Glover, Danny Pudi, and Yvette Nicole Brown. Aired April 14, 2011, on NBC, Sony, 2020, DVD.

Cutler, Emily, and Karey Dornetto, writers. *Community*. Season 1, episode 21, "Contemporary American Poultry." Directed by Tristram Shapeero, featuring Joel McHale, Alison Brie, Donald Glover, Danny Pudi, and Yvette Nicole Brown. Aired April 22, 2010, on NBC, Sony, 2020, DVD.

Dabb, Andrew, writer. *Supernatural*. Season 8, episode 22, "Clip Show." Directed by Thomas J. Wright, featuring Jensen Ackles, Jared Padalecki, Misha Collins, and Mark Sheppard. Aired May 8, 2013, on the CW, Warner Brothers, 2013, DVD.

Day, Richard, and Jim Vallely, writers. *Arrested Development*. Season 3, episode 9, "S.O.B.s." Directed by Robert Berlinger, featuring Jason Bateman, Jessica Walters, Portia de Rossi, and Will Arnett. Aired January 2, 2006, on Fox, Fox, 2006, DVD.

Del Tredici, Luke, writer. *Brooklyn Nine-Nine*. Season 5, episode 14, "The Box." Directed by Claire Scanlon, featuring Andre Braugher, Andy Samberg, Melissa Fumero, Terry Crews, and Chelsea Peretti. Aired April 1, 2018, on Fox, Universal, 2022, DVD.

Donovan, Garrett, and Neil Goldman, writers. *Community*. Season 3, episode 1, "Biology 101." Directed by Anthony Russo, featuring Joel McHale, Alison Brie, Donald Glover, Danny Pudi, and Yvette Nicole Brown. Aired September 22, 2011, on NBC, Sony, 2020, DVD.

Dornetto, Karey, writer. *Community*. Season 1, episode 18, "Basic Genealogy." Directed by Ken Whittingham, featuring Joel McHale, Alison Brie, Donald Glover, Danny Pudi, and Yvette Nicole Brown. Aired March 11, 2010, on NBC, Sony, 2020, DVD.

Dornetto, Karey, writer. *Community*. Season 2, episode 6, "Epidemiology." Directed by Anthony Hemingway, featuring Joel McHale, Alison Brie, Donald Glover, Danny

Pudi, and Yvette Nicole Brown. Aired October 28, 2010, on NBC, Sony, 2020, DVD.

Dornetto, Karey, writer. *Community*. Season 2, episode 22, "Applied Anthropology and Culinary Arts." Directed by Jay Chandrasekhar, featuring Joel McHale, Alison Brie, Donald Glover, Danny Pudi, and Yvette Nicole Brown. Aired April 28, 2011, on NBC, Sony, 2020, DVD.

Downing, Andy. "Dan in Real Life: 'Community' Creator Talks About Creativity on the Show and After." *The Cap Times*, January 17, 2013. https://captimes.com/entertainment/television/dan-in-real-life-community-creator-talks-about-creativity-on-the-show-and-after/article_4f602721-e5e5-5bf9-b64b-c3e58975fc34.html

Duralde, Alonso. "Polly Platt: Accomplished and Forthcoming—Even About 'Irreconcilable Differences.'" *Reuters*, July 27, 2011.

Elias, Michael, and Rich Eustis, writers. *Head of the Class*. Season 3, episodes 3–4, "Mission to Moscow." Directed by Eric Laneuville, featuring Howard Hesseman, Robin Givens, Rain Pryor, and William G. Schilling. Aired November 2, 1988, on ABC, Warner, 2021, DVD.

Elliot, Mary, and Jazmine Hughes. "Four Hundred Years after Enslaved Africans Were First Brought to Virginia, Most Americans Don't Know the Full Story of Slavery." *New York Times Magazine*, August 19, 2019. https://www.nytimes.com/interactive/2019/08/19/magazine/history-slavery-smithsonian.html

Emerson, Jim. "Hot Pick—Life of Peter Bogdanovich Told in Satire." *The Orange County Register*, November 13, 1992, p. 41.

Entertainment Editors. "Family Guy Returns to Production with an Initial Order of 22 New Episodes to Premiere in Early 2005." *Business Wire*, March 26, 2004. https://web.archive.org/web/20090717064830/http://www.allbusiness.com/media-telecommunications/information-services/5639961-1.html

Epstein, Daniel Robert. "Channel 101 Co-Creator Rob Schrab." *Suicide Girls*, June 30, 2005. https://www.suicidegirls.com/girls/anderswolleck/blog/2679269/channel-101-co-creator-rob-schrab/

Eskridge, Sarah K. *Rube Tube: CBS and the Rural Comedy in the Sixties*. Columbia: University of Missouri Press, 2018.

EW Staff. "'Will and Grace': In the Pink," *Entertainment Weekly*, September 10, 1999. https://ew.com/article/1999/09/10/will-and-grace-pink/

Farquhar, Dave, "How Much Did VHS Tapes Cost in the 80s?" *The Silicon Underground*, March 8, 2022. https://dfarq.homeip.net/how-much-did-vhs-tapes-cost-in-the-80s/#ixzz8xkpnTcSG

Feig, Paul, writer. *Freaks and Geeks*. Season 1, episode 18, "Discos and Dragons." Directed by Paul Feig, featuring Linda Cardellini, Seth Rogan, John Francis Daley, Busy Phillips, and Jason Segel. Aired July 8, 2000, on NBC, Shout! Factory, 2004, DVD.

Fernandez, Maria Elena. "'Jericho' Can Thank the Peanut Gallery." *Los Angeles Times*, February 10, 2008. https://www.latimes.com/archives/la-xpm-2008-feb-10-ca-jericho10-story.html

"Fine Writing Spurs Chevy to Move to 'Community.'" *Omaha World-Herald*. October 22, 2009. https://archive.ph/20130104083338/http://www.omaha.com/article/20091022/ENTERTAINMENT/710229873#selection-1949.0-1949.209

Fontana, Tom, writer. *Homicide: Life on the Street*. Season 1, episode 6, "Three Men and Adena." Directed by Martin Campbell, featuring Andre Braugher, Kyle Secor, Yaphet Kotto, and Melissa Leo. Aired March 3, 1993, on NBC, Shout! Factory, 2017, DVD.

Fordham, Debra, writer. *Scrubs*. Season 4, episode 17, "My Life in Four Cameras." Directed by Adam Bernstein, featuring Zach Braff, Donald Faison, Sarah Chalke, Judy Reyes, and John C. McGinley. Aired February 15, 2005, on NBC, Buena Vista, 2006, DVD.

Fritz, Ben. "TV Traumatized by Tech Turmoil: Nets Enthused but Confused by Digital Shifts." *Variety*, November 14–20, 2005:18. https://variety.com/2005/digital/features/tv-traumatized-by-tech-turmoil-1117932834/

Furey, Joe, Brian Kelley, Josh Lieb, and Sam Johnson, writers. *News Radio*. Season 4, episode 22, "Sinking Ship." Directed by Tom Cherones, featuring Dave Foley, Phil Hartman, Maura Tierney, Steven Root, and Vicky Lewis. Aired May 12, 1998, on NBC, Sony, 2008, DVD.

Furey, Joe, Josh Lieb, and Paul Simms, writers. *News Radio*. Season 3, episode 24, "Space." Directed by Tom Cherones, featuring Dave Foley, Phil Hartman, Maura Tierney, Steven Root, and Vicky Lewis. Aired May 21, 1997, on NBC, Sony, 2008, DVD.

Fusfeld, Matt, and Alex Cuthbertson, writers. *Community*. Season 3, episode 21, "The First Chang Dynasty." Directed by Jay Chandrasekhar, featuring Joel McHale, Alison Brie, Donald Glover, Danny Pudi, and Yvette Nicole Brown. Aired May 17, 2012, on NBC, Sony, 2020, DVD.

Ganz, Megan, writer. *Community*. Season 2, episode 8, "Cooperative Calligraphy." Directed by Joe Russo, featuring Joel McHale, Alison Brie, Donald Glover, Danny Pudi, and Yvette Nicole Brown. Aired November 11, 2010, on NBC, Sony, 2020, DVD.

Ganz, Megan, writer. *Community*. Season 2, episode 16, "Intermediate Documentary Filmmaking." Directed by Joe Russo, featuring Joel McHale, Alison Brie, Donald Glover, Danny Pudi, and Yvette Nicole Brown. Aired February 17, 2011, on NBC, Sony, 2020, DVD.

Ganz, Megan, writer. *Community*. Season 3, episode 8, "Documentary Filmmaking: Redux." Directed by Joe Russo, featuring Joel McHale, Alison Brie, Donald Glover, Danny Pudi, Gillian Jacobs, and Yvette Nicole Brown. Aired November 17, 2011, on NBC, Sony, 2020, DVD.

Ganz, Megan, writer. *Community*. Season 3, episode 17, "Basic Lupine Urology." Directed by Rob Schrab, featuring Joel McHale, Alison Brie, Donald Glover, Danny Pudi, and Yvette Nicole Brown. Aired April 26, 2012, on NBC, Sony, 2020, DVD.

Ganz, Megan, writer. *Community*. Season 4, episode 2, "Paranormal Parentage." Directed by Tristram Shapeero, featuring Joel McHale, Alison Brie, Donald Glover, Danny Pudi, and Yvette Nicole Brown. Aired February 14, 2013, on NBC, Sony, 2020, DVD.

Ganz, Megan, writer. *Community*. Season 4, episode 13, "Advanced Introduction to Finality." Directed by Tristram Shapeero, featuring Joel McHale, Alison Brie, Donald Glover, Danny Pudi, and Yvette Nicole Brown. Aired May 9, 2013, on NBC, Sony, 2020, DVD.

Garcia, Greg, writer. *My Name Is Earl*. Season 1, episode 1, "Pilot." Directed by Marc Buckland, featuring Jason Lee, Ethan Suplee, Jaime Pressley, and Eddie Steeples. Aired September 20, 2005, on NBC, Fox, 2006, DVD.

Gates, Henry Louis, Jr. "Did Black People Own Slaves?," *The Root*, March 4, 2013. https://web.archive.org/web/20130308014646/http://www.theroot.com/views/did-black-people-own-slaves

Giannini, Erin. "'And Was There a Lesson in All This?': Weaponizing—and Subverting—the Very Special Episode." In *Very Special Episodes: Televising Industrial and Social Change*, edited by Jonathan Cohn and Jennifer Porst, 145–158. New Brunswick: Rutgers, 2021.

Gonzalez, Sandra. "'Community' Creator Dan Harmon on a Clip Show Like No Other." *Entertainment Weekly*, December 16, 2011. https://ew.com/article/2011/12/16/community-creator-dan-harmon-clip-show-best-of-behind-the-scenes/

Gray, Tim. "At One with the Cult of the DVD." *Variety*, January 6–12, 2003, 52.

Griffiths, Nick. "America's First Family." *The Times Magazine*, April 15, 2000, 25, 27–28.

Guest, Andrew, writer. *Community*. Season 1, episode 5, "Advanced Criminal Law." Directed by Joe Russo, featuring Joel McHale, Alison Brie, Donald Glover, Danny Pudi, and Yvette Nicole Brown. Aired October 15, 2009, on NBC, Sony, 2020, DVD.

Guest, Andrew, writer. *Community*. Season 2, episode 5, "Messianic Myths and Ancient Peoples." Directed by Tristram Shapeero, featuring Joel McHale, Alison Brie, Donald Glover, Danny Pudi, and Yvette Nicole Brown. Aired October 21, 2010, on NBC, Sony, 2020, DVD.

Guest, Andrew, writer. *Community*. Season 1, episode 15, "Romantic Expressionism." Directed by Joe Russo, featuring Joel McHale, Alison Brie, Donald Glover, Danny Pudi, and Yvette Nicole Brown. Aired February 4, 2010, on NBC, Sony, 2020, DVD.

Guest, Andrew, writer. *Community*. Season 2, episode 14, "Advanced *Dungeons and Dragons*." Directed by Joe Russo, featuring Joel McHale, Alison Brie, Donald Glover, Danny Pudi, and Yvette Nicole Brown. Aired February 3, 2011, on NBC, Sony, 2020, DVD.

Guest, Andrew, writer. *Community*. Season 2, episode 23, "A Fistful of Paintballs." Directed by Joe Russo, featuring Joel McHale, Alison Brie, Donald Glover, Danny Pudi, and Yvette Nicole Brown. Aired May 5, 2011, on NBC, Sony, 2020, DVD.

Guterman, Dan, writer. *Community*. Season 5, episode 7, "Bondage and Beta Male Sexuality." Directed by Tristram Shapeero, featuring Joel McHale, Alison Brie, Donald Glover, Danny Pudi, and Yvette Nicole Brown. Aired February 27, 2014, on NBC, Sony, 2020, DVD.

Guthrie, Marisa. "'Live-Plus-Three' Wins Upfront Fans." *Broadcasting and Cable*, June 18, 2007, 26.

Harmon, Dan, writer. *Community*. Season 1, episode 1, "Pilot." Directed by Anthony and Joe Russo, featuring Joel McHale, Alison Brie, Donald Glover, Danny Pudi, and Yvette Nicole Brown. Aired September 17, 2009, on NBC, Sony, 2020, DVD.

Harmon, Dan, writer. *Community*. Season 1, episode 2, "Spanish 101." Directed by Joe Russo, featuring Joel McHale, Alison Brie, Donald Glover, Gillian Jacobs, Danny Pudi, and Yvette Nicole Brown. Aired September 24, 2009, on NBC, Sony, 2020, DVD.

Harmon, Dan, writer. *Community*. Season 3, episode 5, "Horror Fiction in Seven Spooky Steps." Directed by Tristram Shapeero, featuring Joel McHale, Alison Brie, Donald Glover, Danny Pudi, and Yvette Nicole Brown. Aired October 27, 2011, on NBC, Sony, 2020, DVD.

Harmon, Dan, and Chris McKenna, writers. *Community*. Season 5, episode 1, "Repilot." Directed by Tristram Shapeero, featuring Joel McHale, Alison Brie, Donald Glover, Danny Pudi, and Yvette Nicole Brown. Aired November 12, 2009, on NBC, Sony, 2020, DVD.

Harmon, Dan, and Chris McKenna, writers. *Community*. Season 6, episode 1, "Ladders." Directed by Rob Schrab, featuring Joel McHale, Alison Brie, Donald Glover, Danny Pudi, and Yvette Nicole Brown. Aired March 17, 2015, on Yahoo! Screen, Sony, 2020, DVD.

Harmon, Dan, and Chris McKenna, writers. *Community*. Season 6, episode 13, "Emotional Consequences of Broadcast Television." Directed by Rob Schrab, featuring Joel McHale, Alison Brie, Danny Pudi, Gillian Jacobs, and Keith David. Aired June 2, 2014, on Yahoo! Screen, Sony, 2020, DVD.

Hatton, Briggs, writer. *Community*. Season 6, episode 12, "Wedding Videography." Directed by Adam Davidson, featuring Joel McHale, Alison Brie, Danny Pudi, Gillian Jacobs, and Keith David. Aired May 26, 2015, on Yahoo! Screen, Sony, 2020, DVD.

Hettrick, Scott. "So They Just Discovered DVD? Studio Data Suggest No Clear Consumer Switch." *Variety* (Special section: DVD Exclusive), July 2005: 1

Hills, Matthew. *The Pleasures of Horror*. London: Continuum, 2005.

Hilmes, Michele. *Only Connect: A Cultural History of Broadcasting in the United States*, 3rd ed. Boston: Wadsworth Cengage Publishing, 2011.

Hinds, Julie. "Broadcast vs. Cable vs. Streaming: The Future of Television Is a Confusing Maze for Viewers." *Detroit Free Press*, March 4, 2024. https://www.freep.com/story/entertainment/television/2024/03/04/the-future-of-tv-chaos-confusion-and-a-war-for-eyeballs/72805782007/

Hobert, Tim, writer. *Community*. Season 1, episode 9, "Debate 109." Directed by Joe Russo, featuring Joel McHale, Alison Brie, Donald Glover, Danny Pudi, and Yvette Nicole Brown. Aired November 12, 2009, on NBC, Sony, 2020, DVD.

Hobert, Tim, and Jon Pollack, writers. *Community*. Season 1, episode 3, "Introduction to Film." Directed by Anthony Russo, featuring Joel McHale, Alison Brie, Donald Glover, Danny Pudi, and Yvette Nicole Brown. Aired October 1, 2009, on NBC, Sony, 2020, DVD.

Holston, Noel. "Hooterville's Head Hillbilly Henning Put Rural Life on a Television Pedestal." *Orlando Sentinel*, August 3, 1986.

Hong, Gene, writer. *Community*. Season 4, episode 9, "Intro to Felt Surrogacy." Directed by Tristram Shapeero, featuring Joel McHale, Alison Brie, Gillian Jacobs, Danny Pudi, and Yvette Nicole Brown. Aired April 11, 2013, on NBC, Sony, 2020, DVD.

Hughes, Sarah Anne. "'Community' Fans Hold Protest Outside Rockefeller Center [Video]." *Washington Post*, December 23, 2011. https://www.washingtonpost.com/blogs/celebritology/post/community-fans-hold-protest-outside-of-rockefeller-plaza-video/2011/12/23/gIQAaqRgDP_blog.html

Hunter, Blake, writer. *Diff'rent Strokes*. Season 5, episodes 16–17, "The Bicycle Man, Parts 1 and 2." Directed by Gerren Keith, featuring Gary Coleman, Conrad Bain, Shavar Ross, and Gordon Jump. Aired February 5 and 12, 1983, on NBC, Shout! Factory, 2017, DVD.

Hyden, Steven. "Interview: How Dan Harmon Went From Doing Comedy Sportz in Milwaukee to Creating NBC's *Community*." *The AV Club*, October 19, 2009. https://web.archive.org/web/20091023172513/http://www.avclub.com/milwaukee/articles/how-dan-harmon-went-from-doing-comedysportz-in-mil,34126/

"I Am Dan Harmon, Creator of Community, Writer of Monster House, and Executive Producer of the Upcoming Charlie Kaufman Stop Motion Animated feature Anomalisa, Ask Me Anything!" r/IAmA, Reddit, August 22, 2012. https://www.reddit.com/r/IAmA/comments/yne9x/i_am_dan_harmon_creator_of_community_writer_of/ https://www.reddit.com/r/IAmA/comments/yne9x/i_am_dan_harmon_creator_of_community_writer_of/

Itzkoff, David. "'Community Creator Writes to Child, Disses Spielberg and Wins Our Hearts." *New York Times*, March 29, 2010. https://archive.nytimes.com/artsbeat.blogs.nytimes.com/2010/03/29/community-creator-writes-to-child-disses-spielberg-and-wins-our-hearts/

Johnson, Derek. "Inviting Audiences In: The Spatial Reorganization of Production and Consumption in 'TVIII.'" *New Review of Film and Television Studies* 5, no. 1 (2007): 61–80.

Jowett, Lorna, and Stacey Abbott. *TV Horror: Investigating the Dark Side of the Small Screen*. London: IB Tauris, 2013.

Jude, Tamara. "9 Craziest Fan Campaigns That Actually Worked (And 6 That Failed)." *Screen Rant*, July 30, 2017. https://screenrant.com/9-craziest-fan-campaigns-that-actually-worked-and-6-that-failed/

Kane, Joel, writer. *The Many Loves of Dobie Gillis*. Season 2, episode 20, "The Second Childhood of Herbert T. Gillis." Directed by Robert Gordon, featuring Dwayne Hickman, Frank Faylen, Florida Friebus, and Bob Denver. Aired March 7, 1961, on CBS, Shout! Factory, 2013, DVD.

Kapinos, Tom, and Gina Fattore, writers. *Dawson's Creek*. Season 3, episode 23, "True Love." Directed by James Whitmore Jr., featuring James Van Der Beek, Katie Holmes, Michelle Williams, and Joshua Jackson. Aired May 24, 2000, on the WB, Sony, 2004, DVD.

Kasdan, Jon, writer. *Freaks and Geeks*. Season 1, episode 17, "The Little Things." Directed by Jake Kasdan, featuring Linda Cardellini, Seth Rogan, John Francis Daley, Busy Phillips, and Jason Segel. Aired July 8, 2000, on NBC, Shout! Factory, 2004, DVD.

Keeley, Pete. "'Parker Lewis Can't Lose' at 25: Like 'Going to the Juilliard School of Cinema.'" *The Hollywood Reporter*, June 14, 2018. https://www.hollywoodreporter.com/tv/tv-news/parker-lewis-cant-lose-directors-talk-shooting-innovative-series-1120072/

Kelley, David E., writer. *Boston Public*. Season 1, episodes 18, "Chapter Eighteen." Directed by Elodie Keene, featuring Chi Mcbride, Anthony Heald, Jessalyn Gilsig, and Nicky Katt. Aired April 23, 2001, on Fox.

Kelly, Keegan. "The Awful 'Ferris Beuller' Show Opened With the New Ferris Chainsawing Matthew Broderick in Half." *Cracked*, June 17, 2024, https://www.cracked.com/article_42529_the-awful-ferris-bueller-tv-show-opened-with-the-new-ferris-chainsawing-matthew-brodericks-likeness-in-half.html

Kendall, David, writer. *Growing Pains*. Season 4, episode 20, "Second Chance." Directed by John Tracy, featuring Tracey Gold, Kirk Cameron, Alan Thicke, and Matthew Perry. Aired April 12, 1989, on ABC, Warner, 2015, DVD.

Kilkenny, Katie. "Writers Guild Calls First Strike in 15 Years: Picketing by Hollywood Scribes Is Slated to Begin at 1 pm PT in Los Angeles at Production Sites across the City with Simultaneous Demonstrations Occurring in New York." *The Hollywood Reporter*, May 1, 2023. https://www.hollywoodreporter.com/business/business-news/wga-writers-strike-moves-forward-contract-negotiations-1235404087/

King, Stephen. *Danse Macabre*. New York: Scribner, 2010.

Klein, Paul. "Why You Watch What You Watch When You Watch." *TV Guide*, July 24, 1971: 6–9.

Kohan, David, and Max Mutchnick, writers. *Will & Grace*. Season 2, episode 14, "Acting Out." Directed by James Burrows, featuring Debra Messing, Eric McCormack, Sean Hayes, and Megan Mullaly. Aired February 22, 2000, on NBC, Lions Gate, 2004, DVD.

Kott, Gary, writer. *The Cosby Show*. Season 3, episode 6, "The March." Directed by Tony Singletary, featuring Bill Cosby, Phylicia Rashad, and Malcolm Jamal-Warner. Aired October 30, 1986, on NBC, Mill Creek, 2008, DVD.

Kula, Chris, writer. *Community*. Season 3, episode 9, "Foosball and Nocturnal Vigilantism." Directed by Anthony Russo, featuring Joel McHale, Alison Brie, Donald Glover, Danny Pudi, and Yvette Nicole Brown. Aired December 1, 2011, on NBC, Sony, 2020, DVD.

Leavitt, Ron, and Michael G. Moye, writers. *It's Your Move*. Season 1, episodes 12–13, "The Dregs of Humanity, Parts 1 and 2." Directed by Jim Drake, featuring Jason Bateman, Caren Kaye, Adam Sadowsky, and David Garrison. Aired January 2 and 9, 1985, on NBC.

Leitch, Will. "The Poehler Effect: Can Amy Poehler's *Parks and Recreation* Resurrect NBC? No Pressure or Anything … " *New York Magazine*, April 5, 2009. https://web.archive.org/web/20120413052905/http://nymag.com/arts/tv/features/55851/

Liebmann, Norm, and Ed Haas, writers. *The Munsters*. Season 1, episode 2, "My Fair Munster." Directed by David Alexander, featuring Fred Gywnne, Beverely Owen, and Al Lewis. Aired October 1, 1964, on CBS, Universal, 2008, DVD.

Lomartire, Paul. "Have I Got News for You about Molly." *The Palm Beach Post*, June 18, 1994, 1D.

Maddox, David. "A Conversation With Rob Schrab." *SF Site*, March 2008. https://www.sfsite.com/05a/rs271.htm

Marc, David. "Origins of the Genre: In Search of the Radio Sitcom." In *The Sitcom Reader: America Re-viewed, Still Skewed*, 2nd ed., edited by Mary M. Dalton and Laura R. Linder, 1–12. Albany: SUNY Press, 2016.

Markus, John, Carmen Finestra, and Gary Kott, writers. *The Cosby Show*. Season 5, episode 15, "The Lost Weekend." Directed by Tony Singletary, featuring Bill Cosby, Phylicia Rashad, and Malcolm Jamal-Warner. Aired February 2, 1989, on NBC, Mill Creek, 2008, DVD.

Martin, Michael. "Dan Levy Discusses *Schitt's Creek*, His Eyebrows and Being a Sex Object: When You're Born into Comedy Royalty, Just Grab the Crown and Run with It." *Out Magazine*, March 9, 2015. https://www.out.com/television/2015/3/09/dan-levy-discusses-schitts-creek-his-eyebrows-being-sex-object#toggle-gdpr

Masius, John, writer. *Ferris Bueller*. Season 1, episode 1, "Pilot." Directed by Jonathan Lynn, featuring Charlie Schlatter, Richard Riehl, Jennifer Aniston, and Ami Dolenz. Aired August 23, 1990, on NBC.

McKenna, Chris, writer. *Community*. Season 1, episode 22, "The Art of Discourse." Directed by Adam Davidson, featuring Joel McHale, Alison Brie, Donald Glover, Danny Pudi, and Yvette Nicole Brown. Aired April 29, 2010, on NBC, Sony, 2020, DVD.

McKenna, Chris, writer. *Community*. Season 2, episode 1, "Anthropology 101." Directed by Joe Russo, featuring Joel McHale, Alison Brie, Donald Glover, Danny Pudi, and Yvette Nicole Brown. Aired September 23, 2010, on NBC, Sony, 2020, DVD.

McKenna, Chris, writer. *Community*. Season 2, episode 2, "Accounting for Lawyers." Directed by Joe Russo, featuring Joel McHale, Alison Brie, Donald Glover, Danny Pudi, and Yvette Nicole Brown. Aired September 30, 2010, on NBC, Sony, 2020, DVD.

McKenna, Chris, writer. *Community*. Season 2, episode 21, "Paradigms of Human Memory." Directed by Tristram Shapeero, featuring Joel McHale, Alison Brie, Donald Glover, Danny Pudi, and Yvette Nicole Brown. Aired April 21, 2011, on NBC, Sony, 2020, DVD.

McKenna, Chris, writer. *Community*. Season 3, episode 4, "Remedial Chaos Theory." Directed by Jeff Melman, featuring Joel McHale, Alison Brie, Donald Glover, Danny Pudi, Chevy Chase, Gillian Jacobs, and Yvette Nicole Brown. Aired October 13, 2011, on NBC, Sony, 2020, DVD.

Miller, Liz Shannon. "'Community' Creator Dan Harmon Is Not Ashamed, and Yahoo Doesn't Mind." *IndieWire*, October 2, 2014, https://www.indiewire.com/features/general/community-creator-dan-harmon-is-not-ashamed-and-yahoo-doesnt-mind-69471/

Minear, Tim, writer. *Firefly*. Season 1, episode 8, "Out of Gas." Directed by David Solomon, featuring Nathan Fillion, Gina Torres, Alan Tudyk, Ron Glass, and Summer Glau. Aired October 25, 2002, on Fox, Fox, 2003, DVD.

Molloy, Tim. "'Community Canceled by NBC After 5 Seasons of Critical Acclaim, Low Ratings: Goodbye, Paintball, Animation and Tributes." *The Wrap*, May 9, 2014. https://www.thewrap.com/community-canceled-nbc-5-seasons-critical-acclaim-low-ratings/

Murphy, Morgan, writer. *Abbott Elementary*. Season 1, episodes 3, "Wishlist." Directed by Randall Einhorn, featuring Quinta Brunson, Tyler James Williams, Janelle James, and Sheryl Lee Ralph. Aired January 11, 2022, on ABC, Warner, 2022, DVD.

Murray, Matt, writer. *Community*. Season 3, episode 6, "Advanced Gay." Directed by Joe Russo, featuring Joel McHale, Alison Brie, Donald Glover, Chevy Chase, Danny Pudi, and Yvette Nicole Brown. Aired November, 2011, on NBC, Sony, 2020, DVD.

Murray, Matt, writer. *Community*. Season 3, episode 16, "Virtual Systems Analysis." Directed by Tristram Shapeero, featuring Joel McHale, Alison Brie, Donald Glover, Danny Pudi, and Yvette Nicole Brown. Aired April 19, 2012, on NBC, Sony, 2020, DVD.

Navar-Gill, Annemarie. "The Fan/Creator Alliance: Social Media, Audience Mandates, and the Rebalancing of Power in Studio-Showrunner Disputes." *Media Industries* 5, no. 2 (2018). Accessed December 1, 2024. https://quod.lib.umich.edu/m/mij/15031809.0005.202/–fan-creator-alliance-social-media-audience-mandates?rgn=main;view=fulltext#N35-ptr1

Nelson, Jenny. "Talking to Broken Lizard's Jay Chandrasekhar about 'Freeloaders' and the Chevy Chase N-Word Thing." *Vulture*, May 16, 2013. https://www.vulture.

com/2013/05/talking-to-broken-lizards-jay-chandrasekhar-about-freeloaders-and-the-chevy-chase-n-word-thing.html

Newman, Michael Z., and Elana Levine. *Legitimating Television: Media Convergence and Cultural Status*. New York: Routledge, 2012.

Nielsen Media. "Nielsen Reports DVR Playback Is Adding to TV Viewing Levels" [press release]. *Nielsen Media*, February 14, 2008. http://www.nielsen.com/media/2008/pr_080214.html

Nussbaum, Emily. "Cahiers Du Buffy." *The New Yorker*, March 28, 2014. https://www.newyorker.com/culture/culture-desk/cahiers-du-buffy

Oberman, Margaret, and Rosie Shuster, writers. *Square Pegs*. Season 1, episode 9, "Muffy's Bat Mitzvah." Directed by Kim Friedman, featuring Sarah Jessica Parker, Amy Linker, Jami Gertz, and Tracy Nelson. Aired November 29, 1982, on CBS, Sony, 2008, DVD.

Ocko, Peter, and Adam Barr, writers. *Parker Lewis Can't Lose*. Season 2, episode 22, "Geek Tragedy." Directed by Larry Shaw, featuring Corin Nemec, Billy Jayne, Troy Slaten, and Melanie Chartoff. Aired April 18, 1993, on Fox, Shout! Factory, 2015, DVD.

O'Neal, Sean. "The Tortured Mind of Dan Harmon." *GQ*, May 30, 2018. https://www.gq.com/story/dan-harmon-rick-and-morty-profile

O'Neil, Megan. "Dan Harmon Screens 'Community' at GCC." *Los Angeles Times*, November 5, 2010. https://www.latimes.com/socal/glendale-news-press/news/tn-gnp-screening-20101105-story.html

Owen, Rob. "Comedy in 'Parks' Gets Lost in Translation." *Pittsburgh Post-Gazette*, April 9, 2009. http://www.post-gazette.com/pg/09099/961595-67.stm

Paez, Zack, writer. *Community*. Season 1, episode 10, "Environmental Science." Directed by Seth Gordon, featuring Joel McHale, Alison Brie, Donald Glover, Danny Pudi, and Yvette Nicole Brown. Aired November 19, 2009, on NBC, Sony, 2020, DVD.

Panos, Sona, writer. *Community*. Season 2, episode 19, "Critical Film Studies." Directed by Richard Ayoade, featuring Joel McHale, Alison Brie, Donald Glover, Danny Pudi, and Yvette Nicole Brown. Aired March 24, 2011, on NBC, Sony, 2020, DVD.

Parker, Ryan. "Will Smith Calls Dramatic Fan-Made 'Bel-Air' Trailer 'Brilliant.'" *The Hollywood Reporter*, April 26, 2019. https://www.hollywoodreporter.com/lifestyle/lifestyle-news/will-smith-calls-fan-made-bel-air-trailer-brilliant-1205187/

Paste Staff. "Catching Up With … *Community* Creator Dan Harmon." *Paste Magazine*, May 5, 2010. https://www.pastemagazine.com/tv/dan-harmon/catching-up-with-communitys-creator-dan-harmon

Petski, Denise. "Netflix & Hulu Pull Episode of 'Community' Due to Blackface Scene." *Deadline*, June 26, 2020. https://deadline.com/2020/06/netflix-hulu-pull-episode-community-due-to-blackface-scene-1202971493/

Phillips, Clyde, writer. *Parker Lewis Can't Lose*. Season 3, episode 15, "Write or Die." Directed by Larry Shaw, featuring Corin Nemec, Billy Jayne, Troy Slaten, and Melanie Chartoff. Aired April 18, 1993, on Fox, Turbine Medien, 2015, DVD.

Pollack, Jon, and Tim Hobert, writers. *Community*. Season 1, episode 13, "Investigative Journalism." Directed by Joe Russo, featuring Joel McHale, Alison Brie, Donald Glover, Danny Pudi, and Yvette Nicole Brown. Aired January 14, 2010, on NBC, Sony, 2020, DVD.

Pollock, Isaac. "Fifteen Years Later: A Retrospective on the '07 Writers Guild Strike." *34th Street*, June 16, 2023. https://www.34st.com/article/2023/06/writers-guild-strike-chat-gpt-friday-night-lights-reality-tv-equal-pay

Polygon Staff. "How a Rick and Morty Joke Led to a McDonald's Szechuan Sauce Controversy." *Polygon*, February 21, 2018. https://www.polygon.com/2017/10/12/16464374/rick-and-morty-mcdonalds-szechuan-sauce

Pomerantz, Lauren, writer. *Community*. Season 1, episode 14, "Interpretive Dance." Directed by Justin Lin, featuring Joel McHale, Alison Brie, Donald Glover, Gillian Jacobs, Danny Pudi, and Yvette Nicole Brown. Aired January 21, 2010, on NBC, Sony, 2020, DVD.

Poniewozik, James. "The Decency Police." *Time*, March 20, 2005. https://time.com/archive/6671688/the-decency-police/

Pritzker, Steve, writer. *The Mary Tyler Moore Show*. Season 3, episode 11, "You've Got a Friend." Directed by Jerry Belson, featuring Mary Tyler Moore, Ed Asner, and Valerie Harper. Aired November 25, 1972, on CBS, 20th Century Fox, 2006, DVD.

Raftery, Brian. "How Dan Harmon Drives Himself Crazy Making *Community*." *Wired*, September 22, 2011. https://www.wired.com/2011/09/mf-harmon/

Rash, Jim, writer. *Community*. Season 4, episode 11, "Basic Human Anatomy." Directed by Beth McCarthy-Miller, featuring Joel McHale, Alison Brie, Donald Glover, Danny Pudi, and Yvette Nicole Brown. Aired April 25, 2013, on NBC, Sony, 2020, DVD.

Richardson, Randi. "'Living Single' Fans React to Jennifer Aniston Downplaying 'Friends' Being Offensive: 'Living Single' Was a Trending Topic on Twitter March 30." *Today*, March 31, 2023. https://www.today.com/popculture/tv/living-single-fans-react-jennifer-aniston-downplaying-friends-offensiv-rcna77434

Richter, Paul. "Sony to Buy Columbia, Says Americans Will Run Studio: 1st Sale of Film Maker to Japanese." *Los Angeles Times*, September 27, 1989. https://www.latimes.com/archives/la-xpm-1989-09-27-mn-335-story.html

Roller, Matt, writer. *Community*. Season 5, episode 10. "Advanced Advanced *Dungeons and Dragons*." Directed by Joe Russo, featuring Joel McHale, Alison Brie, Danny Pudi, Jonathan Banks, and Yvette Nicole Brown. Aired March 20, 2014, on NBC, Sony, 2020, DVD.

Rose, Lacey. "'Community's' Dan Harmon Reveals the Wild Story Behind His Firing and Rehiring." *The Hollywood Reporter*, July 17, 2013. https://www.hollywoodreporter.com/news/general-news/communitys-dan-harmon-reveals-wild-586084/

Rose, Lacey. "Donald Glover and Maya Erskine on Real-Life Marriage, Professional Divorce and When to Walk Away." *Hollywood Reporter*, February 7, 2024. https://www.hollywoodreporter.com/tv/tv-features/donald-glover-maya-erskine-interview-marriage-mr-and-mrs-smith-1235817327/

Rossen, Jake. "The Tommy Westphall Theory of a Unified TV Universe, Explained." *Mental Floss*, January 21, 2024. https://www.mentalfloss.com/article/500756/tommy-westphall-theory-unified-tv-universe-explained

Rubens, Alex, writer. *Community*. Season 5, episode 4, "Cooperative Polygraphy." Directed by Tristram Shapeero, featuring Joel McHale, Alison Brie, Donald Glover, Danny Pudi, and Yvette Nicole Brown. Aired January 16, 2014, on NBC, Sony, 2020, DVD.

Rubens, Alex, writer. *Community*. Season 6, episode 2, "Lawnmower Maintenance and Postnatal Care." Directed by Jim Rash and Nat Faxon, featuring Joel McHale, Alison Brie, Gillian Jacobs, Danny Pudi, and Keith David. Aired March 17, 2015, on Yahoo! Screen, Sony, 2020, DVD.

Rubenstein, Brian, writer. *Abbott Elementary*. Season 2, episode 19, "Festival." Directed by Randall Einhorn, featuring Quinta Brunson, Tyler James Williams, Janelle James, and Sheryl Lee Ralph. Aired March 15, 2023, on ABC, Warner, 2023, DVD.

Russell, M. E. "The Browncoats Rise Again: The Best Sci-fi Series You've Never Seen Has Gone from Cancellation to the Big Screen. Will a Never-Tried Marketing Strategy Work for 'Serenity'?" *The Weekly Standard*, June 25, 2005. http://www.weeklystandard.com/Content/Public/Articles/000/000/005/757fhfxg.asp

Ryan, Maureen. *Burn It Down: Power, Complicity, and a Call for Change in Hollywood*. New York: HarperCollins, 2023.

Ryan, Maureen. "'Parks and Recreation': Less Funny than 'Joey'?" *Chicago Tribune*, May 13, 2009. http://featuresblogs.chicagotribune.com/entertainment_tv/2009/05/parks-recreation-amy-poehler-nbc.html

Saccardo, Tim, writer. *Community*. Season 3, episode 18, "Course Listing Unavailable." Directed by Tristram Shapeero, featuring Joel McHale, Alison Brie, Donald Glover, Danny Pudi, and Yvette Nicole Brown. Aired May 3, 2012, on NBC, Sony, 2020, DVD.

Saccardo, Tim, writer. *Community*. Season 4, episode 7, "Economics of Marine Biology." Directed by Tricia Brock, featuring Joel McHale, Alison Brie, Donald Glover, Danny Pudi, and Chevy Chase. Aired March 21, 2013, on NBC, Sony, 2020, DVD.

Saccardo, Tim, writer. *Community*. Season 5, episode 5, "Geothermal Escapism." Directed by Joe Russo, featuring Joel McHale, Alison Brie, Donald Glover, Danny Pudi, and Yvette Nicole Brown. Aired January 23, 2014, on NBC, Sony, 2020, DVD.

Santamaria, Vera, writer. *Community*. Season 3, episode 11, "Urban Matrimony and the Sandwich Arts." Directed by Kyle Newacheck, featuring Joel McHale, Alison Brie, Donald Glover, Danny Pudi, and Yvette Nicole Brown. Aired March 15, 2012, on NBC, Sony, 2020, DVD.

Sayre, Carolyn. "10 Questions for Chevy Chase." *Time*, April 11, 2007. https://content.time.com/time/subscriber/article/0,33009,1609793,00.html

Schneider, Michael. "'Community' Movie Is Finally Happening, at Peacock, Fulfilling the Show's Prophesy." *Variety*, September 30, 2022. https://variety.com/2022/tv/news/community-movie-peacock-dan-harmon-joel-mchale-1235389233/

Scovell, Nell, writer. *Sabrina the Teenage Witch*. Season 1, episode 1, "Pilot." Directed by Robby Benson, featuring Melissa Joan Hart, Caroline Rhea, Beth Broderick, and Soleil Moon Frye. Aired September 27, 1996, on ABC, CBS Home Media, 2007, DVD.

Sepinwall, Alan. "For 'Community', How Much Meta Is Too Much?," *Uproxx*, May 5, 2010. https://uproxx.com/sepinwall/for-community-how-much-meta-is-too-much/

Sepinwall, Alan. "Parks and Recreation: Interviewing Co-creator Mike Schur." *New Jersey Star-Ledger*, September 17, 2009. http://www.nj.com/entertainment/tv/index.ssf/2009/09/parks_and_recreation_interview.html

Shales, Tom. "NBCees Paul Klein to the Door: NBC's Paul Klein: Out in the Shuffle." *Washington Post*, March 5, 1979. https://www.washingtonpost.com/archive/

lifestyle/1979/03/06/nbcees-paul-klein-to-the-door/998c31db-7e66-4bc0-bbd3-b3090f0b97d1

Sheldon, Sidney, writer. *I Dream of Jeannie*. Season 1, episode 1, "The Lady in the Bottle." Directed by Gene Nelson, featuring Barbara Eden and Larry Hagman. Aired September 18, 1965, on NBC, Sony, 2006, DVD.

Sherman, Amy, and Jennifer Heath, writers. *Roseanne*. Season 4, episode 1, "A Bitter Pill to Swallow." Directed by Andrew D. Weyman, featuring Roseanne Barr, John Goodman, Lacy Goranson, and Sara Gilbert. Aired March 1, 1995, on ABC, Mill Creek, 2013, DVD.

Simms, Paul, writer. *News Radio*. Season 3, episode 7, "Daydream." Directed by Tom Cherones, featuring Dave Foley, Phil Hartman, Maura Tierney, Steven Root, and Vicky Lewis. Aired November 13, 1996, on NBC, Sony, 2008, DVD.

"Sitcom Character Archetypes." *TV Tropes*. Accessed October 14, 2024. https://tvtropes.org/pmwiki/pmwiki.php/Main/SitcomCharacterArchetypes

Sommers, Erik, writer. *Community*. Season 5, episode 3, "Basic Intergluteal Numismatics." Directed by Tristram Shapeero, featuring Joel McHale, Alison Brie, Donald Glover, Danny Pudi, and Yvette Nicole Brown. Aired January 9, 2014, on NBC, Sony, 2020, DVD.

Spangler, Todd. "Off-Peak TV: Number of Scripted Shows Fell 24% in 2023, Study Finds." *Variety*, January 19, 2024. https://variety.com/2024/tv/news/us-scripted-tv-shows-2023-peak-tv-study-1235877669/

Spangler, Todd. "Why Yahoo's Foray Into Original TV Series Failed." *Variety*, October 27, 2015. https://variety.com/2015/digital/news/yahoo-community-other-space-money-loss-1201627039/

Sridhar, Priya. "The Good Parts of *Community*, Season Four." *Medium*. February 4, 2001. https://medium.com/permanent-nerd-network/the-good-parts-of-community-season-four-ff8455d00014

Stabile, Carol A. *The Broadcast 41: Women and the Anti-Communist Blacklist*. London: Goldsmiths Press, 2018.

Stack, Tim. "Ryan Murphy Says the WB Was Homophobic during *Popular*: The Creator of the Teen Comedy Reveals the Network Would Give Him Notes to Make the Series 'Less Gay.'" *Entertainment Weekly*, September 26, 2016. https://ew.com/article/2016/09/26/ryan-murphy-wb-popular-homophobic/

Stamatopoulos, Dino, writer. *Community*. Season 5, episode 11, "G. I. Jeff." Directed by Rob Schrab, featuring Joel McHale, Alison Brie, Donald Glover, Danny Pudi, and Yvette Nicole Brown. Aired March 20, 2014, on NBC, Sony, 2020, DVD.

Stamatopoulos, Dino, and Dan Harmon, writers. *Community*. Season 2, episode 11, "Abed's Uncontrollable Christmas." Directed by Duke Johnson, featuring Joel McHale, Alison Brie, Donald Glover, Danny Pudi, and Yvette Nicole Brown. Aired December 9, 2010, on NBC, Sony, 2020, DVD.

Stevens, Bob, writer. *Night Court*. Season 3, episode 12, "Dan's Escort." Directed by Jeff Melman, featuring Harry Anderson, Markie Post, Charles Robinson, John Larroquette, and Richard Moll. Aired January 9, 1986, on NBC, Warner Brothers, 2023, DVD.

Stevens, Hampton. "The Meta, Innovative Genius of *Community*: It's One of the Most Innovative Shows in Sitcom History. But Can It Make Us Care about the Characters?" *The Atlantic*, May 12, 2011. https://www.theatlantic.com/entertainment/archive/2011/05/the-meta-innovative-genius-of-community/238740/

Svetkey, Benjamin. "The 'Enterprise' Turns 25: A Look Back at 'Star Trek''s History." *Entertainment Weekly*, September 27, 2001. https://ew.com/article/1991/09/27/enterprise-turns-25/

Sweeten, Julia. "'Gilmore Girls': Dragonfly Inn and Scenes from Stars Hollow." *Hooked on Houses*, May 16, 2010. https://hookedonhouses.net/2010/05/16/gilmore-girls-dragonfly-inn-and-scenes-from-stars-hollow/

Sweeting, Paul. "DVD Warrior Makes the Case for VOD." *Variety*, March 25–April 1, 2001: 26.

Sweeting, Paul. "PCs, Vidgames Give DVD Plenty of Drive in Rental." *Variety*, October 2–8, 2000: 12.

Tan, Justin, writer. *Abbott Elementary*. Season 3, episode 9, "Alex." Directed by Randall Einhorn, featuring Quinta Brunson, Tyler James Williams, Janelle James, and Sheryl Lee Ralph. Aired April 10, 2024, on ABC, Warner, 2025, DVD.

Tucker, Ken. "The Chevy Chase Show." *Entertainment Weekly*, October 8, 1993. https://ew.com/article/1993/10/08/chevy-chase-show/

Ulin, Rob, and Perry Dance, writers. *Roseanne*. Season 7, episode 19, "All About Rosey, Part 1." Directed by Gail Mancuso, featuring Roseanne Barr, John Goodman, Sarah Chalke, and Sara Gilbert. Aired March 1, 1995, on ABC, Mill Creek, 2013, DVD.

Ulin, Rob, and Perry Dance, writers. *Roseanne*. Season 7, episode 20, "All About Rosey, Part 2." Directed by Gail Mancuso, featuring Roseanne Barr, John Goodman, Sarah Chalke, and Sara Gilbert. Aired March 1, 1995, on ABC, Mill Creek, 2013, DVD.

VanArendonk, Kathryn. "What Is a Bottle Episode? The People on the Internet Are Wrong. Or Are They?" *Vulture*, February 7, 2025. https://www.vulture.com/article/what-is-a-bottle-episode-meaning.html

Venable, Nick. "*Community* Is Everyone's Latest Netflix Obsession, and Fans Can't Get Enough." *Cinema Blend*, April 12, 2020. https://www.cinemablend.com/television/2494328/community-is-everyones-latest-netflix-obsession-and-fans-cant-get-enough

Voger, Mark. "'Dobie Gillis': The Complete Series on DVD." *NJ.com*, July 5, 2013. https://www.nj.com/entertainment/2013/07/dobie_gillis.html

Wallenstein, Andrew. "Yahoo Shutters Video Service Yahoo Screen." *Variety*, January 4, 2016. https://variety.com/2016/digital/news/yahoo-shutters-video-service-yahoo-screen-exclusive-1201671374/

Warburton, Matt, writer. *Community*. Season 3, episode 20, "Digital Estate Planning." Directed by Adam Davidson, featuring Joel McHale, Alison Brie, Donald Glover, Chevy Chase, Danny Pudi, and Yvette Nicole Brown. Aired May 17, 2012, on NBC, Sony, 2020, DVD.

Weithorn, Michael J, writer. *Family Ties*. Season 2, episode 12, "Go Tigers." Directed by Will Mackenzie, featuring Michael J. Fox, Meredith Baxter, Justine Bateman, and Michael Gross. Aired January 12, 1984, on NBC, Paramount, 2007, DVD.

Werts, Diane. "Review: CBS' 'Viva Laughlin' a Train Wreck." *Newsday*, October 18, 2007. https://web.archive.org/web/20071020034800/http://www.newsday.com/entertainment/tv/ny-ettell5415699oct18,0,5351094.story

Wilcox, David, writer. *Law & Order*. Season 17, episode 7, "In Vino Veritas." Directed by Tim Hunter, featuring Sam Waterston, Jesse L. Martin, Milena Govich, Alana de la Garza, and Chevy Chase. Aired November 3, 2006, on NBC, Universal, 2011, DVD.

Winston, Hilary, writer. *Community*. Season 1, episode 6, "Football, Feminism and You." Directed by Joe Russo, featuring Joel McHale, Alison Brie, Donald Glover, Danny Pudi, and Yvette Nicole Brown. Aired October 22, 2009, on NBC, Sony, 2020, DVD.

Winston, Hilary, writer. *Community*. Season 1, episode 25, "Pascal's Triangle Revisited." Directed by Joe Russo, featuring Joel McHale, Alison Brie, Donald Glover, Gillian Jacobs, Danny Pudi, and Yvette Nicole Brown. Aired May 20, 2010, on NBC, Sony, 2020, DVD.

Winston, Hilary, writer. *Community*. Season 2, episode 13, "Celebrity Pharmacology." Directed by Fred Goss, featuring Joel McHale, Alison Brie, Chevy Chase, Danny Pudi, and Yvette Nicole Brown. Aired January 27, 2011, on NBC, Sony, 2020, DVD.

Winston, Hilary, writer. *Community*. Season 2, episode 24, "For a Few Paintballs More." Directed by Joe Russo, featuring Joel McHale, Alison Brie, Donald Glover, Danny Pudi, Chevy Chase, and Yvette Nicole Brown. Aired May 12, 2011, on NBC, Sony, 2020, DVD.

Wittler, Wendall. "Television Grapples with a Weighty Matter." *Today*, October 5, 2004. https://www.today.com/popculture/television-grapples-weighty-matter-wbna5991977

"The X-Files." Fanlore. Accessed December 31, 2024. https://fanlore.org/wiki/The_X-Files

Zoglin, Richard. "Late-Night Mugging." *Time*, September 20, 1993. https://web.archive.org/web/20101028054014/http://www.time.com/time/magazine/article/0,9171,979242,00.html

INDEX

Abbott Elementary 1, 4, 73, 77–8, 82
ABC 12, 16–7, 18–19, 23, 24–7, 41, 77, 81, 88, 134, 137
The Addams Family 13–15, 79
Air Conditioning Repair School 56, 65, 97, 98
Angel 46, 146
Arrested Development 27, 69, 94, 138
Austerlitz, Saul 94, 103, 157

Baby Boomer 16, 61, 119, 165
Bareilles, Sara 117, 162
Barnes, Troy 54–6
Bel-Air 149
Bennett, Andre 66–67, 109
The Bernie Mac Show 27
Better Off Ted 27, 101
The Bill Cosby Show 76, 79
Black, Jack 34, 35, 105
Bloodworth-Thomason, Linda 18, 172n15
The Boondocks 136
Boston Public 4, 77
bottle episodes 2, 108–11, 114–15, 124
Boy Meets World 24, 79, 81
The Brady Bunch 17, 41
Brooklyn Nine-Nine 30, 108, 132, 133
Brown, Yvette Nicole 50, 67, 163–4
Buffy the Vampire Slayer 25, 42–3, 46, 73, 78–9, 131, 137
Bush, George H. W. 44, 90

cable television 78, 83, 88, 102, 118, 129–31, 137–9, 144
   HBO 88, 129, 130, 135
CafePress 44
Cannell, Stephen J. 40–1, 83
The Cape 118, 145–6
Carsey-Werner Productions 89
Carter, Chris 41
CBS 1, 10, 11–12, 16, 17–18, 20, 25–6, 40, 79, 88, 89, 92, 129, 135, 138, 146, 172n15

Chandrasekhar, Jay 61
Chang, Ben 5, 62, 67, 97, 98, 107, 109, 118–19, 141, 145, 157, 160
Channel 101 32, 34–5, 47, 147
Chase, Chevy 3, 5, 37, 49–50, 58–9, 158
Cheers 2, 19, 20, 23, 32, 89, 105
Claymation 62, 117, 123, 160
clip shows 2, 108, 115–20
Columbia Pictures 134–6
"Comedy Night Done Right" 2
Comedy Sportz 3, 31, 32–3
Community: The Board Game 127–8, 141–2
Connor, Alan 52, 53
The Cosby Show 2, 15, 19–20, 22, 88, 89, 91, 102
Cousin Oliver trope 104
CW 12, 28, 37, 81, 131, 138, 149

darkest timeline 65, 114, 148
Dawson's Creek 25, 42, 78, 79, 131, 137
David, Keith 99, 124, 132, 146, 165
Dead Alewives 33
Dead Like Me 116
Degrassi (franchise) 84
Designing Women 18, 128
Desilu Productions 39–40
A Different World 20, 85, 89
Digital Video Recorder/DVR 23, 144
Doctor Who 55, 124
the Dreamatorium 65, 127
DuMont Network 9, 11–12, 41, 129, 130
Duncan, Ian 36, 51, 96, 153
Dungeons and Dragons 33, 37, 55, 84, 109–10, 161
DVD format 31, 84, 115, 143–5

Edison, Annie 56–8
Ellen (sitcom) 23–5
episodes, Community
   "Abed's Uncontrollable Christmas" 117, 123, 160, 164; "Advanced Dungeons

and Dragons" 37, 59–60, 109–10, 160–1; "Applied Anthropology and Culinary Arts" 109; "Basic Intergluteal Numismatics" 122, 167; "Basic Lupine Urology" 123, 165–6; "Basic Rocket Science" 122; "Contemporary American Poultry" 4, 52–3, 96, 102, 121, 156–57, 162; "Cooperative Calligraphy" 108–9, 117–18; "Critical Film Studies" 121–2, 161–2; "Curriculum Unavailable" 116, 118–20, 124, 166; "Documentary Filmmaking Redux" 149, 163; "Emotional Consequences of Broadcast Television" 5, 50, 54, 106–7, 151, 169; "Foosball and Nocturnal Vigilantism" 67–8, 163–4; "G. I. Jeff" 53–4, 123; "Horror Fiction in Seven Spooky Steps" 97, 123, 163, 169; "Intermediate Documentary Filmmaking" 149, 167; "Modern Warfare" 62, 121, 157; "Paradigms of Human Memory" 86, 116–18, 119, 146, 164, 166; "Pillows and Blankets" 99, 123–4, 165; "Regional Holiday Music" 86, 105, 119, 123, 151, 164–5; "Remedial Chaos Theory" 110–15, 146, 148, 152, 162; "Wedding Videography" 149, 168
"ethnic sitcoms" 10–11
Everybody Hates Chris 22, 28, 42, 76, 81–2

The Facts of Life 32, 88, 99
Family Ties 19, 22, 88, 89, 99
fanbase 44, 47, 128, 142, 144
Federal Communications Commission 12
Ferris Bueller (TV series) 82
fin-syn/financial incentive and syndication 16, 40, 41
Firefly 108, 132, 143, 147–8
Fox Network 12, 20–1, 26, 28, 33–4, 41–2, 82, 83, 91, 123, 130, 133, 143
Fraiser 23, 26, 28, 88, 91, 92, 150–1
Freaks and Geeks 80, 83–4
Friends 2, 22–3, 26, 28, 87, 92, 101, 145
Fuller House 151

Ganz, Megan 3, 46
"gas leak year" 5
Gilmore Girls 39, 44, 45, 83, 133, 150
Glee 84–5, 105, 123, 151, 164
Glover, Donald 3, 5, 50, 93–4, 148–9, 168
The Goldbergs (1950s) 9, 10, 11, 85
GoodFellas 2, 4, 52, 102, 121, 156
The Good Place 69, 75, 133

Halpern, Justin 97
Hangin' With Mr. Cooper 24, 77
Hanna-Barbera 135
Hawthorn, Pierce 37, 50, 59, 110
Harmon, Dan 1, 2, 30, 31–47, 50–1, 61, 64, 101, 102, 106, 116–17, 128, 132, 141–2, 146–7, 151, 167
Head of the Class 19, 77, 78–9, 80
Heat Vision and Jack 34, 47
Hendrix, Leslie 123, 166
Henning, Paul 13
Hickey, Buzz 64, 97
Hilmes, Michele 130
House Un-American Activities Committee 11
high-concept 34, 138, 156, 160
Hulu 145, 147

I Love Lucy 1, 9, 10, 11, 40, 103
Inspector Spacetime 55, 65, 124
internet 4, 31, 41–2, 47, 112, 127, 128
Interview With a Vampire 150
Irreconcilable Differences 39
It's Your Move 80–1, 90, 91

Jacobs, Gillian 5, 50–1
Jeong, Ken 5, 62
Jericho 146
Johnson, Derek 142

Keaton, Alex P. 89, 99
Klein, Paul L. 87
Kripke, Eric 44

The Larry Sanders Show 88, 136, 171n3
LaserDisc 143
Law & Order 58–9, 123, 165–6
Lawson, Gilbert 61, 98, 167
Lear, Norman 23, 31, 40, 88, 89, 135, 149
least objectionable programming (LOP) 87

Leave It to Beaver 10, 14, 31, 43, 79, 116
Levy, Dan 103
Lieberfarb, Warren 143
lineup 19–20, 30, 77, 89, 93, 131
Littlefield, Warren 22, 42
Living Single 22, 24, 28, 42, 91
Lorre, Chuck 2, 26, 141

Magnitude (character) 95–6
Malcolm in the Middle 27, 83
The Many Loves of Dobie Gillis 79, 81
Marc, David 9
Marvel Cinematic Universe 2–3, 151–2
Mary Kay and Johnny 3, 9, 11
*M*A*S*H* 16, 65, 102, 103–4
McHale, Joel 2, 37, 141
McKenna, Chris 3
metatextual/meta 2, 3, 34, 64, 66, 83, 101, 104, 108, 116, 120, 123, 130, 131, 139, 144, 151–2, 156, 162, 169
Monster House 35
Moonlighting 130, 160
Mr. Novak 73, 75–6
Mr. Peepers 11, 75, 79
MTM 16, 17, 40, 88, 89
multicamera 26, 37, 51, 69, 89, 92, 103, 105–6, 149, 151
The Munsters 13–14
Murphy Brown 18, 25, 44, 143
Murphy, Ryan 84
"Must-See TV" 2, 22–3
My Dinner With Andre 99–100, 122, 161–2
My Name Is Earl 4, 28–30, 92–3, 104

Nadir, Abed 2, 64–6
Navar-Gill, Annemarie 46
Netflix 86, 132–3, 145, 147, 148, 150, 151
News Radio 91, 136, 137–8
Nielsen ratings 10, 16, 17, 20, 128, 144
Night Court 19, 20, 89–90, 109

The Office (US) 28, 30, 31, 69, 78, 88, 92–5, 101, 102, 131, 145
Osbourne, Alex ("Star Burns") 52, 86, 96, 121
Our Miss Brooks 4, 75, 77, 79

paintball 55, 62, 99, 119, 121, 149, 157, 168
Paramount Decree 38
Parker Lewis Can't Lose 21, 27, 30, 82–3, 91, 104–5, 137, 138, 139
Parks and Recreation 2, 30, 69, 88, 93–5, 100, 102, 131
Patashnak, Elroy 99, 132
PBS/National Education Television 74, 84
Peacock 133, 145, 148, 150
Pen 15 1
Perry, Britta 61–4
PixelDrip Gallery 142, 146–7
Popular 84–5
public service announcement (PSA) 74

Rash, Jim 96
Reilly, Kevin 92–3
Rhimes, Shonda 44
Rick and Morty 2, 3, 35, 44–5, 142
Room 222 76, 77
Roseanne 2, 21, 23, 44, 89, 91, 94, 116
rural sitcoms 11, 13–14, 16
"rural purge" 16
Russo, Anthony and Joe 3, 151
Ryan, Maureen 45–6

The Sarah Silverman Program 35–6
Saturday Night Live 30, 46, 49, 79, 93, 138
Saved By the Bell 80, 87, 109
Schrab, Rob 32–6
Schur, Michael 30, 93
Screen Gems 135
Scrubs 30, 83, 92, 99, 104–5
Scud, the Disposable Assassin 33–4
Seinfeld 4, 22, 23, 28, 91–2, 94, 95, 101–2, 136
Sepinwall, Alan 102
Serenity 143, 147–8
Sherman-Palladino, Amy 2, 44, 45, 133, 150
showrunners 37, 38–47, 80, 133
The Simpsons 20–1, 27, 83, 90–1, 101–2, 138
Sony Television 3, 5, 35, 37, 50, 127–8, 134–9
Spelling, Aaron 40–1, 42, 88

Square Pegs 79–80
Star Trek 40, 41, 146
The Steve Harvey Show 21–2, 42, 77, 92
story circle 32, 36–7
streaming 49, 78, 81, 84, 85, 93, 102, 115, 128, 131, 132–3, 138–9, 144–9
superhero 53, 137, 145–6
Supernatural 44, 116, 128, 132, 133

Tandem Productions 16, 17–18, 40, 89, 135
Telecommunications Act of 1996 134
30 Rock 2, 4, 30, 69, 88, 93–5, 100, 102, 131, 135, 141
thirtysomething 130
Thomas, Rob 44
timeslot 22–3, 88
Tommy Westphall Universe 127
Twin Peaks 137, 143

UPN 12, 21, 22, 28, 41–2, 78, 81–2, 130, 131

very special episode 18, 43, 74, 108
video game 137, 147, 166–7

WB/Warner Brothers 12, 21, 28, 41–2, 74, 78, 81, 84–5, 130–1, 133
   Midwest Street 39
Welcome Back, Kotter 75, 76–7, 78, 88
WGA Strike (2007) 43, 144
WGA/SAG Strike 139, 149
Whedon, Joss 2, 31, 42–4
The White Shadow 4, 76, 77
Winger, Jeff 51–4

The X-Files 41, 143

Yahoo! Screen 93, 132–3, 141, 144, 147–8, 168

ABOUT THE AUTHOR

Erin Giannini, PhD, is an independent scholar who has written numerous articles about topics from corporate culture in genre television to production-level shifts and their effects on television texts. She is also the author of *Supernatural: A History of Television's Unearthly Road Trip* (2021) and *The Good Place* [TV Milestones] (2022) and the coeditor of the book series "B-TV: Television Under the Critical Radar," for Bloomsbury. She lives in Albuquerque, New Mexico.